Inside the Radical Right

What explains the cross-national variation in the radical right's electoral success over the past several decades? Challenging existing structural and institutional accounts, this book analyzes the dynamics of party building and explores the attitudes, skills, and experiences of radical right activists in eleven countries. Based on extensive field research and an original data set of radical right candidates for office, David Art links the quality of radical right activists to broader patterns of success and failure. He demonstrates how a combination of historical legacies and incentive structures produced activists who helped party building in some cases and doomed it in others. In an age of rising electoral volatility and the fading of traditional political cleavages, *Inside the Radical Right* makes a strong case for the importance of party leaders and activists as masters of their own fate.

David Art is Associate Professor of Political Science at Tufts University. He is the author of *The Politics of the Nazi Past in Germany and Austria* (Cambridge, 2006), as well as articles on the radical right in such journals as *Comparative Politics*, *German Politics and Society*, and *Party Politics*. Art is co-convenor of the European Consortium for Political Research's Standing Group on Extremism and Democracy. During 2008–2009, he was a Max Weber Fellow at the European University Institute, and he has been awarded grants from the Fulbright Program, the German Academic Exchange Service, and the Minda de Gunzburg Center for European Studies at Harvard University.

Inside the Radical Right

The Development of Anti-Immigrant Parties in Western Europe

DAVID ART

Tufts University

 CAMBRIDGE
UNIVERSITY PRESS

CAMBRIDGE UNIVERSITY PRESS
Cambridge, New York, Melbourne, Madrid, Cape Town,
Singapore, São Paulo, Delhi, Mexico City

Cambridge University Press
32 Avenue of the Americas, New York, NY 10013-2473, USA

www.cambridge.org
Information on this title: www.cambridge.org/9780521720328

First published 2011
Reprinted 2012

A catalog record for this publication is available from the British Library.

Library of Congress Cataloging in Publication Data
Art, David, 1972–
    Inside the Radical Right : The Development of Anti-Immigrant Parties in
    Western Europe / David Art.
      p. cm
    Includes bibliographical references and index.
    ISBN 978-0-521-89624-5 – ISBN 978-0-521-72032-8 (pbk.)
    1. Political parties – Europe, Western. 2. Right-wing extremists – Europe,
    Western. 3. Radicalism – Europe, Western. 4. Europe, Western – Emigration
    and immigration – Political aspects. I. Title.
    JN 94.A979A78   2011
    324.2'13094–dc22   2010046685

ISBN 978-0-521-89624-5 Hardback
ISBN 978-0-521-72032-8 Paperback

For Henry

Contents

Preface

This book is about people who join radical right parties in Western Europe. Its central claim is that the qualities of these individuals determine whether such parties develop into major players or remain marginal forces. In contrast to most studies of the radical right, and indeed of political parties in general, it focuses on agency rather than structure and demonstrates that political choices – sometimes choices that seem insignificant at the time – can produce radically different outcomes in societies that are all facing the same basic set of large-scale transformations. That a micropolitical turn provided the key to understanding the development of anti-immigrant parties in Western Europe first occurred to me as I was conducting interviews with radical right politicians in Austria and Germany. So it is appropriate to begin with them.

In 2000, the editor-in-chief of the left-liberal weekly *Falter*, Armin Thurnher, coined a new term for some members of the radical right Austrian Freedom Party (FPÖ) that combined the German *Faschisten* (fascists) with the Austrian-German *fesch* (good looking): the *Feschisten*. The thirty-one-year-old FPÖ finance minister, Karl-Heinz Grasser, always dressed to the nines, was the unofficial leader of this new breed of Freedom Party politician. A number of highly educated, ambitious, and capable people had entered the party since Jörg Haider had come to power in 1986. Members of the older cohort remained as well, but these were generally respectable people in their communities. During my interviews – which I arranged by phone and email – I came across a few odd characters. By and large, however, Freedom Party politicians struck me as individuals who quite easily could have become Social Democrats or Christian Democrats. If they held overtly racist opinions, they were sophisticated enough not to reveal them to me.

In Germany, locating members of the Republikaner (REP) party proved to be a challenge. Their office in Berlin was open only on Tuesday mornings, and no one ever seemed to pick up the phone. After several weeks of trying, I finally coaxed the telephone number of the head of the Berlin REP organization out of the party's only (unpaid) staff member. When I visited the REP leader at his home, he spent most of the time defending the Waffen-SS. He was good enough to personally put me in touch with several other party members, explaining that efforts to reach them on my own were doomed because they were highly distrustful of anyone who wanted to talk with them. It quickly became apparent why. Several interviews lasted three hours or more, most of which were devoted to anti-Semitic and anti-Mason conspiracy theories. Racial slurs were tossed around with abandon. That I might not share these opinions never seemed to occur to my interviewees, and I had the distinct feeling that they were suffering from intense loneliness. When the head of the Bavarian wing of the REP told me later that the party attracted only those "who had nothing else to lose," I knew exactly what he was talking about.

As these two anecdotes suggest, there are major differences in the personnel of radical right parties. This is not to deny that parties are heterogeneous or that one could find seemingly moderate and competent members of the REP, and extremist members of the FPÖ, if one looked hard enough. Yet this book will demonstrate that the activists of successful radical right parties tend to look a lot like those from the FPÖ and that the anecdote about REP members captures an essential feature of failed radical right parties. On the basis of their attitudes and motivations, I develop a tripartite typology of radical right activists: *moderates*, *extremists*, and *opportunists*. I show, first theoretically and later empirically, how different distributions of these activists matter for party development. I also demonstrate how some parties are able to attract highly educated and experienced activists, while other parties mostly recruit activists with low socioeconomic status, little to no political experience, and "nothing else to lose." Why some parties are able to attract activists that are a net benefit to party building, while others seem to attract only people that doom such an endeavor, is one of the central questions of this book.

Radical right parties have captured enormous academic and media attention over the past quarter-century. Although some of the best known of these parties – such as the French National Front – may be in electoral decline, others appear poised to rise and occupy a new generation of scholars and journalists. Indeed, it is now difficult to imagine West European politics without radical right parties. While the cases of success and failure will undoubtedly look different in five or ten years, I believe that the basic developmental patterns that this book uncovers will be repeated in the future. For those who want to understand where radical right parties are headed, it is important to understand where they have been.

But this book is really about more than radical right parties, important as they are for party politics and policy making, and integral as they are to basic structural transformations in European politics, such as immigration, European integration, and globalization. It is a study of party building in an age when the major social cleavages that had structured partisan competition in Europe for decades began to decline in importance. One of the chief consequences of electoral dealignment and rising electoral volatility is that the political parties are masters of their own fate to an even greater extent than before. And as it becomes harder to read off the success of political parties from the basic contours of societies, the organizational choices that parties make and the quality of people that they attract are likely to matter even more. Radical right parties certainly faced a unique set of hurdles in these respects, but new types of political parties, as well as mainstream parties that are still trying to adapt to the new electoral environment, are faced with broadly similar challenges.

I benefited from the counsel of many people while writing this book. Going back a ways, Ivo Banac, David Cameron, and Juan Linz at Yale first sparked my interest in European politics and in challenges to liberal democracy. Suzanne Berger at MIT taught me a great many things about comparative politics, the two most important being that structure does not always overwhelm agency and that empirical reality is usually more interesting than deductive theorizing. I am grateful to the following colleagues for reading parts of the project as it evolved: Ben Ansell, Tim Bale, Tor Bjørklund, Judith Chubb, Consuelo Cruz, Jennifer Fitzgerald, Mark Franklin, Matthew Goodwin, Wade Jacoby, Elizabeth Remick, Jens Rydgren, Debbie Schildkraut, Chris Wendt, and Daniel Ziblatt. Those who went beyond the call of duty and suffered through the entire manuscript include Erik Bleich, Elisabeth Carter, Antonis Ellinas, Jane Gingrich, Sarah de Lange, Peter Mair, Cas Mudde, Oxana Shevel, Amos Zehavi, and Adam Ziegfeld. Yannis Evrigenis deserves special mention, as his office ceiling collapsed on him during a rainstorm as he was penning one critical comment after another in the margins. Although the manuscript was perhaps physically intact after this onslaught, it was really never the same again. Two anonymous reviewers at Cambridge University Press provided yet another round of very constructive criticism. I also benefited from conversations and email exchanges with the following people: Kai Arzheimer, Uwe Backes, Simon Bornschier, Jean-Yves Camus, Dirk De Bièvre, Pascal Delwit, Bruno De Wever, Lieven De Winter, Jørgen Elklit, Meindert Fennema, Peter Gundelach, Bernt Hagtvet, Gilles Ivaldi, Chantal Kesteloot, Valérie Lafont, Annete Linden, Nonna Mayer, Teun Pauwels, Alban Perrin, Jens Rydgren, Rinke van den Brink, Wouter van der Brug, Joost van Spanje, Stefaan Walgrave, and Lien Warmenbol.

I began this book at the College of the Holy Cross, finished it at Tufts University, and had the luxury of working on it for an entire year at the European University Institute (EUI). All three institutions provided generous intellectual and financial support. Several Research and Publication Grants from Holy Cross, combined with the helpful intercession of Chick Weiss, helped me get the project off the ground. At Tufts, support from the Faculty Research and Awards Committee and from Rob Hollister at the Tisch College of Citizenship gave me the opportunity to conduct as much fieldwork as I could manage. A Max Weber Fellowship from the EUI allowed me to concentrate on writing in an idyllic environment, where Ramon Marimon and Peter Mair were gracious hosts. I also benefited enormously from the intellectual camaraderie of many friends that I made at the EUI. In addition to those whose labors have already been mentioned, I would like to acknowledge Joshua Derman, Isabelle Engeli, Simona Grassi, Silja Häusermann, Stephanie Hofmann, Paolo Masella, Eleonora Pasotti, Miriam Ronzoni, Roger Schoenman, Violet Soen, and Simon Levis Sullam.

I am grateful for the able research and editorial assistance of Richard Ammerman, David Attewell, Stephanie Coutrix, and Daniel Ferry at Tufts, and Jean-Thomas Arrighi, Theresa Kuhn, Helene Lund, Julie Nielsen, Maarit Ströbele, and Carolien Van Ham at the EUI. It goes without saying that I could not have completed the research for this book without the politicians who agreed to be interviewed and gave generously of their time. I also thank the journal *Comparative Politics* for granting permission to use material originally published as "The Organizational Origins of the Contemporary Radical Right: The Case of Belgium" (July 2008). Eric Crahan at Cambridge University Press was enthusiastic about this project from start to finish and has been a pleasure to work with.

I am fortunate to come from a family where writing is celebrated and where the struggle that accompanies it is understood. My father, mother, and sister continue to provide encouragement at every turn. I don't say often enough how much they mean to me, so here it is in print. My wife, Julija, deserves a footnote on every page of this book, if only to remind me that her unrelenting emotional, intellectual, and spiritual support that I have come to take for granted is extraordinary. I dedicate this book to Henry, for all that he gave us in his short time with us.

Abbreviations

AN	National Alliance (Italy) / Alleanza Nazionale
BNP	British National Party
BZÖ	Alliance for the Future of Austria / Bündnis Zukunft Österreich
CD	Center Democrats (the Netherlands) / Centrumdemocraten
DF	Danish People's Party / Dansk Folkeparti
DVU	German People's Union / Deutsche Volksunion
FN	National Front (France) / Front National
FNb	National Front (Belgium) / Front National
FPÖ	Austrian Freedom Party / Freiheitliche Partei Österreichs
FrP	Progress Party (Norway) / Fremskrittspartiet
FRPd	Danish Progress Party / Fremskridtspartiet
LN	Northern League (Italy) / Lega Nord
LPF	List Pim Fortuyn (the Netherlands) / Lijst Pim Fortuyn
MSI	Italian Social Movement / Movimento Sociale Italiano
ND	New Democracy (Sweden) / Ny Demokrati
NF	National Front (UK)
NPD	National Democratic Party of Germany / Nationaldemokratische Partei Deutschlands
ÖVP	Austrian People's Party / Österreichische Volkspartie
PVV	Freedom Party (the Netherlands) / Partij Voor de Vrijheid
REP	The Republicans (Germany) / Die Republikaner
SD	Sweden Democrats / Sverigedemokraterna
SPÖ	Social Democratic Party of Austria / Sozialdemokratische Partei Österreichs

SVP	Swiss People's Party / Schweizerische Volkspartei
VB	Flemish Bloc / Flemish Interest (Belgium) / Vlaams Blok / Vlaams Belang
VdU	League of Independents (Austria) / Verband der Unabhängigen

1

Introduction

In March 1984, a foreign correspondent for the *Washington Post* tracked down Pierre Poujade, the stationery salesman who had led a political revolt of French shopkeepers three decades earlier. Poujade's movement, the Union de Défense Commerçants et Artisans (Union for the Defense of Tradesmen and Artisans, UDCA), did not survive beyond a single parliamentary term in the French National Assembly and serves as a classic example of a "flash" party. But the ideology of Poujadism – the defense of small business interests and traditional values against the forces of modernization – appeared to be making a comeback in the form of Jean-Marie Le Pen's Front National (National Front, FN). Le Pen had first entered parliament as a twenty-eight-year-old deputy of the UDCA, and although he was now well into his sixth decade, Poujade still spoke of him as a protégé. "A handsome kid with a fine gift of gab" was his estimation of the FN's leader. Le Pen was attracting national attention after his party, with the cooperation of two mainstream conservative parties, won several council seats in the town of Dreux. This led to a series of television appearances and increased visibility, and by the time of the interview with Poujade the FN was polling between 10% and 15% for the upcoming elections to the European Parliament. Nonetheless, Poujade foresaw a bleak future for Le Pen: "Take my word for it: by 1988, he will be down to 1 or 2 percent of the vote."[1]

Poujade's prediction may have been colored by his own meteoric rise and fall, but the overwhelming majority of commentators at the time also viewed the FN's success as ephemeral. Most were unwilling to believe

[1] *Washington Post*, March 18, 1984.

that the party represented anything more than a hodgepodge of political cranks riding a momentary wave of protest. When Le Pen and the other elected FN parliamentarians took their seats in the European Parliament in July 1984, an article in the *Guardian* described them as the "Strasbourg Cuckoos" and argued that French voters would soon toss them out.[2] This view persisted four years later, even after Le Pen had captured 14% of the vote in the 1988 presidential election. "So far," the *Economist* reminded its readers, "Europe's post-Hitler experience has been that far-right parties wane almost as quickly as they wax."[3] There was thus no reason to believe that Le Pen would not become the next Poujade.

The media's tone, however, had changed markedly by the early 1990s. Not only had the FN consolidated its electoral position and established a national organization, but other parties that railed against immigration and the political establishment had also begun to do surprisingly well across Western Europe. Journalists started to juxtapose quaint, travel-book descriptions of small European states with this new wave of xenophobia. "The gentle face of Belgium, affectionately teased as the home of beer, chips and Tintin, had turned ugly overnight," reported one after the Vlaams Blok's breakthrough in the 1991 municipal elections in Antwerp.[4] "The photograph shows three young, handsome Austrians with wind-blown hair and open collars, laughing at the camera as they pose for a picture high in the Alps," wrote another of an Austrian Freedom Party poster in 1990.[5]

By the turn of the twenty-first century, it had become clear that many of these parties, which I will refer to as radical right parties, were here to stay. They had participated in national governments in Austria, Italy, the Netherlands, and Switzerland, supported minority governments in Denmark and Norway, and won representation in state parliaments and local councils across Europe. Several had approached 30% of the vote in national elections. The French National Front never reached the latter mark, but Jean-Marie Le Pen's entrance into the second round of the 2002 presidential election, despite no meaningful chance of winning the contest, marked the culmination of his political career.

Poujade obviously failed to predict the rise of the FN, and a plethora of other parties like it, nor did he foresee how their emergence would reshape

---

[2] *Guardian*, July 26, 1984.
[3] *Economist*, April 30, 1988.
[4] *Independent*, November 26, 1991.
[5] *New York Times*, October 7, 1990.

European party systems. Some observers, frightened by the electoral success of the radical right, went to the other extreme, predicting fundamental political change from what proved to be only transitory electoral breakthroughs. Many scholars of German politics, for example, believed in the early 1990s that the radical right Republicans (Republikaner, REP) would become a permanent fixture in the party landscape. They have, to an extent, but given their underwhelming electoral performance since then (0.4% in the last federal election), the party can hardly be considered a meaningful presence. When New Democracy (Ny Demokrati, ND) became the third-largest party in the Swedish parliament (Riksdag) in 1991, many argued that Sweden was simply following in the steps of Denmark and Norway, where anti-tax parties had converted themselves into successful radical right ones several years earlier. But ND imploded after its electoral breakthrough, and by 2000 it was defunct. The attention lavished on parties like the FN, the Vlaams Belang (VB, formerly the Vlaams Blok), and the Austrian Freedom Party (FPÖ) has obscured the inability of other radical right parties to capture more than a couple of percentage points in national elections or even to survive after a particularly impressive electoral showing. The development of the radical right in Western Europe over the past quarter-century has thus been a story of failure as well as success.

That scholars and pundits were unable to predict with any accuracy in the 1980s, and even in the 1990s, the trajectories of radical right parties is not surprising. European states underwent a more or less common set of structural changes – the most important being an increase in ethnic heterogeneity – over this time period. And while these states and societies differed in important ways, they did possess enough in common for reasonable people to believe that they would respond to these changes in parallel ways. Hence, the success of a radical right party in one presaged consistent victories elsewhere. That this did not occur is puzzling.

Furthermore, when one looks more closely at the trajectories of radical right parties in particular sets of cases, it becomes clear that existing theories – which I review at length later – cannot account for the variation in their success across different regions or countries. For example, some theorize that specific electoral systems or economic crises act as catalysts for radical right success. Yet the same electoral rules in Flanders and Wallonia have not produced the same outcome: the radical right is strong in Flanders but weak in Wallonia. The latter has also been mired in a permanent economic crisis, while the former has done relatively well. Yet another theory suggests that rates of immigration in a given country determine the electoral fortunes of radical right parties. However, the theories of both electoral systems and immigration rates are contradicted by the example of the three Scandinavian countries, which use similar electoral systems and whose basic commonalities often make them the subject of structured-focused comparison. It is far from obvious why the radical right has thus far failed in Sweden, which has nearly twice the percentage of foreign-born residents as neighboring Norway and Denmark, where the radical right has succeeded.

The goal of this book is to explain the variation in the success of radical right parties across Western Europe. Although there are many ways of conceiving of success and failure, I use electoral persistence as my dependent variable and define success as receiving more than 5% of the vote in three successive national parliamentary elections.[6] This means that I am not concerned with explaining how radical right parties achieve their initial electoral breakthrough.[7] The reasons for these breakthroughs, however defined, have been so varied that they are probably better viewed as contingent events rather than the result of similar processes.[8] Since every party I examine in this book has experienced some form of electoral breakthrough, I take this event as my starting point rather than my outcome of interest. Electoral persistence does not overlap perfectly with other possible measures of success, such as representation in parliament, government participation, or influence on mainstream parties.[9] Yet since

---

[6] The election results for radical right parties since 1980 can be found in Appendix A. The reader will see that changing the 5% barrier by a couple of points in either direction, or looking at two national elections rather than three, does not lead to different codings.

[7] There is no common definition in the literature of what constitutes an electoral breakthrough. For some scholars, such as Mudde (2007: 301), it means winning enough votes to enter parliament. My view is that this is too restrictive a definition, as it would exclude cases such as the municipal elections in Dreux in 1983 that most scholars would agree represented a "breakthrough" for the FN. I would therefore define a breakthrough as an election in which a party receives enough votes to attract the attention of the media and other political parties.

[8] For example, the REP owed its breakthrough in the West Berlin elections of 1989 to a xenophobic television commercial that the local media seized upon and amplified. The FN's success in the town of Dreux in 1983 can be attributed largely to the efforts of Jean-Marie Stirbois and his wife, Marie-France, who had campaigned there for five years. The German DVU won nearly 13% in state elections in Sachsen-Anhalt in 1998 through an unprecedented mass mailing of propaganda material. The BNP won local representation in 2002 in towns that had recently experienced ethnic riots.

[9] For example, in France the FN has persisted electorally despite being effectively denied representation in the National Assembly. The VB is one of the largest parties in Flanders but has been shut out from government at every political level. Alternatively, the LPF did not persist electorally but certainly reshaped the public debate over immigration and integration.

electorally persistent parties also tend to succeed on these other dimensions, it makes sense to focus on this variable rather than on something else. Moreover, looking at persistence (or lack thereof) allows us to analyze the trajectories of radical right parties over the past quarter-century and to avoid overemphasizing any particular election result. While we are thus unable to fully account for the occasionally wild swings in their electoral support, taking the long view brings into sharp relief those forces that have created strong radical right parties in some countries and weak ones in others. A decade from now, the list of successes and failures might look very different: some of the parties I code as successes here (such as the Front National) appear to be in decline, and some new parties (perhaps the Party of Freedom in the Netherlands) may have consolidated themselves in their party systems. But while comparative historical analysis is obviously backward looking, my hope is that the lessons that emerge from this book will help us to understand future patterns. The case selection is explained toward the end of this chapter, but the cases themselves – eight cases of success and nine of failure – are summarized in Table 1.1.

Some of these parties will be familiar to anyone who has followed European politics over the past several decades. Others – particularly the ones that have failed – are more obscure, and one might wonder why I have spilled so much ink over parties that have left such a small political footprint. The reason, aside from the obvious methodological imperative in case study research of including variation on the dependent variable, is that unless the failures are examined, the success of radical right parties appears to be almost natural, and even theoretically uninteresting. Indeed, one could tell a relatively simple story about the rise of the radical right in which massive structural transformations – primarily postindustrialization, immigration, globalization, and European integration – generated a predictable and uniform backlash. Looking at cases in which radical right parties should have done well, but did not, helps us dismiss such deterministic arguments.

This book breaks with much of the literature on the radical right by taking a careful look at the parties themselves. Once we begin to look inside them, dramatic differences emerge between successful and unsuccessful cases. To put it bluntly, failed radical right parties have adhered to the so-called Pogo principle: "We have met the enemy, and it is us." Bitter factionalism, incompetence, criminal activity, organizational chaos, and a host of other internal pathologies have led to party implosion, oftentimes at the very moment that these parties had registered a large electoral gain.

TABLE 1.1. *Successful and Unsuccessful Radical Right Parties, 1980–2009*

Country	Party	Outcome
Austria	Austrian Freedom Party (FPÖ)	Success
Belgium (Flanders)	Vlaams Belang (VB)	Success
Denmark	Danish People's Party (DF)	Success
France	National Front (FN)	Success
Italy	National Alliance (AN)	Success
Italy	Northen League (LN)	Success
Norway	Progress Party (FrP)	Success
Switzerland	Swiss People's Party (SVP)	Success
Belgium (Wallonia)	Belgian National Front (FNb)	Failure
Germany	German National Party (NPD)	Failure
Germany	German People's Union (DVU)	Failure
Germany	Republicans (REP)	Failure
Great Britain	British National Party (BNP)	Failure
Netherlands	Center Democrats (CD)	Failure
Netherlands	List Pim Fortuyn (LPF)	Failure
Sweden	New Democracy (ND)	Failure
Sweden	Sweden Democrats (SD)	Failure

Note: Successful parties are those that received 5% in three successive national parliamentary elections. Unsuccessful parties are those that did not.

The radical right parties that persisted have not been entirely immune to these types of problems. Yet they not only have managed to weather them, but have also developed organizational capacities that rival, or even surpass, those of mainstream parties.

The question, of course, is what accounts for these differences. This book claims that the internal life of radical right parties – and, indeed, political parties in general – is shaped by the nature of their activists. While we know a great deal about radical right voters, we know extremely little about those people whose commitment to radical right politics goes far beyond casting a ballot every couple of years. With a few notable exceptions, scholars have treated the individuals who work on behalf of radical right parties as either homogeneous fanatics or the docile followers of a powerful, and often charismatic, leader. Yet radical right activists hold different ideas about immigration and parliamentary democracy. They have different visions of their parties and different levels of commitment to them. They come with different levels of education and political experience. Through a combination of comparative historical analysis, ethnographic research, and an analysis of an original data set of radical right candidates for office, this book demonstrates how the types of activists a party attracts ultimately determine its success or failure. Most important, it offers an explanation of why radical right parties attract the types of activists they do.

Although this book focuses on a particular type of political party, both the rise of these parties and my argument for their diverse trajectories have broader implications for the study of party politics in advanced industrial societies. This is not the place to recapitulate the debate over whether the political cleavages that Lipset and Rokkan (1967) described as "frozen" have thawed to the point where they are no longer useful in predicting contemporary voting behavior (for a review see Bornschier 2009) or whether new cleavages have replaced them (Kriesi et al. 2008; Van der Brug and Van Spanje 2009; Bornschier 2010). One thing, however, is clear: electoral volatility in Western democracies has increased over the past several decades (Drummond 2006). Party fortunes and individual electoral behavior have become far less predictable than in the past, and the effective number of parties has increased across advanced industrial societies (Dalton, McAllister, and Wattenberg 2002). Radical right parties – particularly those that use populist appeals – may be uniquely positioned to take advantage of this fluid electoral environment, since skillful use of the media and ideological flexibility have become two of their hallmarks (Poguntke 2002). Yet they are clearly not the only type of new party, even if they currently receive more academic attention than all other types of new parties combined. Green, regionalist, far left, center, liberal, and now even pirate parties have contested elections across Western Europe, and many have won seats in national legislatures.

Most of the literature on new parties is concerned with explaining their emergence (Harmel and Robertson 1985; Hug 2001; Tavits 2006) and, to a lesser extent, their electoral success. Given their novelty, it is not surprising that few scholars have tried to explain why some of them disappear while others persist or why their participation in government has thus far received little attention (an exception is Deschouwer 2008). If the argument in this book is correct, the electoral persistence of new parties will have less to do with sociostructural or institutional factors than with their ability to navigate successive developmental stages in their political life cycle (Pedersen 1982). Put another way, changes in the basic political cleavages of advanced industrial societies may have given new parties the opportunity to prosper in a more volatile electoral environment, but it is up to them to take advantage of this opportunity. In this less predictable world, agency matters more.

Over the past several decades, the personalization of elections – and, indeed, of politics writ large – across advanced industrial societies has produced a wave of research on its causes and consequences for democracy. The simple insight that some candidates for office are of higher quality than others has generated a large literature in the field of U.S. elections (Jacobson and Kernell 1983; Krasno 1994; Carson, Engstrom, and Roberts 2007). That campaigns are becoming more candidate centered, and that parliamentary systems are increasingly taking on some of the key features of presidential systems, has attracted the attention of scholars of European electoral behavior as well (Poguntke and Webb 2005; McAllister 2007). Radical right parties would seem to fit particularly well into this literature on the personalization of politics. Indeed, perhaps the most popular explanation for the rise of radical right parties is that they are led by charismatic personalities who exert nearly dictatorial control over their organizations. Although I, like others (Van der Brug and Mughan 2007), take issue with the charismatic leader thesis, this book looks closely at the difference that individuals make in both winning elections and building viable parties.

In sum, the study of the radical right is important for understanding broader trends in contemporary party politics. Yet because this book deals exclusively with radical right parties, it is also necessary to justify their real-world importance. This is something that scholars studying the radical right have not often paused to consider, in part because there have always been enough politicians and commentators warning, in apocalyptic fashion, that its rise prefigures a return to the politics of the interwar period or, somewhat less hysterically, that it threatens to undermine the quality of European democracy. The fourteen member states of the European Union appeared to endorse the latter view when they placed sanctions on Austria after a radical right party (the Austrian Freedom Party) joined a coalition government in February 2000. But after six months of refusing to appear in photos with their Austrian counterparts, EU politicians dispatched a crew of three "wise men" to determine whether minorities were suffering under the new government. They were not, the report concluded, nor was the FPÖ dismantling Austrian democracy. Radical right parties that have been parts of governments elsewhere in Europe, or who have propped up minority governments in Denmark and Norway, have not behaved much differently. Moreover, since radical right parties have been denied the reins of government even in places where they are electorally strong, like France and Flanders, it is reasonable to ask whether and how they matter.

Yet the fact that radical right parties are not threatening to overturn liberal democracy does not mean that they are not important or that their differential success across Europe will not produce lasting consequences. Indeed, they have been both the products and agents of some of the most fundamental changes in European politics over the past several decades. Most strikingly, immigration has turned nation-states that were formerly homogeneous into ones with large minority populations; the rise of the radical right would have been inconceivable without this basic social transformation. At the same time, the radical right is profoundly influencing how European states and societies negotiate the issues that immigration has introduced. Even when they have not been in power, radical right parties have shown a startling ability to set the agenda on issues such as asylum, immigration quotas, integration requirements, and citizenship laws (Williams 2006; Howard 2009). Mainstream parties seeking to co-opt the radical right have instituted policies that they otherwise might not have. Furthermore, in the cases where they have exercised power at the national level – such as Austria, Denmark, and Italy – radical right parties have largely succeeded in making immigration policies more restrictive (Van Spanje 2010). Since these policies will shape the nature and pace of immigration over the coming decades, it is likely that variation in radical right success will produce enduring differences in the ethnic composition of European societies.

In addition to policy changes, the radical right influences the ongoing public debates in European states about immigration, integration, and national identity. Politicians facing strong radical right parties have often tried to co-opt them by integrating elements of their discourse. Jacques Chirac's references in the 1980s to the "smells" emanating from immigrant households was in part a response to Le Pen, as was Nicolas Sarkozy's tough talk on law and order and preserving national identity in the 2007 presidential election. Pim Fortuyn's attacks on Islam provoked an intense public debate in the Netherlands about the compatibility between it and Dutch political culture that continues to this day.

As noted earlier, the growth of the radical right, along with the libertarian left (or the Greens), also marked a historic transition in European party systems that had been "frozen" since before the Second World War (Lipset and Rokkan 1967). The ties that had inextricably bound certain social groups to specific political parties loosened for many reasons: postindustrialization and the growth of the service sector eroded the power of unions and, by extension, the link between workers and Social Democratic parties; secularization cut into the base of Christian

...ocratic parties; new forms of mass media (particularly television) rendered voters less dependent on all types of political parties for information while simultaneously promoting more candidate-centered political campaigns. The radical right has been a beneficiary of this electoral dealignment and has at the same time accelerated it. By providing parties on the right with another coalition partner, the radical right has led to the bipolarization of party systems (Bale 2003; Mair 2008). In so doing, it has helped to alter patterns of policy making in European countries. The growth of the Austrian Freedom Party was aided by Austria's specific form of consociationalism, but has also undermined it. The politics of consensus in Denmark, and to a lesser extent in the Netherlands, has not been able to coexist with large radical right parties. Switzerland's "Magic Formula," under which four parties form a national coalition government, was first altered, and later broken, by the Swiss People's Party.

Finally, the radical right also clearly matters for the course of European integration. Although their positions toward the European Union have shifted over time, most of these parties have become deeply skeptical of the integration process. In France, the National Front played an important role in helping to defeat the referendum on the EU constitution in 2005. One can imagine radical right parties mounting similar campaigns if, and when, EU member states call on their citizens to vote on future issues. Some scholars have even argued that the rise of the radical right is a by-product of European integration itself (Berezin 2009).

Defining the Radical Right

The term "radical right" requires an immediate definition, particularly since scholars have used a number of designations – extreme right, right-wing populist, far right, to name a few – to refer to the same basic party family. In this book, I use "far right" as an umbrella term for any political party, voluntary association, or extraparliamentary movement that differentiates itself from the mainstream right. The term is problematic for a number of reasons, but given its wide usage it is a convenient way of referring to political movements across time and space. "Radical right" refers to a specific type of far right party that began to emerge in the late 1970s. This term, too, is potentially misleading because parties that have carried the adjective "radical" include left-liberal parties in nineteenth-century France and Italy, as well as anticommunist conservative movements in the postwar United States. However, since there has been a convergence around the term in the literature, I will use it rather than invent another.

My definition draws from Betz (1994) and Mudde (2007), who both identify an ideological core of this party family.[10] For Betz, these parties are on the right because they reject individual and social equality, oppose the integration of marginalized groups, and make xenophobic appeals. Neoliberalism is the economic dimension of this ideology, while nativism forms its cultural component. For reasons that will become clear later, culture has trumped economics as the signature feature of the radical right. A minority of these parties adhere to a biological form of racism, which holds that some ethnic groups are genetically superior to others. The majority tend more toward ethnopluralism, which does not posit a racial hierarchy but holds that the mixing of ethnic groups creates insurmountable problems. But they all see ethnic differences as basic, immutable, and impervious to political projects that seek to change them. From this follows their demand that immigration be dramatically reduced or even reversed through deportation, which has led some scholars to describe these parties simply as anti-immigrant (Van der Brug, Fennema, and Tillie 2005). The subtitle of this book recognizes the centrality of this idea to radical right parties. Yet it is important to note that radical right parties also seek to defend the nation from forces other than immigration, such as globalization and European integration.

The foregoing features are clearly not confined to radical right parties: mainstream conservative parties, and even some social democratic ones, have made nationalist and xenophobic appeals. To further distinguish them, we need to focus on their "radical" nature. There is clearly a discursive component here: radical right parties use language that mainstream parties would normally shy away from. But there is a deeper critique of liberal democracy in this radicalism as well. Although they regularly pledge their allegiance to the democratic system, in some cases to avoid being banned by state authorities, they are clearly at odds with its central liberal features, such as pluralism, the protection of minorities from the will of the majority, and checks on executive authority (Mudde 2007).

Although both Mudde and Betz view populism as a defining feature of this party family, I choose not to limit my definition in this way, for two reasons. First, since radical right parties have been part of national coalitions or supported minority governments in six European states (Austria, Denmark, Italy, the Netherlands, Norway, and Switzerland), it

---

[10] The two authors use different terms, however: "right-wing populist" (Betz) and "radical right-wing populist" (Mudde).

has become increasingly difficult for them to claim that they are not part of the governing elite, as populists normally do.[11] Second, while it is true that most radical right parties divide their societies into the "people," who are wise, authentic, and honest, and the elite, who are intellectual, degenerate, and corrupt, this bifurcation of society constitutes an explicit critique of parliamentary democracy and is therefore already implied in the "radical" nature of these parties.

Defining the radical right broadly means that I treat parties like the Norwegian Progress Party (FrP) and the British Nationalist Party (BNP) as different manifestations of the same basic phenomenon. This may strike specialists as odd. After all, the FrP has arguably downplayed nativism and stressed neoliberalism, while the BNP is biologically racist and anti-capitalist. Yet in order to understand why the radical right has succeeded in some places and not in others, we need to explain why these parties have taken different forms in different contexts. By adopting a broad definition and allowing for a high degree of internal variation within it, we are able to address this question, one to which there is no shortage of possible answers. Fortunately, there has been a progression in the field, as some initially plausible hypotheses that did not withstand empirical tests were subsequently rejected by most specialists. To clear space for my own explanation, it is important to first review these alternatives.

Demand Factors: Necessary but Not Sufficient

The initial wave of literature on the radical right tried to explain why parties that "mobilize resentment" (Betz 1994) emerged at around the same time in some of the world's wealthiest and best-governed democracies. Most of these studies argued that societal changes were responsible for the regeneration of the postwar far right. Some authors claimed that postindustrialization had created a reservoir of "modernization losers" who suffered from the status anxieties that Lipset saw as crucial to the rise of fascist parties (Lipset 1960). Others argued that the rise of post-materialist values (Inglehart 1977) had provoked a backlash, or "silent counterrevolution" (Ignazi 1992), among those who disagreed with the ideology of the new left. The massive increase in immigrant populations and asylum seekers contributed to both these trends; immigrants increased the sense of insecurity among the so-called modernization losers and made the core issues of the radical right more politically salient.

---

[11] It is true that some of these parties have adopted strategies for appearing to be outsiders while in – or close to – government. See Albertazzi and McDonnell (2005).

With these macrosocial changes in mind, scholars then turned to the microlevel to identify the characteristics of the radical right electorate. As a result of these studies, we now know a great deal about the "median" radical right voter. *He* (there is a large gender gap; for analysis see Givens 2004; Arzheimer and Carter 2006) possesses some education but not an advanced degree (Lubbers, Gijberts, and Scheepers 2002; Arzheimer and Carter 2006), is employed in either a low-skilled or semiskilled industry in the private sector (Evans 2005), and has negative attitudes toward foreigners and a low degree of trust in the political system (Norris 2005).

What this literature failed to do, however, was to create any scholarly consensus about the relationship between sociostructural variables and cross-national variation in the radical right's electoral performance (see Arzheimer 2009 for a review). For example, while some scholars discovered a positive relationship between unemployment and votes for the radical right (Jackman and Volpert 1996), others found that correlation to be negative (Knigge 1998; Lubbers et al. 2002; Arzheimer and Carter 2006). Similarly, while several scholars identified a positive correlation between high levels of immigration and support for radical right parties (Knigge 1998; Gibson 2002; Lubbers et al. 2002), others discovered no relationship whatsoever (Kitschelt 1995; Norris 2005).

Although these disputes were in part the product of different research designs and codings of cases, the more recent literature on the radical right has largely rejected the proposition that "demand-side" variables (the factors that shape the electorate's demand for radical right parties) provide sufficient explanations for cross-national variation. According to Van der Brug et al. (2005: 563), "[S]ociostructural developments within the European Union are so similar in all member states that those developments cannot explain the enormous differences in aggregate support for anti-immigrant parties." Mudde (2007), Norris (2005), Givens (2005), and Carter (2005) reach a similar conclusion. Thus, while demand-side factors – particularly immigration – appear to be necessary for the rise of the radical right, they are certainly not sufficient for electoral success. Although most authors have used statistical techniques to demonstrate the insufficiency of demand-side explanations, even a brief survey of the cases suggests that there are simply too many outliers – given the small number of cases – to make demand-side explanations compelling. For example, if rates of immigration are fundamentally important, how can we explain the lack of a successful radical right party over the long term in high-immigration countries like Germany, the Netherlands, or Sweden? If unemployment is crucial, why have these same countries not produced durable radical right parties, given that each has suffered from long periods of high unemployment over the past several decades? And why have radical right parties succeeded in states where unemployment has been quite low since the early 1980s, such as Austria, Norway, and Switzerland?

Rather than varying from country to country, it thus appears that there is a persistent demand among voters for radical right parties across Europe, both in states where they have achieved success and in those where they have not. For a generation of Europeans, and for many scholars of European politics, the appeal of parties that mobilize nationalist, xenophobic, and populist sentiment may seem surprising. But there are a number of reasons for rejecting the view that individual preferences for radical right politics are puzzling at all. First, both common sense and scholarly research tell us that there are a certain number of individuals in any society who possess authoritarian attitudes (Stenner 2005). Although reasonable people can disagree over whether they constitute 5% or 15% of the population, and whether that percentage might be slightly higher in some European states than in others, the important point is that there are enough of them to make a party that expresses their attitudes viable.

Second, public opinion polls consistently reveal high levels of racism and xenophobia across Europe. A *Eurobarometer* poll released at the end of the European Union's "European Year Against Racism" in 1997 found that the public relations campaign had most likely been in vain: 65% of Europeans agreed with the statement that "our country has reached our limits; if there were to be more people belonging to these minority groups we would have problems."[12] Nearly one-third of Europeans described themselves as "quite racist" or "very racist," and one in five believed that all non-EU immigrants (including legal immigrants) should be sent back to their country of origin.[13] A *Eurobarometer* survey in 2000 recorded no change in views on deportation, but also found that more than 50% of Europeans agreed with the statements that minority groups "abuse the system of social welfare," "are a reason for unemployment," and "are more involved in criminality than average."[14] Although there is some variation between European states in mass attitudes toward immigrants, it is clear that a significant percentage of Europeans tend to support positions on immigration that are close to those of the radical right. One

[12] *Eurobarometer* 47.1 (1997).
[13] *Eurobarometer* 47.1 (1997). Since the European Union didn't conduct a similar study before the campaign began, it is difficult to measure its effects.
[14] *Eurobarometer* 53 (2000).

reaches the same basic conclusion when evaluating the results of several questions from the European Social Survey (ESS) of 2002, the only wave thus far to ask questions about immigration.[15]

Third, is it at all puzzling that the losers of postmodernization or globalization may harbor resentment toward the political establishment? In times of rapid change, would we not expect that political parties that lambaste the elite and offer simple solutions to complex problems would emerge as representatives of the "common man"? While populism is a concept that defies easy definition, it is a timeless element of democratic politics, and waves of populist mobilization have occurred in the United States, Latin America, and now Europe. Moreover, as mass party organizations have disappeared and partisan loyalties have declined, is it any wonder that voters are attracted to the boisterous, and often entertaining, radical right leaders who routinely outperform their rivals in what have become permanent, media-dominated election campaigns?

Finally, the rise of cartel parties that collude with each other, and the state, to ensure their own survival (Katz and Mair 1995) has not been lost on European voters, and it is not surprising that they may be attracted to new parties that promise to break up such cozy arrangements.

Indeed, it was the first three decades of the postwar period, rather than the previous three, that were anachronistic, in that far right parties were, with several notable exceptions, marginal players.[16] The "thirty glorious years," as the French refer to the period from the end of the war to the 1970s, was a historical epoch whose defining economic and political features are unlikely to be reproduced. A period of rapid economic growth, a dramatic increase in living standards across social classes, an expansion of the welfare state, and the insulation of national economies from international economic forces are each exceptional events; their concurrence is historically unique. Far right parties have been a feature of party systems since the beginning of mass politics; there is no reason to believe that they will not continue to be in the future.

Once we shift our perspective and assume that radical right parties *should* win a sizable share of the vote in Western European states, it is their failure to do so that becomes the interesting question. There are clearly a number of factors other than voter demand that influence the success and failure of the radical right. These have been termed "supply-side" explanations and come in several forms.

---

[15] See Rydgren (2008) for a cross-national analysis of the relevant ESS questions.
[16] Hossay and Zolberg (2002: 304) make a similar point.

Electoral Institutions

Many scholars have turned to electoral institutions to explain cross-national variation in the radical right's success (Jackman and Volpert 1996; Golder 2003). The basic idea is that systems with high effective thresholds make it difficult for small parties to win seats and votes. The clearest difference is obviously between majoritarian systems with single-member districts (SMD) and systems that use proportional representation (PR). Not surprisingly, if one defines seats won by radical right parties as the dependent variable, majoritarian systems have a straightforward mechanical effect (Norris, 2005). For example, despite consistently winning around 10% of the vote, the French National Front has won only a couple of seats in the National Assembly since 1988. France's two-round majoritarian system allows other parties to coordinate in the second round to prevent FN candidates from winning seats. However, France's majoritarian system has clearly not prevented the FN from winning a significant percentage of votes. In fact, several studies have found that there is no statistically significant relationship between the type of electoral system (SMD or PR) and voteshare for the radical right (Carter 2005; Norris 2005; Van der Brug et al. 2005).

Comparisons among PR systems also do not confirm the conventional wisdom that systems with greater disproportionality decrease votes for the radical right (Carter 2002). Using the cases of Austria, Belgium, Denmark, France, Germany, Italy, and Norway in their analysis, Arzheimer and Carter found that the chances of voting for the extreme right actually *increase* as the disproportionality of the electoral system increases (Arzheimer and Carter 2006). Excluding France, and thus including only PR systems, did not change the results. To explain this counterintuitive finding, the authors suggest that radical right voters either are not aware of the consequences of electoral systems or do not care about them.

Finally, it bears emphasizing that political actors can change electoral institutions. There are certainly cases in which politicians have altered the rules of the game and produced the desired effect on radical right parties. The most well known example of this occurred in 1986 when France's Socialist president, François Mitterrand, seeking to strengthen the National Front and thereby damage his conservative competitors, changed the electoral system from two-round majoritarianism to PR. While it is unclear whether this increased the National Front's voteshare, it certainly increased its seats, and thereby its presence and legitimacy in the French political system (Schain 1987). A less well known example of institutional tweaking occurred in the Netherlands when the government raised the number of signatures required to contest districts from 190 to 570. In contrast to the situation in France, this change was designed to weaken the radical right. The new rules did prevent the Center Democrats (CD) from running in two electoral districts and pushed their voteshare below the 0.67% threshold required for representation in parliament (Van Donselaar 2000: 37–9). In these and other cases, institutional changes reflected the broader strategies of mainstream political actors toward the radical right, either in attempts to deny them power or, alternatively, to use them to divide and weaken more moderate conservative electoral competitors.

The Winning Formula

Rejecting institutional and demand-side explanations, Kitschelt (1995) focuses on the policies of radical right parties to explain what looked like emerging patterns of success and failure in the early 1990s. Specifically, Kitschelt argues that electoral success was the result of radical right parties following a "winning formula" that combined xenophobia with economic liberalism. This created a cross-class constituency of anti-immigrant blue-collar workers and certain white-collar workers who wanted less state intervention in the economy. Only by mobilizing both groups, Kitschelt argues, could radical right parties be successful. Although it gained wide currency in the field, one problem with this theory soon became apparent as most radical right parties jettisoned their neoliberal elements in favor of welfare chauvinism (Mudde 2000; Lubbers 2001). It is also questionable whether economics was ever central to these parties' programs and whether neoliberalism was just one of multiple economic programs – in addition to protectionism and welfare chauvinism – that radical right parties promised in order to maximize their votes (Mudde 2007).

One could still claim that this neoliberal rhetoric, even if it was less salient than Kitschelt implies, was enough to win the votes of a constituency that favored less state intervention. One group that fits this profile is small business owners, and there is in fact an abundance of empirical evidence showing that this group, along with blue-collar workers, is overrepresented in the radical right electorate. The strong support of blue-collar workers for a party that, according to Kitschelt, supports neoliberal policies is curious. To explain this unlikely coalition, scholars have argued that workers have become either less connected to (Kitschelt 1994) or disillusioned with (Betz 1998b) the left and their economic views have ted toward neoliberalism. This economic realignment thesis contends that the economic preferences of workers and small business owners have become aligned in recent years, and this explains the success of radical right parties.

Ivarsflaten (2005) tests this argument on the two cases, Denmark and France, that realignment theorists claim best fit their theory. She finds no support for the economic realignment hypothesis at all. Instead, what unites small business owners and blue-collar workers are not economic preferences but agreements on issues regarding law and order and immigration. Since members of both groups tend not to be highly educated, and since education correlates strongly with positive attitudes toward immigration, it is similar educational attainment rather than economic alignment that has created this "unlikely coalition." In more recent work, Ivarsflaten (2008) finds that the only grievances that all successful radical right parties mobilize are those over immigration. In sum, differences in economic policy do not appear to explain patterns of success and failure.

Ideology

One of the merits of Kitschelt's argument is that it considers radical right parties to be masters of their own fate (see also De Lange 2007a). In his view, some parties offered policies that were attractive to a relatively broad section of the electorate, while others were committed to ideological positions that appealed to only a narrow slice of it. Ignazi (1992) also distinguishes between an Old Right, whose primary reference point is either Italian fascism or German Nazism, and a new right, which does not carry such baggage (see also Cole 2005). Given that the former has been electorally insignificant (Golder 2003; Carter 2005), perhaps ideology or policy positioning explains cross-national patterns of success and failure.

I will not challenge the view that biologically racist and/or antidemocratic parties perform poorly in elections, and in this sense ideology does matter. Yet this argument is incomplete, as it does not explain *why* these parties stick with such positions when they are clearly election losers and do not instead adopt the "master frame" of ethnopluralism and antiestablishment populism that has been successful across Western Europe (Rydgren 2005b). Kitschelt (1995) is correct in noting that both history and the preferences of party members prevent parties of the old right from adopting a more "winning" ideology. Put another way, party ideology is a reflection of other underlying variables that we need to explore.

TABLE 1.2. *"New" Radical Right Party Types*

Authoritarian Xenophobic Parties	Neoliberal Xenophobic Parties
Austrian Freedom Party	Danish People's Party
Center Democrats	Northern League
Belgian National Front	*List Pim Fortuyn*
National Front	*New Democracy*
Republicans	Progress Party
Vlaams Blok/Belang	*Sweden Democrats*
	Swiss People's Party

Note: Unsuccessful parties in italic.

But what ideological differences exist within the "New Right" wing of the radical right? Following Carter (2005), one can divide these parties into two types: authoritarian xenophobic parties and neoliberal xenophobic parties. The major difference is that the former subtype seeks more state intervention in the economy and stronger powers for the executive, while the latter calls for less state intervention and tighter links between individuals and their parliamentary institutions. Table 1.2 divides the radical right parties covered in this book according to Carter's subtypes.[17]

The table makes clear that both subtypes include both successful and unsuccessful (in italic) parties, suggesting that ideology cannot explain differences in electoral performance, at least over the longer term. Furthermore, two of the unsuccessful parties clearly imitated the policy positions of their successful counterparts, to no avail. The Belgian Front National took not only the name and symbols of the French original, but its slogans and policies as well. Several members of the Sweden Democrats confided in interviews that they had modeled their party manifesto on that of the Danish People's Party.

The Argument in Brief

In sum, it remains an open question why radical right parties succeed or fail. To answer it, this book focuses on those people who do not just vote for radical right parties, but work actively on their behalf. This group includes everyone from party leaders, to elected representatives in local councils, to ordinary members whose level of involvement exceeds

[17] Carter does not include the SVP and LPF in her chart. These additions are justified in the case studies.

paying their yearly dues. Since there is no precise term for members of this group, I use the umbrella definition of "activist" to distinguish them from voters.

The basic argument is that the trajectories of radical right parties are shaped by the types and number of activists they recruit. On the basis of their attitudes and motivations, I develop a tripartite typology of radical right activists: *moderates, extremists,* and *opportunists.* I show, first theoretically and later empirically, how different distributions of these activists matter for party development. I also demonstrate how some parties are able to attract highly educated and experienced activists, while other parties recruit mostly activists with low socioeconomic status, little to no political experience, and nothing else to lose. The focus is thus on the microdynamics of party building. As scholars of civil war have demonstrated, fine-grained analyses offer distinct advantages over econometric ones when it comes to demonstrating causal mechanisms and testing microfoundations (Peterson 2001; Wood 2003; Kalyvas 2006; Weinstein 2007). This book draws inspiration from those studies, as well as from work in party politics that takes activists – and the skills they possess – seriously (Kitschelt 1989; Gryzmala-Busse 2002).

Both the size and nature of the activist core strongly influence a radical right party's ability to harness voter demand and to persist electorally. The following chapter draws on the literature linking party organization to voting behavior to isolate these general causal mechanisms. I show theoretically how five features of parties – size, cohesion, competence, legitimacy, and ideological flexibility – affect their electoral performance. Given the number of parties and elections this book covers, it was impossible to always demonstrate these links empirically; doing so would have required another book. Fortunately, other scholars have already done much of this work. For example, we have already seen that radical right parties that are not ideologically flexible and cling to fascist ideas have done very poorly at the polls. It also appears that party organization, a concept that includes my features of size, cohesion, and competence, is strongly correlated with electoral performance.[18] In her cross-national analysis, Elisabeth Carter found that party organization accounts for nearly one-half of the variance in the voteshare of radical right parties

---

[18] A number of scholars, such as Betz (1998), Norris (2005), Ellinas (2007), Kitschelt (2007), and Mudde (2007), have called attention to the importance of radical right party organization. Yet Carter's is the only cross-national quantitative study of the topic.

TABLE 1.3. *Expert Assessments of Radical Right Party Organizations: Successful versus Unsuccessful Parties*

	Country	Mean (2000)	Mean (2004)
Successful parties			
Vlaams Belang	Belgium (Flanders)	7.9	8.7
National Alliance	Italy	7.6	7.4
National Front	France	7.4	7.2
Swiss People's Party	Switzerland	6.8	8.6
Austrian Freedom Party	Austria	6.4	2.5
Danish People's Party	Denmark	5.5	8.5
Northern League	Italy	5.5	6.2
Norwegian Progress Party	Norway	5.3	7.4
Mean of successful parties		6.6	7.1
Unsuccessful parties			
Sweden Democrats	Sweden	4.3	3.4
British National Party	Great Britain	3.8	4.0
German People's Union	Germany	2.7	3.3
Belgian National Front	Belgium (Wallonia)	2.7	1.6
Republicans	Germany	2.1	3.6
Mean of unsuccessful parties		3.1	3.2

Note: Experts were asked to assign a numerical score to the strength of the party's organization from 0 (the lowest) to 10. The means are the averages of the experts' assessments.
Source: Lubbers (2001) and Van Spanje, Mair, Van der Brug, and Van der Eijk (2004).

over the past two decades (Carter 2005).[19] In addition, the results of expert surveys, in which respondents rated the strength of organization from 0 (lowest) to 10 (highest), reveal a high correlation between levels of party organization and electoral success.[20] The means for 2000 (overall mean 5.9) and 2004 (overall mean 6.2) are reported in Table 1.3.

While electoral persistence is the ultimate dependent variable, this is a book about the internal life of radical right parties rather than electoral behavior. Its goal is not only to demonstrate how different distributions of activists affect party development, but to account for these differences in the first place. I argue that two master variables explain variation in radical right personnel: both are necessary for electoral persistence, and neither alone is sufficient.

The first is *the nature of preexisting resources for radical right party building*. This variable captures historical legacies and requires us to

[19] Carter codes organizational strength on the basis of the secondary literature.
[20] In Chapter 2, I argue that causation does not run in the opposite direction.

ight landscape in Western European countries from the
the 1970s. The second is *the reaction, and particu-
᷍tion, of other political parties and civil society to the*
ɟ*radical right parties.* It concerns the political opportunity
᷍ure, and more specifically the incentive structure shaping activist
recruitment, and demands a detailed analysis of the interaction between
the radical right and other political and social actors since the early 1980s.
Putting the two variables together, my explanation is similar to that of
Doug McAdam's (1982) for the rise of the civil rights movement in the
United States. For McAdam, social movements require both their own
"indigenous resources" and a degree of cooperation from other political and social actors to succeed.[21] Given that radical right parties often
emerge from social movements, and given that they often view themselves
as challengers to the existing order, it is both useful and appropriate to
apply this broad framework from social movement theory to them.

Historical legacies provided the indigenous resources, or the means, for
radical right party building. This is a fundamental point that most of the
literature on the radical right has overlooked.[22] Indeed, when they first
appeared, most scholars were quick to point out that radical right parties did not represent a revival of interwar fascism. Although this was an
important public service in the context of magazines juxtaposing pictures
of Jörg Haider and Adolf Hitler on their covers, the rejection of misplaced
comparisons has produced a strangely ahistorical view of radical right parties. While these parties were the product of sociostructural changes that
became apparent only in the late 1970s and 1980s, it is wrong to assume
that all of them emerged from thin air. Some did, to be sure, such as the
List Pim Fortuyn in the Netherlands and New Democracy in Sweden. Yet
these "flash" parties, largely because they were required to build organizations de novo, quickly disappeared from the party landscape.

Most other radical right parties tried to build on a preexisting foundation: a foundation that could be either helpful or destructive. Helpful
foundations came in two varieties. The first was another type of political

[21] McAdam also notes the importance of broad socioeconomic processes and cognitive
liberation for the emergence of social movements in his political process model. In my
explanation, immigration constitutes the primary socioeconomic change. Cognitive liberation does not have a functional equivalent, although the rising political salience of
immigration is similar to it. I am grateful to Erik Bleich for pointing out the similarities
between my explanation and McAdam's.

[22] Kitschelt (1995) refers explicitly to the legacies of history in several case studies, a point
that is often lost in the reduction of his study to the "winning-formula" thesis. Mudde
(2007) also mentions the importance of nationalist subcultures.

party that radical right entrepreneurs transformed from within. The second was a strong nationalist subculture that was not confined to a small number of fascist nostalgics. Every single successful radical right party in Western Europe was built using one of these two types of indigenous resources. Destructive foundations also took two forms. The first, which was unique to Germany, was a large extremist subculture that handicapped efforts to build a modern radical right party. The second, which prevailed in several countries in Western Europe, was a tiny and balkanized extremist subculture that nonetheless managed to derail radical right party building in spite of its small size. Thus history mattered, but not because a strong fascist heritage translated into a strong radical right party. The story, as we shall see, was more complex.

At some point, the initial reservoir of activists was more or less exhausted, and parties needed to attract new people in order to survive. Their ability to do this depended on the interaction between mainstream actors and the radical right, another factor that most of the literature on the radical right has overlooked.[23] These reactions differed dramatically across both time and space. When parties erected so-called *cordons sanitaires* (agreements not to cooperate with them) and groups in civil society made life for their members difficult, radical right parties had a great deal of trouble attracting both the number and type of people necessary to build a viable party. In fact, these reactions created an incentive structure whereby only activists who either were extremist or had nothing to lose were willing to bear the costs of membership. When potential radical right activists faced neither political marginalization nor social stigmatization, however, parties were able to recruit the type of people they needed.

The initial reaction of the mainstream to a radical right electoral breakthrough was more important – at least for the internal development of the party – than subsequent ones. For example, when cordons sanitaires were constructed from the moment a radical right party became visible, they were very effective. However, when parties decided to institute a cordon sanitaire after a radical right party had already established itself as a force in the political landscape, as in Flanders and France, they were not able to effectively marginalize it, as it was difficult to retroactively discredit its legitimacy. Moreover, it was entirely possible for a cordon

---

[23] Although still underresearched, the effects of the cordon sanitaire and the interaction between mainstream parties and radical right challengers have been explored in several studies. See, e.g, Kestel and Godmer 2004; Meguid 2005; Van Spanje and Van der Brug, 2007.

sanitaire to exist alongside a social environment in which radical right activists were treated as normal and legitimate members of society.

To summarize, a combination of historical legacies and the costs and benefits of radical right activism determined both the number and nature of radical right activists. Depending on the distribution of activists within them, radical right parties were either able to transform voter demand into sustained electoral success or completely unable to harness this demand over the longer run. Successful radical right parties were thus not the automatic products of socioeconomic change, favorable electoral institutions, or any other set of factors that can be easily disaggregated from the particular histories and political cultures in which they operated. Understanding the radical right requires us to look closely at these historical legacies and incentive structures in search of common patterns.

Concepts, Cases, and Sources of Evidence

I use this argument to explain the development of radical right parties in twelve polities in Western Europe: Austria, Denmark, Flanders, France, Germany, Great Britain, Italy, the Netherlands, Norway, Sweden, Switzerland, and Wallonia. I have restricted my cases to Western European states that share the following characteristics: (1) the percentage of the immigrant population within them has averaged more than 2% between 1990 and 2002, (2) they have been democratic since 1945, and (3) they have a population greater than 1 million.

Restricting the cases to those with "significant" immigration is necessary because an anti-immigrant platform is a defining feature of radical right parties. Immigration is thus a necessary condition for radical right success, although it is clearly not a sufficient one. Setting the threshold of significant immigration at a 2% average between 1990 and 2002 excludes those states – Finland, Ireland, Spain, and Portugal – that are generally perceived to have experienced little immigration over this time period. While it is true that immigration has been increasing in all of these states, it is too soon to analyze the success or failure of radical right parties in them. I have also excluded the European microstates on the grounds that they are not inherently comparable with larger states. Finally, I have excluded Greece because it, along with Spain and Portugal, has enjoyed uninterrupted democracy for only about three decades. Although these are certainly consolidated democracies today, they were not during the period when radical right parties emerged in the advanced industrial democracies of Northern and Western Europe. I have also added a case by splitting Belgium into Flanders and Wallonia. This is necessary because Belgium lacks a national party system and parties compete exclusively in one region or the other, aside from the complex situation in Brussels.

This book does not consider cases from Central and Eastern Europe, even though radical right parties have emerged as major players there in the past two decades (Ramet 1999; Lewis 2001; Mudde 2005, 2007). The primary reason for this omission is that the fluidity of party systems in the region makes it difficult to compare them with those in the West. In addition, parties in general are far less organized in Central and Eastern European countries (CEECs), rendering it difficult to apply any explanation that privileges organizational attributes to that context. Moreover, although Mudde is correct in noting that their nativism places them in the radical right party family (Mudde 2007), they do not share the anti-immigrant positions that have been the defining feature of their counterparts in the West. Thus while it is possible that the thesis I develop in this book can help explain variation in the strength of radical right parties in the CEECs, these cases lie outside the bounds of this study.

Although national context is central to my argument, it is the party rather than the country that is the unit of analysis. There is a broad consensus about most of the parties that scholars place in the radical right family. There are some borderline cases, however, that raise questions about comparing apples and oranges. Most of these fall under the category of what Carter (2005) terms neoliberal xenophobic parties and Mudde (2007) calls neoliberal populist parties.[24] The debate, as the difference in terms reveals, is whether such parties hold strong enough anti-immigrant positions to qualify for membership in the radical right family.

The results of an expert survey demonstrate that Carter's view is the dominant one.[25] Experts were asked in 2004 to rank the immigration positions of political parties on a scale from 0 to 10, with 0 being the least restrictive and 10 being the most restrictive. This study replicated the question Lubbers posed in his 2001 expert survey, and the results are reported in Table 1.4.

Although these surveys unfortunately do not cover all the parties in this book, they make clear that the various types of neoliberal parties have a strong nativist streak, given that the means of all political parties

[24] See Table 1.2.
[25] The survey is titled "Party Politics in Contemporary Western Europe: An Expert Survey Replicating Marks and Steenbergen (1999) and Lubbers (2001)" and was conducted by Joost van Spanje, Peter Mair, Wouter van der Brug, and Cees van der Eijk. I thank Joost van Spanje for providing me with the data.

TABLE 1.4. *Expert Survey of Party Positions in Immigration:*
Neoliberal Radical Right Parties versus Authoritarian
Xenophobic Radical Right Parties

	Mean (2000)	Mean (2004)
Neoliberal parties		
Danish People's Party	9.7	9.4
Norwegian Progress Party	9.2	8.4
Northern League	9.0	9.5
Sweden Democrats	9.7	9.8
Swiss People's Party	9.1	8.9
Group mean	9.3	9.2
Authoritarian parties		
Austrian Freedom Party	9.1	9.6
Belgian Front National	9.8	9.8
British National Party	9.9	9.7
Front National	9.6	10.0
German People's Union	9.8	9.8
National Alliance	7.9	7.8
Republicans	9.4	9.6
Vlaams Belang	9.8	9.9
Group Mean	9.4	9.5

Note: Experts were asked to assign a score to the positions of radical
right parties toward immigration, with 10 being the most restrictive. The
means are the averages of the experts' scores.
Source: Lubbers (2001) and Van Spanje, Mair, Van der Brug, and Van der
Eijk (2004).

in 2000 and 2004 were 5.42 and 5.44, respectively. Only the National
Alliance (AN) in Italy was significantly less restrictive than other parties,
but this was because it had migrated from a radical right family to a
mainstream conservative one several years before.

The data for this book come primarily from three sources. First, it
draws on 140 interviews that I conducted with radical right activists across
Western Europe. Like the very few scholars who have spoken extensively
with activists (Ivaldi 1996; Klandermans and Mayer 2006; Goodwin
2007a), I found no support for the common perception that radical right
parties deny access. Given the dearth of information on the internal lives
of many radical right parties, the interviews were critical for constructing
case studies of their development. Potential biases and validity questions,
of course, are inherent in political interviewing. Randomness was simply

not feasible, particularly in cases such as Wallonia, in which the hard core of the Belgian National Front consisted of a dozen or so individuals and tracking them down was a major undertaking. Nor was randomness desirable when I wanted to learn about specific events in the party's history from the participants themselves.

Second, I compiled an original data set of radical right candidates for office, which I supplemented with data on radical right activists from other sources, to construct a social profile of radical right parties. To make comparisons across cases, I used the International Standard Classification of Occupations, 1988 (ISCO-88) to code professions. While these data do not allow us to distinguish activists on the basis of ideology or political experience, they do demonstrate that radical right activists differ along at least one important dimension.

Third, this book draws on individual case studies of radical right parties. I use this secondary literature for cases in which it is particularly rich, such as the French Front National or the Italian Lega Nord, and for cases in which I could no longer interview the participants, such as the Dutch Center Party and the German National Democratic Party of the 1960s. In addition, I conducted several dozen interviews with specialists on the radical right. This group included scholars, but also journalists who have covered these parties in their respective countries for years. The secondary literature and my interviews with specialists serve as an additional check on the reliability of my other data.

Road Map

This introductory chapter has introduced the central puzzle, critiqued existing solutions to it, and outlined the research design. Chapter 2 develops the theoretical argument, while the rest of the book consists of case studies. Rather than adopting a country-by-country approach, which would require awkwardly grouping very different radical right parties – such as the Dutch Center Democrats and the List Pim Fortuyn – I structure the cases around different combinations of the two master variables of historical legacies (means) and reactions to the radical right (opportunity). Chapter 3 deals with failed parties that possessed neither means nor opportunity: the Belgian National Front, the Dutch Center Democrats, the Sweden Democrats, and the British National Party. These parties drew on small, extremist networks to construct their parties and faced highly repressive social and political environments. The analysis of these failures sets the stage for Chapter 4, which demonstrates how the combination of large nationalist subcultures and a (at least initially) permissive environment led to the success of the Vlaams Belang, Austrian Freedom Party, and French National Front. Chapter 5 examines radical right parties that had no connection to previous far right organizations and that were not marginalized. The difference was whether they had a means in the form of a preexisting political party, as was the case with the Danish People's Party, the Norwegian Progress Party, and the Swiss People's Party, or lacked any indigenous resources and tried to build a party from scratch, like the List Pim Fortuyn and New Democracy. Chapter 6 analyzes the two cases – Germany and Italy – in which the residue of indigenous fascist movements in the postwar period was much stronger than in other countries. It demonstrates how repression, both immediately after the war and when radical right parties appeared in the 1980s, produced extremist, balkanized, and generally incompetent parties in West Germany, while a more permissive environment has allowed the radical right to gain a foothold in the East. The Italian case documents changes in the opportunity structure over time, and how those changes affected the fortunes of the Italian Social Movement, the National Alliance of Italy, and the Lega Nord. The book concludes by placing the contemporary radical right in the broader context of extremist political movements and suggests how the arguments and methods adopted here can be applied to a wider range of cases.

2

Activists and Party Development

What are the critical differences among radical right activists? How do different types of activists influence a party's development and its electoral performance? What explains the variation in the number and type of activists across parties and across countries? This chapter addresses these three questions in turn and in so doing lays out the theoretical model that the case studies illustrate.

Although the argument is specific to radical right parties, it both draws from studies of other types of political parties and develops a set of general propositions that are also relevant to them. Rather than viewing parties through the lens of the unitary rational actor or the dichotomy of "leaders" and "followers," I divide activists into three ideal types based on their ideological motivations: extremists, moderates, and opportunists.[1] I also distinguish among activists on the basis of both their education and their political experience, under the assumption that some people bring

---

[1] My analysis of these activists resembles Kitschelt's (1989) theory of left-libertarian party behavior, which in turn follows Anthony Downs's (1967) analysis of bureaucracy. According to Kitschelt, whether left-libertarian parties decide to follow a "logic of constituency representation," and express the values and ideology of their organization regardless of electoral success, or a "logic of electoral competition" depends on the relative strength of three types of activists: ideologues, lobbyists, and pragmatists (49–55). The balance of power among these groups in turn depends on the political environment in which the party operates. My tripartite division of radical right activists is clearly different from Kitschelt's of left-libertarians, but the method of theory construction is similar. Kitschelt, it should be noted, does make a distinction between different kinds of radical right activists in his work on the radical right (1995), particularly in the German case, although party organization is not his primary concern.

a wider set of skills to party politics than do others.[2] The general distribution of activists within parties, I then argue, helps determine their ability to mount effective electoral campaigns, manage factionalism, exhibit
competence, gain legitimacy, and offer a message that maximizes the party's appeal among voters. Activists thus provide the microfoundations for
a theory of radical right party development. As stated previously, I take
it as a given that a combination of sociostructural changes in the 1970s
and 1980s – particularly the rising salience of immigration – led both to
voter demand for radical right parties and to the formation, or transformation, of parties to fill that demand. All of the parties that I cover in this
book benefited from an electoral breakthrough that gave them visibility, oftentimes out of proportion to what their electoral tallies deserved.
In addition, the dramatic success of some of these parties – particularly
the French National Front – provided models for party organization and
electoral strategy that could in principle be adopted. Yet it was the nature
of the activists that determined whether the opportunity could be seized
and the model successfully imitated.

After linking activists to electoral performance, this chapter analyzes
the two independent variables that influence the distribution of activists
within radical right parties. The first is the "indigenous resources" – other
political parties, voluntary organizations, social movements, informal networks – from which radical right parties recruited their initial core of personnel. In drawing on preexisting organized groups in society, radical right
parties were no different from Social Democratic, Christian Democratic,
and Green parties. And like parties in general, the origins of radical right
parties cast a long shadow over their subsequent development (Panebianco
1988). Absent certain historical legacies, it was simply not possible for
radical right parties to find the activists they needed to succeed. But these
initial means were not enough: radical right parties needed an opportunity
as well. This opportunity was supplied, or denied, by mainstream political
parties and social actors. By influencing the costs and benefits of radical
right activism, the external environment determined the number and type
of activists that radical right parties attracted.

The central argument is straightforward: a combination of historical legacies (the means) and actions by other political and social actors
(the opportunity) determines the building blocks of radical right parties,

---

[2] The argument here is similar to that of Gryzmała-Busse (2002), who claims that the
presence, or absence, of elites with "portable skills" explains the success and failure of
postcommunist parties in Central and Eastern Europe.

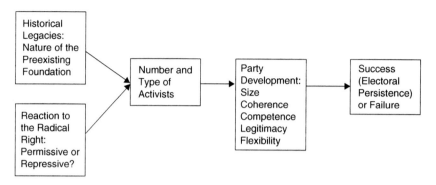

FIGURE 2.1. A model of radical right party development.

which in turn shape their internal development and ability to persist electorally. Yet because the argument has a number of moving parts, and because I begin with the activists and their effects before turning to the conditions that produced them, Figure 2.1 might prove a useful reference for the rest of this chapter.

Radical Right Activists

During my interviews and participant observations, I was constantly reminded of how poorly the world of radical right activism conforms to its popular perception as an undifferentiated mass of racists and street thugs. To be sure, I did meet a number of individuals who fit popular stereotypes: war veterans who made yearly pilgrimages to Waffen-SS reunions, conspiracy theorists who tried to convince me that Jews were in complete control of the international financial regime, and angry young men who boasted about their violent confrontations with left-wing activists. But I also met local politicians who had become concerned about the changing complexion of their neighborhoods, spouses who followed their partners into politics without developing deep political convictions of their own, and many people who had originally joined their party before it adopted an anti-immigrant program but who now agreed with its outlines. To this eclectic mix one could add sports stars and minor television celebrities looking to begin a political career, political wanderers who had burned their bridges with other parties, adventurers looking for a thrill, and people who possessed virtually no interest in politics whatsoever but were attracted by the small salary that often came with the post of communal councilor.

The world of radical right activism is thus heterogeneous: the multiple paths to activism, the various levels of commitment, and the diverse views and attitudes cannot be fully captured by any simple categorization. Yet an ideal typology can help preserve the essential variation among the population of radical right activists while allowing us to make certain generalizations. Although in practice many radical right activists possess attributes of the three types below, this tripartite typology provides the foundation for the general argument.

Extremists come in several forms, but what unites them is their hostility to, or outright rejection of, parliamentary democracy. Many of them are revolutionary and believe in the possibility of building a new authoritarian order. In the immediate postwar era, most extremists were unreconstructed fascists or Nazis. As this generation began to wane in the 1960s, a new cohort of militants mobilized against a rising tide of left-wing activism and resuscitated fascist and Nazi discourses and symbols. Since the 1970s, neo-Nazi youth movements have produced a third and fourth generation of extremists. These activists tend to subscribe to biological racism and condone, or even embrace, the use of violence against their purported enemies, particularly leftists and immigrants. They are also likely to be venomously anti-Semitic and to deny or trivialize the Holocaust. Extremists thus represent the most radical element within the far right landscape. Some have spent years reading and developing their political views, while others are motivated by simple, brute prejudice.

Moderates accept the democratic rules of the game. Although they may want to alter democratic institutions – by creating a presidential system or more direct democracy through referenda – they differ fundamentally from extremists in this respect. And although the designation may seem oxymoronic for radical right party members, the political views of this group in other matters are moderate compared with those of extremists. The defining characteristic of moderates is an adherence to ethnopluralism rather than to biological racism. Most are very careful to point out that they have nothing against other ethnic groups, but stress that the cohabitation of established native populations with new, culturally distinct immigrant groups inevitably leads to a host of irreconcilable problems.[3] They view themselves as defenders of their nation and culture rather than of their race. Unlike extremists, moderates outwardly reject any form of violence. They also normally condemn Nazism and fascism,

---

[3] Moderates are thus similar to the "immigration skeptics" that Rydgren (2008) differentiates from "racists" and "xenophobes" among radical right voters. Extremists are clearly closer to the latter two categories.

although their interpretations of the period often exonerate most of the population (including themselves and their predecessors) from massive violations of human rights. While not denying the Holocaust, they may often compare atrocities committed by other states, particularly Stalinist Russia, to those of the Nazis and their collaborators in an effort to release their nations from a singular burden.

Opportunists differ from extremists and moderates in that they do not generally emerge from far right subcultures. They may be political novices attracted by the radical right's general message or, more likely, by its electoral success. They may also be politicians from other parties that have failed to advance within them or have seen their star fall. Whatever their path to activism, opportunists tend to hold less coherent attitudes than either extremists or moderates. They are more interested in power, material benefits, visibility, and career advancement than they are in ideology.

In addition to their attitudes and motivations, activists differ along two other important dimensions. The first is their socioeconomic status (SES), which is a composite of their education, income, and occupation. Not only have radical right parties tried to recruit activists with the same SES as their median voters; they have also sought to attract their share of university-educated professionals and to place these activists in high-profile positions. This does not mean that activists with lower SES cannot make good candidates or leaders: Pia Kjaersgaard of the Danish People's Party, for example, has no university education and worked as a nurse before entering politics. Yet to the extent that education is correlated with a general set of skills that are helpful for party organization, campaigning, and parliamentary work, radical right parties benefit from having members with high SES.

The second dimension is political experience. Some radical right activists have long political careers that include service in national parliament or government. Others have no political experience whatsoever. To some extent, levels of experience are endogenous to electoral success: parties that win representation and participate in government obviously end up having members with a higher level of political experience than those that do not. Yet radical right parties also began their lives with different levels of experience among their activist core, and these initial differences affected their trajectories.

Activists, Parties, and Voters

The distribution of activists within radical right parties shapes their internal development, and ultimately their electoral performance, in four ways. But before we explore these mechanisms, it is important to note why the *number* of activists – irrespective of their type – matters as well. Some radical right parties are, in fact, empty shells with a miniscule number of active members, while others possess a genuine rank and file. To take two extreme cases, the French National Front was estimated to have close to forty thousand members in the mid-1990s, while the German People's Union could probably count only several hundred after its 1998 breakthrough in Sachsen-Anhalt.

The number of party activists matters for electoral performance, even in an age when parties rely increasingly on the media and public relations professionals to communicate with the public. The view that new technologies made parties less reliant on their members dates from at least V. O. Key's observation in the late 1950s that "the door-bell ringers have lost their function of mobilizing the vote to the public-relations experts, to the specialists in radio and television, and to others who deal in mass communication" (Key 1958: 376; quoted in Scarrow 1996: 88). Yet while technology has undoubtedly affected party organization, parties still count on their members to perform a number of crucial tasks. Scarrow finds that parties value the "outreach benefits" that members provide, and her description of these is worth quoting at length:

Party leaders may value members for the support they can mobilize by means of everyday contacts. For instance, those under the influence of theories such as Paul Lazarsfeld's two-step communication model may consider members who are local notables ("opinion leaders") to be particularly valuable, because such citizens are thought to routinely influence the political views of those in their communities [footnote in original text]. Others may view even non-notable members as potentially valuable ambassadors to the community, as people who can multiply votes through their willingness openly to declare, and even to explain, their personal allegiances. *Party members' everyday contacts may be especially valued in parties which are struggling to gain, or regain, public recognition and acceptance.* (Scarrow 1996: 46, emphasis mine)

Members are also important in producing the "campaign effects" that influence both voter turnout and vote intention in the United States (Iyengar and Simon 2000). Since mobilization efforts also appear to matter in Britain (Whiteley and Seyd 1994, 2003), Germany (Finkel and Schrott 1995), and Japan (Cox, Rosenbluth, and Thies 1998), there is reason to believe that campaigns matter in general. Hillygus (2005) argues that while mobilization efforts have only a marginal influence on those already planning to vote, they do raise turnout among those who had not planned on voting. This finding is potentially important for radical right parties, since they do better than most other parties among previous nonvoters.

While mobilization efforts include activities such as canvassing, direct mailing, and making telephone calls, Gerber and Green's (2000) experimental study suggests that only personal canvassing increases turnout. Empirical studies also show that canvassing raises voter turnout (Huckfeldt and Sprague 1992; Wielhouwer 1999; Niven 2004). If we assume that the reach of canvassing increases with the size of the party rank and file, which appears to be a safe assumption, then we can say that radical right parties with a large activist base possess a greater ability to mobilize potential radical right voters than do parties with a smaller rank and file. In other words, someone still has to put up the signs, man the information booths, and knock on doors. Elections can occasionally be won without a party rank and file, but as recent U.S. elections have shown, the "ground game" still matters.

One thing that parties absolutely cannot do without, however, is candidates. Radical right parties often have difficulty finding people to stand for office, and this problem is magnified when the party has only a small pool of activists from which to recruit them. Under such circumstances, it becomes very difficult to contest enough constituencies to mount a truly national campaign and to overcome any hurdles required for parliamentary representation.

Numbers matter in yet another way. Parties with many activists can afford to be choosy about whom they allow to stand for office and whom they put in important positions. They can select from among the best available alternatives. Parties with few members do not have this luxury. For example, when Hans Janmaat, the leader of the Dutch Center Democrats, was asked why his party was filled with criminals, his telling reply was "because I can't find anyone else."[4]

Cohesion

Let us now turn to how the attributes of activists, and different distributions of activists, affect four other dimensions of party development. The first is the degree of cohesion. All party leaders live with the fear that they will be unable to reconcile their internal divisions, that their private conflicts will become public, and that splinter groups will form. While some degree of factionalism is unavoidable in any political party, intense and chronic infighting is enervating in multiple ways. Splinter

---

[4] Meindert Fennema, personal communication.

parties may compete for the same slice of the electorate and draw votes away from the original party. Large splits threaten the party's survival, and it can take years to recover the organizational resources that were lost. Even defections by individuals can be costly, particularly when they hold elected office and their actions deprive the party of state funds. Any type of infighting – which the media will most likely report – signals to both voters and potential coalition partners that the party is unstable and perhaps unreliable. More generally, any time a party is consumed with putting out its own fires, it has fewer resources to devote to other necessary tasks. For all these reasons, preventing internal conflicts from becoming severe is one of the central tasks that all parties face.

Although most successful radical right parties have experienced periods of intense internal conflict, these have generally been exceptional episodes. Indeed, observers often note that successful radical right parties maintain a degree of internal discipline that few other types of parties have been able to achieve. Cohesion also matters more during the consolidation phase of party development than thereafter. The French National Front, Norwegian Progress Party, and Austrian Freedom Party have all survived major party splits, yet these occurred after they had already qualified as successful parties. By contrast, factionalism, as we shall see, has prevented other parties from capitalizing on their initial electoral breakthroughs.

Although factionalism within radical right parties has many possible sources, three particular distributions of activists are especially likely to produce chronic infighting. The first is a party with many extremists. For a variety of psychological and ideological reasons, extremists tend to be as hostile to one another as they are to established political parties and to parliamentary democracy.[5] When radical right parties draw from extremist subcultures, the fragmentation and personal rivalries that characterize these subcultures are reproduced in party politics.

The second is a party with many opportunists. Since most opportunists, and particularly those whom the party recruits for high places on its electoral lists, have not worked their way up through the ranks, they have experienced none of the socialization rituals that could potentially create loyalty to the organization. Because they are careerists rather than ideologues, they will quit the party or defect to another if the opportunity

---

[5] This dynamic is similar to the "cliquish politics" that Kitschelt (1989) found to be prevalent in left-wing subcultures and that then reappeared within left-libertarian (Green) political parties.

presents itself. They may also try to quickly establish their own power bases within the party. Finally, since there is unlikely to be any ideological glue or set of shared experiences binding opportunists together, it will be difficult for them to find any common ground.

The third is a party that is divided between extremists and moderates. These two groups differ fundamentally in terms of both ideology and tactics, and a significant number of splits within radical right parties can be attributed to conflict between these two types of activists. Opportunists normally cannot consistently mobilize as a group and can be expected to side with moderates in any conflict because the domination of the party by extremists would rule out the electoral growth and government participation that opportunists seek.

Competence

A second way that activists matter is by determining the party's level of competence. Radical right voters do not differ fundamentally from voters of other parties, in the sense that they care both about policies and about the ability of parties to implement them (Van der Brug and Fennema 2003). The notion that radical right voters are simply "protest voters" has been abandoned. Thus voters will desert radical right parties that prove incapable of handling their functions, whether in municipal councils or in government cabinets. They will also be unwilling to put their trust in parties that signal incompetence in other areas.

Although they provide no guarantee, both general analytical skills and political experience help activists perform their duties competently. When either of these is lacking, activists tend to struggle, particularly if installed in political office. Many radical right elected representatives who lacked a university education reported feeling overwhelmed in their new roles: some claimed that they were afraid to speak in front of their better-educated colleagues, let alone offer their own proposals. Even those activists who have achieved a high level of professional success initially find parliamentary work daunting. As one of the former members of the List Pim Fortuyn's parliamentary faction put it, this party of real estate developers, entrepreneurs, lawyers, and doctors came to government with little knowledge of how it operated. "A lot of people didn't know what a second chamber was and what they were supposed to do." By the time they began to figure it out, their inexperience had helped seal their demise. Parties can and do train their personnel, and these courses have been critical in raising their overall competence level. Yet for these courses to function, parties need to have a preexisting cohort of skilled and experienced politicians.

Legitimacy

The nature of the activists matters in a third way by influencing the legitimacy of the radical right party. Although some voters delight in voting for a party perceived to be beyond the political pale, it follows from the previous point about competence that most radical right voters want to see their preferred policies implemented, or at least want their views to have some influence (Kedar 2005). If the radical right is an outcast, and thus has no hope of forming coalitions with other parties or contributing constructively to policy making, some voters will consider a vote for it to be wasted (Cox 1997). They will instead cast ballots for parties that are farther from their ideal preferences but more likely to influence policy. Givens (2005) indeed finds that other parties affect the level of strategic voting for radical right parties by signaling their coalition intentions beforehand.

On the one hand, the openness or closure of coalition markets depends on the behavior of other political parties, as I explain more later. Yet the behavior and structure of radical right parties affect this decision as well. When extremists occupy key positions in the party, they make it difficult for other parties to consider it a viable coalition partner, even if it would be in their own strategic interest to do so. The individual behavior of extremists and unsavory characters can also damage a party's coalition potential. Holocaust denial, violence, and petty crime damage the party's reputation and block its path to legitimacy. For example, it would be very difficult for any other British party to treat the British National Party as a legitimate actor so long as its higher ranks are populated with the likes of a former editor of an overtly anti-Semitic magazine who was convicted of possessing explosives and allegedly tried to hire a hit man to murder a rival politician.[6] We will see in the empirical chapters that this is an extreme but by no means isolated example.

Flexibility

Ideological flexibility is the fourth variable linking activists to voters. On one side of the spectrum are those parties that adopt what Kitschelt (1989) has termed the logic of electoral competition and tailor their message to appeal to as many voters as possible. While these parties retain their nativist core, they are flexible when it comes to a host of other issues. Most important, these parties have dropped the biological racism of the old right in favor of ethnopluralism. This language of cultural

---

[6] Tony Lecomber, second in command of the BNP from the late 1990s until 2006.

difference, as opposed to that of innate genetic hierarchies, not only makes it more difficult to brand radical right parties as fascist or racist, but also appeals to "immigration skeptics" in the voting population who do not consider themselves xenophobic but believe that immigration must be dramatically curtailed if the character of their societies is to be preserved (Rydgren 2008). On the other side of the spectrum are those parties that, again according to Kitschelt, pursue the logic of constituency representation: they value ideological purity over vote maximization. They are thus unwilling to compromise their essential principles, even when such intransigence drastically limits their appeal among voters. The British National Party, for example, still refuses to let nonwhites become members, despite the fact that an overwhelming number of voters believe that such a policy is offensive and has gotten the party into serious legal trouble with the courts.

As Rydgren (2005b) and others have argued, there has been an international diffusion of the radical right's "master frame" of ethnopluralism, along with a general recognition that this discourse provides the key to electoral success. We will see how the leaders of parties with extremist pasts, such as the British National Party and the Sweden Democrats, tried to imitate the successful models of the French National Front and Danish People's Party, respectively. However, these so-called modernizers (moderates, in my terminology) found their attempts to follow the logic of electoral competition stymied by an extremist base. Radical right parties were thus constrained from meeting voter demand by the extremism of their own activists, in turn a product of their own histories (Goodwin 2007a).

Several general conclusions emerge from the foregoing discussion. The first is that moderates with general skills and political experience are essential for radical right party building. One of their primary virtues is that they decrease the party's reliance on both extremists and opportunists, whose presence can hinder long-term electoral success. Although extremists are deleterious in many respects, a small number of them can be useful because they are often highly motivated and willing to volunteer a significant amount of their time to help the party. Yet they have to be controlled by moderates and, if necessary, ejected if their behavior becomes too damaging. Opportunists bring more advantages than do extremists: minor celebrities can help improve the party's image, as can high-profile defectors from other parties. Opportunists can also potentially be transformed into loyal activists. Yet opportunists also bring inexperience and naked ambition, and a party can contain only a certain number of these individuals without breaking apart.

To summarize the argument to this point: radical right activists are heterogeneous, but one can categorize them on the basis of their ideological motivations, their SES, and their political experience. While a party needs a certain number of activists for electoral persistence, it also needs certain types of activists to keep the party unified, make it appear competent and legitimate, and develop a program that potentially appeals to a wide sector of the electorate. It now remains to explain why some radical right parties attracted these types of activists while others did not.

Historical Legacies

It is often assumed that in the wake of the Second World War the far right was obliterated across Western Europe and that those parties that emerged in the 1980s and 1990s marked a fundamental discontinuity with previous far right parties and movements. Yet this view is at best only half right. There were indeed countries in Western Europe in which the postwar far right was tiny, fragmented, and marginalized. Yet there were others in which the far right, while admittedly a shadow of its interwar and wartime self, survived as a coherent political actor. Moreover, in some places radical right parties built on the foundations of preexisting far right movements, while in others they did not. Although no two postwar histories were the same, several distinct patterns emerge.

The first is one in which radical right parties built on a relatively strong far right foundation. Political parties, voluntary associations, and informal social networks that were originally dominated by collaborators or former fascists after the Second World War persisted in these cases. These organizations possessed some degree of legitimacy in politics and society, and even after the war were not universally treated as pariahs. These groups adopted other issues in order to recruit new members from a nationalist subculture, thereby adapting to changing conditions in the 1960s and 1970s while retaining their links to the past. This describes the legacy of far right activity in Austria, Flanders, and Italy. France was slightly different, in that the far right parties, organizations, and voluntary networks that would provide the building blocks for the National Front were less the product of the immediate postwar period than they were the residue of decolonization and the lost cause of Algérie Française. In the French case as well, however, one could discern a nationalist subculture that, while certainly on the defensive in the immediate postwar decades, was large enough to provide resources for the radical right when the time came.

What explains the persistence of nationalist subcultures in these four cases after the Second World War? The common thread was an outstanding national grievance, the substance of which differed mark-edly but which allowed some space for far right politics in these systems. In Flanders, the postwar purge of Flemish collaborators was understood to be yet another episode of repression by the dominant Francophones. Thus the "misguided patriots" who sided with the Germans to achieve independence acquired the status of martyrs for many within the Flemish nationalist movement. In Austria, the issue was not latent ethnic conflict but rather pan-Germanism. A significant minority of Austrians rejected the legitimacy of the Austrian nation and identified culturally and ethni-cally with Germany. This issue, along with amnesty for collaborators, was the defining feature of the Austrian far right for several decades. France was the only country in Europe in which decolonization produced a large collective actor (the *pieds-noirs*) that was unwilling to accept the end of empire and was openly hostile to a republic that it felt had betrayed it. The loss of Algeria reshaped the French far right in the late 1950s and early 1960s, and provided it with a nationalist grievance that could be repackaged into anti-immigrant and anti-Islamic messages in the 1980s. In Italy, fascism was never dismembered and delegitimated to the same extent that it was in Germany, allowing an isolated but nevertheless sig-nificant subculture – and political party – of self-identified neofascists to persist for five decades. In addition, the legacy of incomplete national integration was the necessary condition for the generation of the vari-ous regionalist leagues in the north of the country: the Northern League would identify southern Italians as the primary cause of the country's woes years before it turned its attention to immigrants.

Nationalist subcultures in these four countries certainly comprised both extremists and moderates. The French Organisation de l'Armée Secrète used bombings and assassinations to try to derail Algerian independence, while sectors of the Italian far right embraced terrorism during the "years of lead" (*anni di piombo*) of the 1970s. The far right in both Austria and Flanders was less violent, although certainly not entirely peaceful. All four of these nationalist subcultures contained unreformed Nazis and fascists. Yet it is important to note that each also possessed a large number of moderates who accepted parliamentary democracy and, while perhaps defending elements of collaboration, fascism, or Nazism, recognized the need to move beyond old ideologies. This was true even in Italy, where the members of the unabashedly fascist Italian Social Movement quickly perceived the benefits of clientelism over fascist revolution. The political representatives of these nationalist subcultures by and large did not stem from the margins of society: the MSI was dominated by lawyers, while the Austrian Freedom Party contained a higher percentage of university graduates than the two other Austrian parties. Politicians from the far right in these four states were politically experienced (although to a lesser degree in France), and some of them had been in parliament for years or even decades. These moderate, educated, and experienced politicians constituted an essential resource for radical right party building in the 1970s and 1980s. So too did the nationalist subcultures themselves, which, particularly in Flanders, continue to produce both political entrepreneurs and foot soldiers who can be mobilized by the radical right.

Germany constitutes a second, and unique, historical legacy. Aside from Italy, it was the only country in which an indigenous fascist movement came to power itself and created mass organizations with millions of members. The expulsion of several million ethnic Germans from Eastern Europe at the end of the war also left an outstanding nationalist grievance that persisted for decades. The nationalist subculture was thus larger in Germany than anywhere else in Europe. Yet a combination of allied and state policy divided and marginalized the potential leaders of the far right. In contrast to the tolerance of far right parties in Italy, in Germany a party that openly advocated the policies of the old regime was banned outright. Moderates were co-opted into the political mainstream, and those few who wanted to create a nationalist party to the right of the Christian Democrats found themselves perpetually in conflict both with extremists, whose ideological point of reference remained the Third Reich, and with the forces of a "militant democracy." Extremists thus came to dominate the nationalist subculture, and the radical right parties that emerged in Germany – even a party like the Republikaner that initially sought to distance itself from the neo-Nazi milieu – have not overcome this legacy.

In contrast to that in Austria, Flanders, France, Germany, and Italy, the far right in the rest of Western Europe was essentially irrelevant after the Second World War.[7] In Denmark, the Netherlands, Norway, Britain, Sweden, Switzerland, and Wallonia, the reservoir of activists consisted of small, balkanized networks of extremists, many of whom either openly worshipped Nazism and fascism or were otherwise nostalgic for the "good old days" of war and collaboration. As opposed to the hundreds of thousands of potential members in countries with nationalist subcultures,

---

[7] In some countries it was irrelevant before, and even during, the high tide of fascism. Only the Rexists in Wallonia, the NSB in the Netherlands, and various fascist parties in Switzerland registered significant electoral scores in the 1930s.

the far right could probably count at best several thousand members in the latter group of cases.

This legacy hampered radical right party building in two ways. First, as in Germany, members of the extremist subculture flocked to radical right parties and clashed with the few moderates who sought to imitate the discourse and organizational strategies of successful radical right parties elsewhere. Second, even when parties were able to insulate themselves from extremists, they found that, in the absence of a preexisting nationalist subculture, the only activists they could recruit were opportunists. These "flash" parties whose activist bases were dominated by opportunists were soon exposed as empty shells. The choice, simply put, was to build from "poor resources" or to build from scratch. Neither strategy worked.

Yet this does not account for the three successful cases of radical right party building in states without nationalist subcultures: the Danish People's Party, the Norwegian Progress Party, and the Swiss People's Party. In these three states, political parties that had only tenuous links to the far right were transformed into radical right parties.[8] In the two Scandinavian cases, anti-tax parties founded by political renegades increasingly came to rely on the themes of immigration, law and order, and national identity in the mid-1980s. In Switzerland, the Zurich wing of the agrarian SVP was taken over by the populist Christoph Blocher, who steered it in a radical right direction over the late 1980s and early 1990s. A preexisting political party that migrated toward the radical right proved to be the functional equivalent of a strong nationalist subculture in these cases. In fact, it provided even better foundations for party building because a party organization already existed and did not need to be pieced together from different far right parties and voluntary organizations. Since members of these parties did not initially join them because of their stance on immigration, they were dominated by moderates and contained virtually no extremists. These parties would also be less reliant on the opportunists who flooded the parties after their electoral breakthroughs, but would instead be able to use such new recruits for their own purposes.

In sum, either a legitimate nationalist subculture or a preexisting political party was a requirement for successful radical right parties. Yet neither was a sufficient condition. The historical legacies described in this section

---

[8] One could discern rightist ideas in the two Progress parties' libertarian economic policies and in the social conservatism of the Swiss agrarian party. But none of these parties had links with fascism or collaboration.

TABLE 2.1. *Cordons Sanitaires*

Country	Party	Approximate Start
Belgium	Vlaams Belang	1991
Belgium	Belgian National Front	1985
France	National Front	1988
Germany	German National Party	1964
Germany	Republicans	1983
Germany	German People's Union	1987
Netherlands	Center Democrats	1984
Sweden	Sweden Democrats	1988
United Kingdom	British National Party	1982

were powerful, but they were not deterministic. They cannot explain, for example, why some radical right parties were unable to attract a new wave of moderate and educated activists even after their electoral breakthroughs. Nor can they explain how successful radical right parties built upon their initial resources. Finally, as both the French and Italian cases demonstrate, nationalist subcultures did not produce success in the absence of opportunity. We thus need to turn to the political and social reaction that radical right parties generated when they gained visibility in the 1980s and 1990s, as well as the incentive structures that these reactions created.

Reacting to the Radical Right: Permissive and Repressive Environments

Beginning with the political reaction, the key factor was whether mainstream political parties ruled out all forms of cooperation with the radical right or whether they kept their options open. When all political parties adopted the former strategy, a *cordon sanitaire* against the radical right existed and the environment could be considered repressive. Table 2.1 lists the cases of cordons sanitaires covered in this book and the approximate dates when they began.

When political parties did not erect a cordon sanitaire, the environment for radical right parties was permissive. By permissive, I do not mean that mainstream parties necessarily welcomed radical right parties as coalition partners, although this did occur in some contexts and radical right parties did join national governments in some places (see Table 2.2). A permissive environment is rather one in which the radical right has cooperated with one or more political parties, even if this

TABLE 2.2. *Radical Right Parties in National Governments*

Country	Party	Years
Austria	Austrian Freedom Party	2000–2006
Italy	Northern League	1994, 2001–2006, 2008–
Italy	National Alliance	1994[a]
Netherlands	List Pim Fortuyn	2002
Sweden	New Democracy	1991–1994
Switzerland	Swiss People's Party	Mid-1980s–2007[b]

[a] The AN was also a member of the national government between 2001 and 2006, and has been again from 2008 to the present. However, by the late 1990s it had left the radical right party family.

[b] The starting date for the SVP is approximate, for the party's shift from an agrarian party to a radical right one was not instantaneous.

TABLE 2.3. *Cooperation with Radical Right Parties at the Local, Regional, or National Level*

Country	Party
Austria	Austrian People's Party
Denmark	Danish People's Party
France (1983–1998)	National Front
Italy	Northern League, National Alliance
Norway	Progress Party
Switzerland	Swiss People's Party

cooperation (whether in the form of coalitions, joint lists, stand-down agreements, or something else) occurs at the local or regional level (see Table 2.3). When radical parties become members of local or state governments, they acquire a certain recognition and legitimacy in the political system. Efforts by politicians to keep such parties out of national office become increasingly difficult and hypocritical when the radical right is cooperating with their party brethren at the local and/or state level. Also, cooperation at any level (particularly for the first time) is likely to draw enormous media attention and immediately raise the national profile of what may have been an obscure party. One example of this dynamic was the National Front's success in local elections in Dreux in 1983. While the FN's 16.7% in that election was newsworthy, the bigger story was the electoral pact that mainstream conservative parties signed with it. Because even small cracks in the cordon sanitaire can have large consequences, it is possible to define permissive environments as those in which the radical right and its members are not universally treated as pariahs.

The openness or closure of coalition markets affects the number and type of activists that radical right parties can recruit. An airtight cordon sanitaire dissuades ambitious, competent, and educated political entrepreneurs from joining. To illustrate, let us consider the calculation of a politician who is considering running for the lowest level of government in most countries: the municipal council. These positions are often unpaid (or the salary is minimal), and material incentives alone usually cannot explain the candidate's decision to run. However, local office can be an entryway to a political career and can also serve as a training ground for higher office. With a cordon sanitaire in place, it is difficult to imagine why anyone who cares about policy making would run for municipal office on a radical right ticket. With no possibility of forming coalitions and with the expectation that any policy proposal, however mundane, will be voted down because it emerged from a representative of a radical right party, the incentives of far right candidacy are unclear. One could argue that ambitious entrepreneurs could use their office to rise within the party, but if a cordon sanitaire exists at a local level, it is sure to exist at a regional and national level as well. Opportunists and moderates are unlikely to join. There will certainly be some people who are not dissuaded by the cordon sanitaire: extremists, who are less concerned about wielding power than expressing their ideas, and people who, in the words of one of my interviewees, "just like to yell and scream." The prediction is that a strong cordon sanitaire will lead to a larger percentage of extremists within the party, as well as those who have little interest in achieving higher office at all. Moreover, the futility of campaigning without the hope or intention of winning office will eventually lead to disengagement, defections, and low levels of recruitment.

When a cordon sanitaire is not in place, however, joining a radical right party can be an attractive option for moderates and opportunists. Inner-party mobility can be much greater within radical right parties than within traditional Social Democratic or Christian Democratic parties, and both experienced politicians and novices may be attracted by the possibility of rapid advancement. Provided that these opportunists build on a core of loyal moderates, a weak cordon sanitaire is good for party building. The influx of opportunists and moderates may also change the ideology of the party, making it more palatable to a broader electorate. In a cross-national study, Van Spanje and Van der Brug (2007) found that radical right parties that were not ostracized became more moderate, which is consistent with my argument.

The cordon sanitaire is most effective in the period after a radical right party has achieved a measure of visibility. It is likely to be ineffectual, or even counterproductive, however, if it is instituted after a radical right party has won a series of elections and constituted itself in the political system, for several reasons. First, when these parties become relatively large, they can set the political agenda and force other mainstream parties to co-opt their positions. Activists thus feel some sense of efficacy and are far less likely to view their political investment as pointless. Second, large radical right parties have already won paid offices or have, in most countries, received enough public money to employ a permanent staff, and these material incentives certainly help in recruitment. Third, when radical right parties become large, they lead to debates about the future of the cordon sanitaire. When politicians within mainstream parties question its viability and effectiveness, they raise expectations that it may crumble. Sequencing is thus critical: to be effective, cordons sanitaires must be instituted before radical right parties have become electorally strong.

Whereas the effects of cordons sanitaires have received some attention in the literature (Dézé 2004; Kestel and Godmer 2004; Art 2007; Van Spanje and Van der Brug 2007), the reactions of other social actors to the rise of the radical right have been almost completely ignored (but see Klandermans and Mayer 2006). In some states, openly belonging to a radical right organization can result in the loss of one's job, or at least doom one's chances for promotion. It can cost radical right activists their friends, acquaintances, and customers. There are, in short, serious non-political costs in joining a radical right party that dissuade most potential activists from taking that step. Those who do, under such circumstances, normally fall into two categories: extremists, who have no problem flouting social norms, and those who have little to lose in terms of employment and social relations.

While these everyday effects are mostly hidden from view, the actions of so-called antifascist groups are easy to detect. Young leftists form the core of these groups in many European states. Although some scholars consider their vigilance against radical right groups to be counterproductive (Koopmans 2001), my research suggests that their actions in fact disturb radical right organizational efforts to a large degree. Bomb threats and vandalism make regular radical right party meetings problematic. The systematic destruction of campaign posters and literature hampers the dissemination of the radical right's message. Antifascist protests accompany radical right election rallies, and the police often intervene to separate the two groups. Although the radical right has developed evasive tactics (such as keeping the location of meetings secret

until the last minute and hanging campaign posters from high trees)
to circumvent the antifascists, the constant battle with them has been
draining.

These types of activities also undoubtedly affect the calculations of
potential radical right candidates and activists. The risks to life, limb,
and property are not negligible. Menacing phone calls, vandalism, egg
throwing, and verbal berating are all commonplace occurrences. How
many people, considering whether to express their support for the radical
right beyond the private act of voting, have asked themselves, "Is it really
worth it?" and answered negatively? How many, when confronted with
daily harassment, have found that it was too much and either left politics
or joined a different party? While it is impossible to answer this question
definitively, it appears that only the extremists accept, or even welcome,
social exclusion and physical threat.

The empirical evidence from the case studies will show that social
sanctions are strong and antifascist protests are common in Germany,
the Netherlands, Sweden, Britain, and Wallonia. In France and Flanders,
social sanctions are much weaker, and although there has been significant protest, the French National Front and Vlaams Blok had already
built strong organizations before antifascist activity became intense. In
these cases, such antifascism was probably ineffectual, and possibly even
bolstered in-group solidarity. And with hundreds of elected officials,
thousands of candidates, and tens of thousands of members, radical
right parties in France and Flanders were already much larger than in the
other four countries, and the ability of antifascist groups to affect their
recruitment was thus far smaller. In Austria, Denmark, Italy, Norway,
and Switzerland, radical right activists faced few consequences in their
everyday life, which made recruiting and organizing much easier. In these
states, radical right parties were able to attract affluent and educated
members. As more doctors, lawyers, and professors joined the radical
right, any existing social taboos were either irreparably weakened or
evaporated altogether.

In sum, cordons sanitaires and strong social sanctions make it very
difficult for radical right parties to attract activists, and those who do
join under such repressive conditions tend to be extremist, of low SES,
or a combination of the two. Repressive environments thus "work" by
selecting for the types of activists that undermine radical right party
development: they discourage the recruitment of moderates with significant human capital, leaving radical right parties with an extremist

or opportunist composition that is politically unsustainable. Permissive environments, by contrast, not only make recruitment much easier in general, but also allow radical right parties to attract the types of activists they need to succeed.

Radical Right Activists: Cross-National Comparisons

To test a portion of this argument, I collected data on the SES of a subset of radical right activists: candidates for public office. In some of the countries included in this study, candidates for public office are required by law to list their profession. I obtained the party list for an election between 2005 and 2007 from the following eight radical right parties: the Austrian Freedom Party (FPÖ), the Danish People's Party (DF), the Belgian National Front (FNb), the French National Front (FN), the German National Party (NPD), the German Republicans (REP), the Sweden Democrats (SD), and the Swiss People's Party (SVP). The cases include four successful parties (DF, FN, FPÖ, SVP) and four failed parties (FNb, NPD, REP, SD). Candidates were coded using the International Standard Classification of Occupations (ISCO-88), which divides professions into nine major groups.

Table 2.4 reports the percentage of radical right candidates for office according to three categories: the first includes ISCO categories 1 (managers) and 2 (professionals); the second includes ISCO categories 3 (technicians and associate professionals), 4 (clerical support workers), and 5 (service and sales workers); and the third includes ISCO categories 6 (skilled agricultural, forestry and fishery workers), 7 (craft and related trade workers), 8 (plant and machine operators, and assemblers), and 9 (elementary occupations).

The data clearly show that the four successful radical right parties possess a high percentage of managers and professionals and a low percentage of individuals belonging to ISCO categories 6–9. The situation is exactly reversed for the unsuccessful, stigmatized, radical right parties.[9] Figure 2.2 demonstrates these differences in SES profile visually.

[9] One could object that the higher average SES of successful radical right parties is in fact a product of their electoral success. Yet this also implies that members of less successful, smaller parties should have lower average SES. The cases of both the German FDP and Greens, both of which contain individuals with high SES, would suggest that there is not necessarily a general relationship between party size and average SES, although this has to be tested.

TABLE 2.4. *Occupations of Radical Right Candidates for Public Office:*
Percentage of the Party List Belonging to Different ISCO Categories

	Managers and Professionals (ISCO 1–2)	Technicians, Clerks, Service and Sales (ISCO 3–5)	Agriculture, Machine Operators, Crafts and Trades (ISCO 6–9)
Successful parties			
Danish People's Party	50	38	12
Swiss People's Party	45	32	24
French National Front	42	50	9
Austrian Freedom Party	38	50	11
Unsuccessful parties			
Belgian National Front	22	43	35
German National Party	22	44	34
Sweden Democrats	20	39	40
Republicans	18	46	34

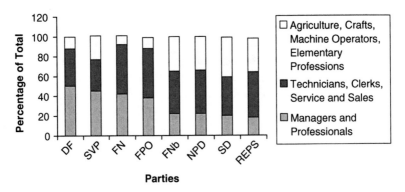

FIGURE 2.2. Occupations of radical right candidates for office.

The gulf between successful and unsuccessful radical right parties in terms of the percentage of manual workers becomes even more pronounced when we ignore agriculture, where only the SVP, for historical reasons, has a significant number of candidates in this category. Table 2.5 presents the percentage of candidates in ISCO categories 7–9.

Unfortunately, the data do not allow us to compare and contrast the number of unemployed and retired persons across the electoral lists. Like individuals working in professions that are less susceptible to employer pressure, these two categories of individuals are less sensitive to threats

TABLE 2.5. *Manual Workers as Radical Right Candidates*

Party	Percentage of Candidates in ISCO Categories 7–9	Outcome
Belgian National Front	35	Failure
Sweden Democrats	34	Failure
Republicans	33	Failure
German National Party	32	Failure
Swiss People's Party	13	Success
Danish People's Party	12	Success
National Front	8	Success
Austrian Freedom Party	6	Success

to their professional advancement. Most electoral lists massively under-report individuals belonging to these two categories, either because individuals were asked to list their previous professions or because they did not want to list themselves as retired or unemployed. Only the electoral list of the FNb contains both categories in significant numbers. Here the numbers are striking: 27% of FNb candidates were retired and 29% were unemployed, meaning that a majority of the electoral list was out of the active workforce entirely. This picture conforms to other scattered evidence on the social profile of highly stigmatized parties, such as the SD, where one-third of party members are receiving unemployment aid from the state.

The foregoing social profile of radical right parties is consistent with the only other existing cross-national data set on radical right activists. Although they did not report data on occupations, members of the research team directed by Klandermans and Mayer coded the activists they interviewed in Flanders, France, Germany, Italy, and the Netherlands according to their level of education, using the categories "low," "medium," and "high." The results are reported in Table 2.6. Grouping the activists into nonstigmatized (France, Flanders, and Italy) and stigmatized (Germany and the Netherlands) cases, the difference in education levels is striking, as Figures 2.3 and 2.4 reveal.

It thus appears that highly repressive environments produce a radical right activist base with lower levels of SES. This is an important finding in its own right, since I have argued that radical right parties need activists with general analytical skills for electoral persistence. But it is also significant because it is the only observable implication of the argument for which there are quantitative data. There are currently no attitudinal

TABLE 2.6. *Education Levels of Radical Right Activists*

Country	High	Medium	Low
France	64	31	5
Flanders	50	50	0
Italy	33	55	12
Germany	28	60	12
Netherlands	16	44	39

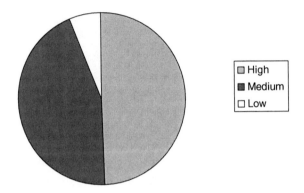

FIGURE 2.3. Education levels of radical right activists: nonstigmatized cases.

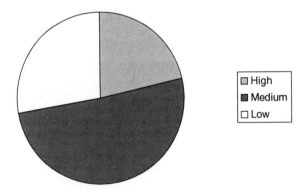

FIGURE 2.4. Education level of radical right activists: stigmatized cases.

surveys of radical right activists that would allow us to divide them into the categories of extremist, moderate, and opportunist. And since radical right parties generally do not respond to written queries (Goodwin 2007b; Mudde 2007), such a survey would probably not be fruitful. The case studies, however, will demonstrate that permissive environments do allow moderates to join the party, while repressive environments select for extremists.

Summarizing the Cases

We are now in a position to summarize the two major independent variables, the intervening variable of party personnel, and the dependent variable for seventeen radical right parties. The rest of this book will flesh out these variables, as well as demonstrate how different combinations of activists produced varying levels of coherence, competence, legitimacy, and ideological flexibility among the parties. But Table 2.7 provides both a road map and quick reference for the case studies.

Critiques and Caveats

There are several possible objections to this book's central argument. The three that I consider the most serious are the possibility of reverse causation, the problem of omitted variables, and the issue of ultimate causation. I shall consider each in turn.

Beginning with reverse causation, what if party organization is simply a result, rather than a cause, of electoral performance? Consider the following scenario. A radical right party achieves an electoral breakthrough for reasons that have nothing to do with organization. Yet this breakthrough helps it achieve visibility and leads to a spike in membership. Ambitious political entrepreneurs who were unwilling to join the party when it was electorally irrelevant – or simply unknown – now climb on board. Depending on the extent of the breakthrough, the party may then receive public funds that permit it to hire permanent staff members and, potentially, open up party offices. This process is repeated so long as the party performs well, and party unity is secured so long as the promise of continued expansion dampens conflicts over key positions and places on party lists. Once it performs badly, however, party membership drops precipitously and conflicts erupt over shrinking opportunities and future strategies.

While it would be disingenuous to deny that there is a feedback loop between electoral performance and party development, there are at least

TABLE 2.7. *Summary of Radical Right Party Development*

Party	Preexisting Foundation	Opportunity Structure	Median Activist	Outcome
National Front	Nationalist subculture	No initial CS, no social sanctions	Moderate, high SES, experienced	Success
Austrian Freedom Party	Nationalist subculture	No CS, no social sanctions	Moderate, high SES, experienced	Success
National Alliance	Nationalist subculture	Change in CS over time, no social sanctions	Moderate, high SES, experienced	Success
Northern League	Nationalist subculture	No CS, no social sanctions	Moderate, high SES, initially inexperienced, now experienced	Success
Vlaams Belang	Nationalist subculture	No initial CS, no social sanctions	Moderate, high SES, experienced	Success
German People's Union	Large extremist subculture	CS, social sanctions, state pressure	Few activists, extremist, inexperienced	Failure
German National Party	Large extremist subculture	CS, social sanctions, state pressure	Extremist, low SES, mixed experience	Failure
Republicans	Large extremist subculture	CS, social sanctions, state pressure	Moderate/extremist, low SES, inexperienced	Failure
British National Party	Small extremist subculture	CS, social sanctions	Extremist/moderate, low SES, inexperienced	Failure

Center Democrats	Small extremist subculture	CS, social sanctions, state pressure	Few activists, Moderate/extremist, low SES, inexperienced	Failure
Belgian National Front	Small extremist subculture	CS, social sanctions	Few activists, Moderate/extremist, low SES, inexperienced	Failure
Sweden Democrats	Small extremist subculture	CS, social sanctions	Moderate/extremist, low SES, inexperienced	Failure
List Pim Fortuyn	No foundation	No CS, no social sanctions	Opportunist, high SES, inexperienced	Failure
New Democracy	No foundation	No CS, no social sanctions	Opportunist, SES unknown, inexperienced	Failure
Danish People's Party	Party transformation	No CS, no social sanctions	Moderate, high SES, experienced	Success
Norwegian Progress Party	Party transformation	No CS, no social sanctions	Moderate, high SES, experienced	Success
Swiss People's Party	Party transformation	No CS, no social sanctions	Moderate, high SES, experienced	Success

Note: CS denotes cordon sanitaire.

three reasons that the simple model is misleading. First, there were several radical right parties that possessed relatively strong organizations but sustained long periods of electoral oblivion, including the Vlaams Blok, the Norwegian Progress Party, the Austrian Freedom Party, and the Italian Social Movement. In this sense, they resembled the German Nazi Party, which constructed a strong party organization years before it registered significant electoral success. Strong organizations were essential to these parties' survival before changes in the political opportunity structure allowed them to grow. This sequencing was also important because organization allowed these parties to absorb new members without succumbing to factionalism and splitting.

This is precisely what occurred in a second set of cases. The empirical record shows that it is often at the peak of their electoral success that radical right parties self-destruct. This is most evident for "flash" parties like New Democracy in Sweden and the List Pim Fortuyn in the Netherlands. But the organizational pathologies of perpetually weak radical right parties like the Belgian National Front and the Dutch Center Democrats also appear to be more severe when these parties do well in elections. The French National Front also suffered its most significant split during a period of electoral strength when Bruno Mégret left the party and founded his own in 1999.

Third, electoral performance is not the only factor that affects recruitment patterns. Even if a radical right party does well at the polls, it is unlikely to attract a significant number of activists if high costs are associated with openly belonging to it. And those activists who do join under such circumstances, as I argued earlier, are precisely the type whose abundance leads to party failure.

In terms of omitted variables, two in particular come to mind. The first is the role of leadership. One of the striking attributes of most radical right party leaders is their longevity. Le Pen (FN), Hagen (FrP), Bossi (LN), and Haider (FPÖ) all stood atop their respective parties for at least a decade and a half. The leaders of unsuccessful radical right parties have also generally held their grip for a long time: Daniel Féret lasted for twenty-two years as leader of the FNb, and Janmaat presided over the CD for eighteen years. Given the concentration of power in their hands and the time they have had to wield it, one might posit that leadership is the key to understanding patterns of success and failure. Indeed, one common hypothesis is that some radical right leaders possess more charisma than others and are thus more appealing to voters. But as several authors have noted (Van der Brug et al. 2005), many of these analyses are tautological, because charismatic leaders are identified as such by their electoral success. For example, the former leader of the German REP, Franz Schönhuber, was a popular journalist and radio host who was widely viewed as charismatic during the brief period when his party was on the rise. When the party stagnated, observers blamed it in part on Schönhuber's lack of charisma. This case is consistent with the findings of a larger cross-national study that found no support for the charismatic-leader thesis at all (Van der Brug and Mughan 2007).

Yet there is another aspect of leadership – "internal leadership" (Mudde 2007: 263–264) – whose influence is somewhat easier to trace. Internal leadership refers primarily to the ability to build a party organization, to recruit capable and talented individuals, and to moderate factionalism. Some radical right party leaders have demonstrated themselves to be much more interested in these tasks than others. Anders Lange, founder of the progenitor to the FrP, and Mogens Glistrup, founder of the DF, were hostile to parties in general and had little interest in building their own. Both Janmaat's and Féret's paranoia militated against party building. On the other side of the spectrum are leaders like Bossi, who was devising organizational flowcharts when his party consisted of only several dozen members; Hagen, who spent years building up local organizations in Norway; and Le Pen, who kept diverse coalitions together within the FN for longer than anyone had thought possible.

The qualities of the "first activist" – the political entrepreneur who either founds the party or takes it over after an initial leadership battle – are particularly important during the period of party formation. If a leader with no interest in building an organization seizes hold of the party, he can effectively block efforts at party building for a long time. Alternatively, the early actions of party builders like Hagen and Bossi can have positive long-term consequences. Leaders do play an important role in setting the course of party development, as the empirical chapters will demonstrate. Yet political entrepreneurs cannot become leaders in the absence of activists. Immediately after they were founded, radical right parties required a core of committed supporters willing to devote their time to a movement whose chances of success were at best uncertain. When this core did not exist or when it consisted of certain types of activists, even the most talented political entrepreneurs would have ultimately failed, or would have failed to emerge in the first place.

A second possible omitted variable is party rules, both formal and informal. Perhaps what really matters is not the number and type of activists a party attracts, but the institutions it develops to manage relations among them. The case studies will indeed demonstrate that radical right politicians did make organizational choices that mattered. Several learned lessons from the past and created mechanisms to vet members, centralize candidate selection, and prevent alternative power bases from forming. They invested in internal training courses to upgrade their human capital, and invented all sorts of events and festivals to create a sense of solidarity. Parties like the French National Front made far more effort than their mainstream competitors to create an alternative political-social world for their members.

Yet if these institutions contributed to electoral persistence, they began to do so only once parties had the requisite personnel. Bossi's flowcharts, for example, had little bearing on the Lega Lombarda's fortunes while the party consisted of a dozen or so activists. When the Lega Nord counted a membership in the tens of thousands, however, his well-designed vetting mechanisms and set of selective incentives began to matter much more. It is also unclear to what extent *formal* party rules differed from party to party. Several scholars have noted that most radical right parties follow the same centralized organizational model (Taggart 1995; Betz 1998b) and, at least on paper, possess institutions like youth wings, auxiliary organizations, and training centers. What really matters is the extent to which actual behavior conforms to party statutes. This not only is very difficult to uncover without extensive fieldwork in every case, but also, and more importantly, is dependent on the more fundamental properties of party organization that I have identified in this chapter.

A third critique of my argument is that I have not traced the causal chain back far enough – that I have left open the questions of *why* historical legacies were favorable in some countries and not in others, and *why* the reaction to the radical right was permissive in some places and repressive elsewhere. I make no claim to have tackled these issues here. But the decision to take these independent variables as givens must be defended, for the worry is that they could be the outcome of a more fundamental factor that I have missed.

Yet it is difficult to see how this could be the case for either variable. There does not appear to be a single factor that accounts for the existence of nationalist grievances in some European countries as opposed to others. Ethnic division in Belgium, late unification in Italy, pan-Germanism in Austria, and decolonization in France suggest no common root causes. Similarly, it is unclear why only a very small number of political parties that could have adopted a radical right ideology actually did so, and why this transformation occurred in Denmark, Norway, and Switzerland. We thus do not need to reach back farther into history to make sense of these historical legacies.

Repressive environments also appear to have multiple causes. In Germany, the process of coming to terms with the Nazi past clearly played a central role. In the Netherlands, it is often suggested that guilt over complicity in the Final Solution led to vigilant antifascism. In Britain, fascism and treason were virtually synonymous. In Sweden, an elite consensus not to politicize immigration underpins the cordon sanitaire against the Sweden Democrats. In Wallonia, the dominance of the Socialist Party is a central factor in the repression of the Francophone radical right. With the exception of the German case (Art 2006), all of these specific explanations must be developed and tested. Yet the point is that it is probably impossible to derive a general explanation for the origins of repressive environments.

Conclusion

Given both the scale of the forces – such as immigration, globalization, and European integration – that have reshaped European states and societies, and the enduring power of nationalism itself, it is not surprising that the radical right's central message is quite popular across Europe. When we couple these factors with rising levels of political distrust and partisan dealignment over the past several decades, the success of the radical right appears to be overdetermined. In this view, the debate about whether people vote for the radical right because they agree with its policies or to register protest misses the broader picture. Because simply voting for a radical right party costs virtually nothing in terms of time and effort, we should expect these parties to capture a significant number of votes, regardless of the reasons.

To understand why this isn't always the case, we need to look inside the radical right, and this chapter has given us the tools for doing so. Absent certain historical legacies and the collusion, or disregard, of political and social forces, radical right party building has not succeeded. In these failed cases, the initial pool of helpful activists was too small, and cordons sanitaires and social sanctions rendered the costs of membership for new recruits too high. These parties, for reasons we have already discussed, were unable to tap into the demand that existed – and continues to exist – for them. Party building, as opposed to short-term electoral success, is a difficult and complicated enterprise, as the next chapter will demonstrate.

3

Parties of Poor Souls

My survey of radical right parties begins with failure. Specifically, it begins with parties that tried to build on a small extremist culture in the face of a highly repressive political and social environment. Since they possessed neither the means nor the opportunity for sustained electoral success, it is no wonder that of the four parties this chapter analyzes, only the British National Party might be familiar to nonspecialists. The Dutch Center Democrats are now a historical footnote, while the Belgian National Front has been perpetually irrelevant. The Sweden Democrats have recently shown signs of escaping from the margins but have yet to win more than 6% of the vote in national elections. Once we begin to look inside these parties, we are immediately reminded of Karl Marx's well-known epigram: "History always repeats itself twice: first time as tragedy, second time as farce." Indeed, it would be tempting to describe activists within these parties as harmless eccentrics were it not for the fact that some of them were involved in hate crimes against foreigners and Holocaust denial. It is also important to bear in mind that things could have turned out differently had history not provided them with such poor resources for party building and had the costs of activism not been so high.

There are several advantages of looking at the failures first. For one, they highlight the fact that neither socioeconomic conditions nor favorable electoral institutions automatically produce a successful radical right party. Beginning with Belgium, where the divergent fortunes of radical right parties have been particularly striking, one observer notes that several existing explanations for the rise of the radical right "would lead us to expect [it] to be stronger in Wallonia than in Flanders" (Hossay

2002: 16). Unemployment has been far higher in the former than in the latter, and Wallonia also possesses nearly twice the number of foreigners. The percentage of Turks and people from Maghreb countries – population groups that are particularly targeted in the radical right's propaganda as scapegoats for a whole range of social problems – is the same in both regions (Coffé 2005). Indeed, Wallonians are no more tolerant of immigrants than the Flemish. Furthermore, feelings of political powerlessness and authoritarian attitudes are more widespread in Wallonia than in Flanders (Coffé 2005). Finally, since the electoral system is the same in the two regions, at least for federal elections, institutional factors cannot account for the divergent development of the radical right.

The Netherlands also ostensibly possessed a fertile breeding ground and favorable institutions for the radical right. In the 1980s, the country suffered from double-digit unemployment and underwent a painful restructuring of the welfare state. Waves of immigration followed decolonization in Indonesia and Suriname, labor shortages resulted in guest worker programs for people from Southern Europe, Turkey, and northern Africa, and foreign ethnic conflicts in the 1990s brought more than 300,000 asylum seekers to the Netherlands (Tillie and Slijper 2007). By 2001, the percentage of Allochtone (people either not born in the Netherlands or with at least one parent not born in the Netherlands) was more than 17%. The percentages were much higher in the major cities: Amsterdam (46.3%), Rotterdam (41.3%), The Hague (41.4%), and Utrecht (28.9%).[1] There was significant demand – particularly in these cities – for an anti-immigrant party, and the lowest electoral threshold in Western Europe (0.67%) all but ensured that they would achieve parliamentary representation and visibility.

Sweden, too, should have produced a successful radical right party if socioeconomic and institutional variables were the most important factors. The country had both significantly higher rates of both immigration and unemployment than either Norway or Denmark, where radical right parties thrived. Its effective threshold for parliamentary representation of 4% is equal to Norway's, and like both Norway and Denmark it uses the St. Laguë formula to distribute seats.

Only in the case of Great Britain does an institutional explanation carry some weight. Yet one should be wary of ending the analysis of the British National Party's weakness there. First, the counterexample of the French National Front, which has flourished in spite of France's majoritarian

---

[1] These data can be found at www.cbs.nl.

system, suggests that at least some people will vote expressively, as opposed to strategically. Second, the BNP long failed miserably in European elections, where seats are assigned according to proportional representation, before winning two seats in 2009. Third, its gains at the local level have been sporadic and seem to depend more on its organizational resources than on the magnitude of the constituency.

In sum, looking at failures first allows us to reject a set of explanations that are still widely purveyed in the literature. But an even more important reason is that the failures draw into sharp relief the intervening variables linking activists to electoral outcomes. Coherence, competence, legitimacy, and flexibility are properties that are much easier to perceive in their absence, and the four case studies in this chapter demonstrate just how absent they were. Not only did these parties have great difficulty recruiting educated activists (a fact I noted in the preceding chapter), but they struggled mightily to find anyone willing to work publicly on their behalf. By taking a detailed look at the repressive environment potential activists faced, it is not difficult to understand why they never expanded beyond a very small number of active members and why the activists they attracted did more harm than good. By examining the historical legacies, we can understand why moderates were unable to overcome extremist pasts and why these parties were constantly tearing themselves apart. Although some of the pathologies of party building were more marked in some cases than others, the four case studies are very much variations on a theme.

The Radical Right in Francophone Belgium

If one were to try to study the Belgian National Front from the outside by analyzing its party program, electoral performance, or social basis of support, one would conclude that it is not significantly different from its counterparts in other European states. It is an anti-immigrant party, supported predominantly by working-class voters, whose electoral scores have varied significantly over its twenty-five-year history. Although certainly less successful than most other radical right parties, the FNb has had its moments: in the 1994 elections it won seventy-two municipal councilors, and in the 2004 elections for the Walloon regional parliament it won 8% of the vote and four seats. It also possesses its strongholds, such as the perpetually declining industrial town of Charleroi, where its 16.6% of the vote in the 2006 local elections made it the third-strongest party.

Yet such an analysis would miss the defining features of the FNb. During my interviews, I asked members of the Vlaams Belang (the successful radical right party in neighboring Flanders) about their opinion of the FNb. The answers I received, which normally followed a chuckle or raised eyebrows, were uniformly blunt. One politician described FNb party members as "too stupid" and a "bunch of poor souls." Another claimed that the party "takes anyone they can get," while still another described it as "lacking leaders and a program." The Flemish politicians also cast considerable doubt on the mental health of their Francophone counterparts. According to one, the FNb consists of a "bunch of lunatics" that are "impossible to take seriously," while another quipped that the party "has just enough members to fit into a wing of a psychiatric ward."

What is remarkable is that current and former members of the party are hardly more charitable. One claimed that "there are very few normal people in the party," while another acknowledged that FNb activists are "not the most balanced." As will become apparent, the internal life of the party has never been healthy. The few academic studies of the FNb all conclude that the party is poorly organized (Rea 1996; Coffé 2005; Delwit 2007). Yet to describe the party as possessing any organization at all is an exaggeration. The party has no building. The party program has never been updated. The "rank and file" consists of perhaps a hundred militants. As one longtime member of the party conceded, "I would like to say that we are a strong, well-organized, highly institutionalized party, but that would not be true."[2]

What accounts for this situation? National Front politicians are quick to blame Dr. Daniel Féret, the party's founder and president from 1985 to 2007. Féret, many claim, blocked all attempts at party organization in order to preserve his hegemony. He treated the party like an ATM, say others. Indeed, most of what his former and current enemies within the party had to say about him cannot be printed. Even his supporters (the so-called Féretistes) admit that the former president is a "difficult personality" who had little interest in sharing power.[3]

Féret is certainly a bizarre politician. But there are good reasons to believe that the causes of the FNb's perpetual weakness run deeper than simple faults of leadership. The FNb is really an amalgamation of the *groupuscules* (small political groups) that turned increasingly violent in the 1970s. They were populated by extremist activists who had little

[2] Interview with Patrick Sessler (FNb), Brussels, February 2007.
[3] Interview with Michel Delacroix (FNb), Brussels, February 2007.

interest in appealing to a broader audience and lacked the skills required for building a party organization. Since the Wallonian far right consisted of a motley crew of violent street fighters, former collaborators, neo-Nazis, and criminals, it is not surprising that the FNb would attract the same type of people. They coexisted uneasily with the few moderates within the party. The intense stigmatization of the FNb from the moment of its founding meant that it was extremely difficult to recruit capable activists, or indeed many activists at all. Only those who were part of the next generation of extremists or who felt they had nothing to lose were willing to bear the costs of membership.

The Walloon case also provides evidence against three rejoinders to my general argument. First, party organization did not improve following the FNb's occasional electoral coup. If anything, the internal life of the party became even more chaotic when it did comparatively well at the polls and received more public funding. Thus organization is not an automatic product of electoral success. Second, the creation of a cordon sanitaire against the FNb demonstrates that this policy is not endogenous to the size of the radical right party. As we shall see in other cases, mainstream parties have sometimes opted to erect cordons against marginal radical right forces. Third, the FNb failed not because its policies were extremist in the sense of the British National Party or the German National Democratic Party. Indeed, Féret took his ideological cues directly from the French original. The problem was that the party could not keep out the extremists, for doing so would have rendered the party practically devoid of members. To understand why this was the case, we need to begin with the history of the Wallonian far right.

Wallonia has never produced a regional movement equivalent to the Vlaamse Beweging in Flanders. As the ruling minority in Belgium, French-speaking Belgians had little need to fight for their interests, and in fact Belgian nationalism was a much stronger force in the region than Wallonian nationalism ever was. The high-water mark of the Francophone far right occurred in the 1930s with the rise of Léon Degrelle and his Rexist Party. Always more of a political opportunist than an ideologue, Degrelle followed the political winds of the 1930s, and the Rexist Party veered toward a redemptive nationalism and corporatism that placed it within the fascist camp. The Rexists gained a surprising 11.5% of the vote and 21 of 202 seats in the elections of May 1936, and appeared unstoppable in the months afterward.

Degrelle's success would be short lived, however, as political forces within Belgium mounted a vigorous defense of democracy (Capoccia

2005). In the 1939 elections, the party gained only 4.4% of the vote after eight Rexist members of parliament and senators had resigned from it. When the German occupiers installed Degrelle, he was very much a marginal figure without any significant basis of support. Given the size of the movement, it was quite easy to destroy the remains of the Rexists after the end of the war. To quote the concluding words of Martin Conway's (1993: 289) study *Collaboration in Belgium*:

Long before the German retreat of September 1944, the movement had become a political irrelevance and the subsequent trials of Rexist militants served merely as the public expression of its demise. Collaboration had become a disaster which not only destroyed the lives of many followers of Rex, but also consigned their movement to a political oblivion from which there was to be no escape.

The Rexists were viewed as utter traitors within Wallonian society. Whereas Flemish politicians, as we shall see later, often took ambiguous positions regarding collaboration, Walloon politicians sharply condemned collaborators and referred to them as criminals (Seberechts 1992; Colignon 1996). Because the environment was so repressive and collaboration was so demonized, Walloon collaborators never created the types of support networks that existed in Flanders. Most Walloons identified collaboration with violent excesses such as the execution of resistance fighters and the persecution of the Jews. Unlike the situation in Flanders, no political parties emerged to represent the interests of former collaborators and to agitate for an amnesty. The remains of the Rexist movement coalesced in a tiny circle around Jean-Robert Debbaudt in the 1950s in what would be the first of many groupuscules to emerge in the Francophone far right landscape (Balace 1994: 128). Degrelle, who had escaped certain death in Belgium by fleeing to Franco's Spain, became a minor figure in the international Holocaust denial scene and occasionally received visitors (several of whom would later join the FNb) until his death in 1994. But within Francophone Belgium, the far right was nearly nonexistent from the liberation to the early 1960s.

During the 1960s and 1970s, a number of groupuscules would come to populate the far right landscape. According to Hossay (2002: 170), the entire Francophone far right probably consisted of only a few hundred activists at its peak in the 1970s. Yet despite their small size, it is important to mention several of these groupuscules, since the FNb tried to integrate them into a radical right party in the 1980s. The story begins in 1960, when the Belgian Congo gained its independence and tens of thousands of Francophone colonists returned to Belgium. Some of these activists formed the Comité d'Action et de Défense des Belges d'Afrique (CAMDA), which was soon renamed the Mouvement d'Action Civique (MAC). In 1963, MAC dissolved itself and became Jeune Europe, and the goals of the movement changed from the defense of Belgian colonial interests to the unification of Europe and the battle against U.S. power. Jeune Europe developed organizations in other European states, including France and Italy, and forged ties with extremist liberation movements worldwide, including the Vietcong and the Black Panthers, before dissolving in 1969. The group was closely connected to many prominent Nazis and neo-Nazis, and many future members of the National Front, including Daniel Féret, were members of it.

In 1974, Emile Lecerf, a collaborationist who had been active in Jeune Europe, founded the Front de la Jeunesse (FJ) at Liège University. Members of the FJ trained in urban commando tactics and launched violent actions against leftist groups and immigrants in the 1970s.[4] Its members included Daniel Gilson, Daniel Leskens, Patrick Cocriamont, and Francis Dossogne, all of whom would later join the FNb.[5] The party was disbanded in 1983 when many of its members were convicted of belonging to a private militia. Its remaining members joined two different organizations: Delta Nord and the Parti des Forces Nouvelles (PFNB). The first was an even more radical splinter group of the FJ that later became the clandestine Westland New Post, a neo-Nazi groupuscule that adopted the structure of the SS. The second was a political party that would fight bitterly against the FNb in the mid-1980s.

While these internecine conflicts within the right-wing extremist scene mattered to only a small number of militants and to the Belgian security services that monitored them, the "Nols phenomenon" created a significantly larger political stir. Roger Nols, a member of the Front Démocratique des Francophones (FDF), had been the mayor of the Brussels suburb of Schaerbaek since 1970. He first gained national attention for refusing to respect the bilingual language laws and for other anti-Flemish positions. Yet in a transformation similar to that of his erstwhile Flemish enemies (the Vlaams Blok), Nols shifted his attention away from the traditional "other" and toward immigrants in the late 1970s and early 1980s. This move toward the contemporary radical right – the first in Francophone Belgium – led to a break with the FDF, but the mayor organized his own

---

[4] "Front de la jeunesse et Parti des forces nouvelles recycles au FN," *ResistanceS*, August 9 2006.

[5] Dossogne would be convicted in January 2001 for working as a private detective without a license. *ResistanceS*. www.resistances.be/dossogne.html.

electoral lists and subsequently won reelection in a landslide (Hossay 2002: 178). Yet Nols soon overreached: in 1984, he invited Jean-Marie Le Pen to speak in Schaerbaek and provoked a powerful antifascist mobilization in the streets that forced him to reconsider his relationship with the radical right (Ignazi 2003: 127). Although several "Nols clubs" were formed by right-wing extremists, Nols himself was brought back, albeit temporarily, into the liberal party (Hossay 2002: 178).

But the Nols phenomenon, combined with the success of Le Pen in the 1984 European elections, convinced members of the Francophone far right scene that the time was ripe for reconstituting the groupuscules under a single banner. Luc Michel, a former member of the Front de la Jeunesse, was behind the founding of the Front Nationaliste–Nationalistisch Front, the first attempt to cash in on the success of Le Pen's movement (Rea 1996: 193). But this party fizzled, and Michel would become a bitter enemy of the founder of the Belgian version of the National Front, Daniel Féret.

Although Féret had been active in Jeune Europe, he was not a well-known figure in the Francophone far right. A physician by profession, Féret was a member of the liberal Union Démocrate pour le Respect du Travail (UDRT), a flash party that won 2.7% of the vote in 1981 but quickly faded. After trying his luck in several far right groupuscules, he founded the Front National–National Front (FNB-NF, hereafter FNb) in May 1985.[6] Féret did not hide the fact that he was copying the National Front of Jean-Marie Le Pen, taking the French party's name along with many of its symbols and slogans. His attempt to integrate different groupuscules proved more successful than any previous one. The PFNB, which never managed an electoral breakthrough, finally gave up its fight against the FNb and dissolved itself in 1991. Many former PFNB members then crossed over to the FNb, including Cocriamont, Leskens, and Daniel Sessler.

Although the FNb has registered occasional electoral gains over the past two decades, it has been perpetually handicapped by its small size, high degree of factionalism, incompetence, and illegitimacy.[7] In terms of size, the small number of activists means that the FNb is, as one former member put it, a "phantom party." As Delwit (2007) observes, "Except, and only partially, at times of elections, the National Front is a political

---

[6] *ResistanceS*, July 24, 2003.
[7] It is difficult to assess the FNb's degree of ideological flexibility because the party program has never been updated.

TABLE 3.1. *Municipal Elections in Wallonia*

Year	Number of Lists (FNb)	Number of Seats (FNb)
1988	9	1
1994	53	72
2000	18	6
2006	23	28

formation which has no visibility and is evanescent in the field. It is exceptional to meet National Front activists and party communications and tracts are rare." The party has also had great difficulty keeping the activists and candidates it succeeds in recruiting. As Table 3.1 shows, its number of party lists has varied wildly from one municipal election to another.

Even more remarkable is the fact that there is little continuity between these lists. Delwit (2007) found that there were only 3 communes out of a possible 19 in Brussels (the FNb's supposed stronghold), where the party presented lists in the communal elections of 1988, 1994, and 2000. If one restricts the time frame to the latter two elections, the list expands by only 5 communes. The FNb has even less continuity in Wallonia: out of 262 communes, the party was able to field lists in only 6 in both 1994 and 2000.

As these data suggest, one reason that the FNb has been unable to build either a party elite or rank and file is that its activists are perpetually leaving it. Indeed, it is no exaggeration to say that the FNb began to split from the moment of its creation. Manuel Abramowicz has documented more than thirty splits and dissident movements emanating from the party.[8] While some of these splits involved only one or two individuals, others have been quite large and have torn the party apart. In 1995, Marguerite Bastien formed her own party after Féret had excluded her from the FNb on the grounds that she "was colluding with an organization whose goals are incompatible with those of the FNB" (Van den Brink 1996: 65). The organization in question was L'Assault, a neo-Nazi groupuscule composed of former FJ and PFNB members. Although Bastien certainly had close contacts with L'Assault, the notion that her relationship with extremists disqualified her from membership in the FNb is difficult to fathom, since the FNb has always been permeated by such individuals. According to Bastien, Féret ousted her from the FNb because she was examining

[8] *ResistanceS*, February 5, 2005.

possible financial improprieties on his part. She also presented the hitherto most formidable challenge to his leadership (Abramowicz 1996).

After leaving the party, Bastien claimed that the FNb was actually an instrument of the Belgian internal security services, designed to divide and disorganize the Francophone far right (Abramowicz 1996: 213). She was neither the first nor last of the FNb politicians to publicly attack their former party, and the regularity of these condemnations is telling. Jacques Hubert, an FNb representative elected to the Wallonian parliament in 1995, left the party in 1996 because of its "management shortcomings, lack of internal democracy, and dubious accounting practices."[9] When Brussels's deputies Juan Lemmens and Roland Frippiat exited the FNb shortly thereafter, they claimed that the party had "entrusted its management to criminals."[10] The complaints remained largely the same a decade later, when Charles Pire, a member of the Wallonian parliament, justified his defection from the FNb by claiming that Féret "continues to block the expansion of the FNb by keeping alive perpetual disputes with deputies and activists and by opposing the creation of local sections."[11]

Bastien brought several enemies of Féret with her into her new party, which she initially named the Front National–National Front. She lost a legal struggle with the FNb over the right to the acronym and renamed the party the Front Nouveau de Belgique (FNB). Although more than half of the FNb's communal councilors followed her into the party (Van den Brink 1996: 67), the FNB was soon to suffer from the factionalism endemic to the Francophone far right. In the communal elections of 2000, the FNB was able to field lists in only four communes in Wallonia and nine in Brussels and elect two councilors overall (both in Wallonia). By 2006, the party appeared to be moribund: it put together a mere seven lists composed of only fifteen candidates (the party had sixty-two candidates in 2000) and won a single seat. The president of the party, François Xavier-Robert, the former partner of Marguerite Bastien who took over the party after her departure in 2001, conceded that there was no party organization: "I do everything myself." With no hope of winning elected office, Robert acknowledged that the only reason he continued at all was "to damage Féret."[12]

In 2005, dissidents from the FNb formed another party that, like the FNB, looked to trade on the party acronym. The Force Nationale

---

[9] *Le Soir*, April 10, 1996.
[10] *Le Soir*, June 6, 1996.
[11] *Le Soir*, January 27, 2005.
[12] Interview with François Xavier-Robert (FNB), Brussels, February 2007.

(FNationale) was created by Paul Arku, Jacqueline Merveille, Francis Detraux (the FNB's only senator who had been elected in 2004), and Juan Lemmens. The FNationale first fielded candidates for the 2006 communal and provincial elections in which four parties from the radical right battled for votes (FNb, FNB, FNationale, and FDB).[13] Like the FNB, however, the FNationale was unable to appeal to former FNb voters: it won only one council seat and two seats in the Wallonian provincial parliament. Juan Lemmens, formerly of the FNb and the FNB, took one of the latter seats, although he had previously been fired by the Belgian Senate for misrepresenting his educational qualifications.[14] The FNationale, like the rest of the Francophone radical right, possesses virtually no organization: the party holds neither rallies nor meetings and advertises solely over the Internet.

None of the parties that split from the FNb have ever won more than a handful of seats in communal and regional parliaments or tallied more than a fraction of a percentage point in federal elections. Since other former politicians have tried and failed to form their own parties, the argument that Féret alone is responsible for the weakness of the FNb loses some weight. One might further argue that the FNb's centrifugal tendencies have not cost it votes. However, the counterfactual to consider is whether the FNb would have performed better electorally had it not been so fissiparous, and there are good reasons for believing that it would have. Consider, for example, the late 1990s, when support for the FNb hemorrhaged after the breakthrough elections of 1994 and 1995. The party suffered a wave of defections in this period: it had lost at least twenty of its seventy-three seats by 1996, as various elected officials formed new parties, were excluded from the FNb, or resigned (Van den Brink 1996: 61). As a result, the FNb was simply unable to find enough candidates to campaign in the next elections: the number of lists for the communal elections dropped from 53 to 18, while the number of candidates in Brussels plummeted from 260 to 121.

The level of acrimony and infighting within the FNb itself remained high a decade later. One deputy in the Walloon regional parliament refers to Cocriamont, the single FNb deputy in the Federal Parliament, as "Mr. Bean." The same deputy also took great pains to point out that his

---

[13] The FDB (Front de Bruxellois) is yet another splinter party from the FNb.
[14] Lemmens had been the parliamentary assistant to Senator Detraux but had failed to inform the Senate that he did not hold a university diploma required for the position. *ResistanceS*, October 21, 2006.

colleague in the regional parliament, Jean-Pierre Borbouse, had not uttered a single word or completed a single parliamentary act during his tenure.[15] Borbouse accused Féret of being a "political gangster" and suggested that he had never actually received a real medical education.[16] Féret described Borbouse as "an accident of democracy" and claimed that Patrick Sessler, Borbouse's parliamentary secretary and longtime activist within the FNb, is "unable to write two lines without making three errors."[17] Sessler, for his part, accused Féret of creating "enormous ethical problems within the FNb."[18] The lone FNb senator aptly described the members of his party as "not the most balanced,"[19] and it is no wonder that an FNb regional deputy likens an FNb meeting to "mental torture."[20]

FNb activists thus regularly accuse one another of incompetence, and it is clear that this had been one of the party's major problems. Lacking a reservoir of potential candidates, the FNb allowed just about anyone who was willing to stand for office in local elections to do so, and hoped for the best. In 1994, for example, Féret wagered that if two-thirds of the candidates proved reasonably competent and stayed with the party, then the elections would be a success.[21] This, however, was an optimistic assessment, as even high-ranking members of the party admit that many of these councilors "didn't understand a thing" about communal politics and "had no idea what they were doing."[22] According to the only current FNb member of the Chamber of Deputies, most FNb candidates have no experience, no education, and "simply lack culture."[23] According to another member of the party, there are perhaps three people in it who have any university education.[24] Given the difficulties of finding candidates for office, the party's "unconventional" recruitment mechanisms may have had something to do with the quality of the recruits. One former party member claimed that Féret found candidates for communal lists by frequenting bars late at night. "He would walk into bars at 3:00 AM and ask, 'Who wants to be on the list?' He put the least intoxicated

---

[15] Interview with Charles Petitjean (FNb), Luttre, February 2007.
[16] Interview with Jean-Pierre Borbouse (FNb), Brussels, February 2007.
[17] Interview with Daniel Féret (Fnb), Brussels, February 2007.
[18] Interview with Sessler.
[19] Interview with Delacroix.
[20] Interview with Charles Pire (FNb), Brussels, February 2007.
[21] Interview with Féret.
[22] Interview with Delacroix.
[23] Interview with Patrick Cocriamont (FNb), Brussels, February 2007.
[24] Interview with Pire.

first on the list, and the drunkest last."[25] This anecdote would be difficult to believe were it not corroborated by several other members and former members of the party.

In any event, the average FNb elected official (who is almost always a communal councilor) does very little. To demonstrate this point, Abramowicz (1996) conducted a survey of council members from the major political parties (the Greens, Socialists, Christian Democrats, and Liberals) in fourteen of the twenty-five communes where the FNb was represented in 1995. Compiling their answers, it turned out that FNb council members were perceived as active in only five of the fourteen city councils. The councilors said that they were aware of a local FNb party section in six communes, claimed that such did not exist in three communes, and did not know in five others. Thus the FNb failed to leave much of a footprint even in those places in which it won elected office, even at the peak of its electoral performance following the 1994 communal elections.

In addition to incompetents, the FNb is populated by extremists who undermine the party's attempts to sanitize its image and render it legitimate. Neo-Nazis, Holocaust deniers, and violent activists were present from the founding of the FNb, but the party became even more radical following the dissolution of the PFN and the incorporation of its members. Daniel Leskens resigned his council seat in the commune of Anderlecht after the Belgian television station RTBF released a video of him urinating on the graves of Jewish victims of the Holocaust at a meeting of former Waffen-SS members.[26] Patrick Cocriamont, a bus driver by profession and the FN's lone representative in the Federal Assembly since 2004, imitated the Nazi salute during his swearing-in ceremony as a city councilor in Anderlecht (Abramowicz 1996: 173). Leading members of the FNb have been convicted of criminal acts, and Féret himself has accumulated a long rap sheet over the years. In 1987, he was convicted of writing a fake medical certificate, which had served as the (unsuccessful) alibi for an individual who had committed a robbery (Abramowicz 1996: 112). Féret was fined and his political and civil rights were suspended for five years for this offense. In 1995, he lost his seat on the city council of Brussels-Ville because he had falsified his residence (Abramowicz 1996: 113). In 2006, he was convicted of spreading racist

---

[25] Interview with Juan Lemmens (FNationale), Corbais, February 2007.
[26] *ResistanceS*, August 27, 2000.

propaganda and election manifestos, and was barred from standing for elected office for ten years. He was also required to complete 250 hours of community service in the immigrant integration sector. In addition, L'Ordre des Médecins suspended Féret for three months on at least two occasions, in 1987 and again in 1995. On the latter occasion, l'Ordre des Médecins in Brabant suspended him for "not respecting the medical code of ethics and for violating the honor, discretion, and probity that doctors impose upon themselves" (Abramowicz 1996: 113).

Other members of the FNb, including many elected officials, have also had legal troubles. Michel Delacroix, the party's lawyer and current member of the Senate, was arrested for possessing illegal firearms and neo-Nazi literature in November 1994 and received a one-year suspended sentence in 1999. Two months after the 1994 communal elections, an FNb city councilor from La Louvière was arrested for armed robbery. A member of the Wallonian provincial parliament was charged with theft after he stole a copy of the statement he gave after being pulled over for speeding (Abramowicz 1996: 130).

The historical legacy of the Francophone far right goes a long way toward explaining why the FNb has attracted these types of activists. Yet the repressive environment also explains why, according to a former activist, "the only people who dare to be candidates are very weak."[27] There has never been any form of cooperation between the radical right and mainstream parties, nor has there ever been any discussion of it. Quite the opposite, mainstream parties established a powerful and enduring cordon sanitaire; in 1993, all Francophone democratic parties with the exception of the Greens signed a charter to publicly emphasize a tacit agreement that had existed for several years (Delwit 2007). In 1998, the presidents of all the Francophone parties signed an updated version of the charter in which they promised not to cooperate with parties "which advocate ideologies or proposals likely to undermine democratic principles." The parties went even farther than merely closing off coalition markets; they also pledged to "refuse any mandate which might have been obtained thanks to the support or abstention of the representatives" of the radical right.[28] Thus the Francophone parties credibly denied the FNb any direct influence in policy making *before* the party had become electorally significant.

There are significant social and economic costs associated with being an open member of the FNb, the FNB, or the FNationale. As Senator Michel

---

[27] Interview with Robert.
[28] *Le Soir*, May 9, 1998.

Delacroix from the FNb put it, "Those who are not financially independent" cannot join the party.[29] It is well known that civil servants, which in a country like Belgium represent a significant percentage of the working population, will lose their jobs if they join or actively support the FNb. Juan Lemmens of the FNationale admitted that "if you have any social stature, you simply cannot come to the FNationale."[30] The FNationale's primary goal is to win a seat in the Federal Chamber or Senate in order to receive public funding and thus be able to provide compensation for people who lose their jobs as a result of their radical right political activity.

The social pressure extends to the families of radical right activists. The mother of one potential candidate for the FNationale worked for the police, and the department reportedly put so much pressure on her that her son took himself off the party's electoral list.[31] Francois Xavier-Robert, the partner of Marguerite Bastien, claims that his superior officers in the army demanded that he leave Bastien if he wanted to keep his position. When he refused, he was quickly pushed into retirement. Robert also relates the sad story of the former Webmistress of the FNB, Martine Slogmeulder. A former professor of information technology, Slogmeulder lost her job when her university learned of her connection to the FNB. Her husband, who was working at NATO, divorced her and she lost custody of her children. After having her house set on fire, Slogmeulder committed suicide. While this is certainly an extreme result of ostracism, one hears other tales of derailed lives when one speaks long enough with Francophone radical right politicians.

There are allegedly repercussions for the simple act of signing the petition that parties require to appear on the ballot. According to every current and former FNb politician I spoke with, it is common practice for the mayors of Wallonian towns (particularly Socialist mayors) to send the police to the homes of people who signed such petitions to "make sure" that they were not coerced into doing so. Many of these people live in state-subsidized housing and are made to understand that they could lose their apartments if they do not retract their signature. It is little wonder that gathering five hundred signatures is "a very difficult job."[32] Given this hurdle, it is not altogether surprising that the FNb has been convicted several times of falsifying signatures and, as a result, was disqualified from standing in certain elections. In 1995, for example, the FNb's list for

[29] Interview with Delacroix.
[30] Interview with Lemmens.
[31] Interview with Lemmens.
[32] Interview with Cocriamont.

the elections for the Senate was invalidated by the courts (Abramowicz 1996: 197).

This social climate, and the mobilization of antifascist activists, makes it exceedingly difficult for the FNb to find places to meet. State facilities are out of the question, and private parties are worried about vandalism. Their fears are justified. One of my interviewees insisted on taking me on a tour of his damaged property, a bar where the FNb had previously held several functions. Some people (most likely antifascist activists) had thrown bricks through the windows, smashed the lights, and spray-painted the walls.[33] The FNb, as well as the FNB (the FNationale apparently does not organize meetings), are forced "not to disclose the location of the meeting until the last moment."[34] Members often congregate in a public space, such as a train station, before receiving maps directing them to a party function. After receiving numerous bomb threats, the FNB gave up entirely trying to hold meetings in Wallonia and met in Flanders instead.[35]

There are few published reports of FNb meetings, but the following by Hugues Dorzee, a journalist at the daily *Le Soir*, encapsulates descriptions I have heard from FNb politicians:

> The Front National is holding a public meeting in a grimy hangar.... The air is dusty. The napkins are paper.... The audience? About a hundred people.... The beers circulate. The Frontists listen without listening. The big agricultural workers snigger coarsely. Not a shadow of a program. No debate. No vote on the electoral lists.[36]

For two decades, Féret succeeded in maintaining his grip on the FNb. Yet he finally lost control of it in October 2007 when the FNb's political bureau voted to dismiss him as president and elected Delacroix, the lone FNb representative in the Belgian Senate, in his place. However, Delacroix was forced to resign the following November after a video of him singing an anti-Semitic song (one that poked fun at a woman sent to Dachau) aired on Belgian public television. Less than a week later, the text of an interview was printed in *Le Soir* in which the FNb's only representative in the Federal Assembly (Cocriamont) openly admitted to being a Holocaust revisionist.[37] These events touched off a new round of inner-party struggle, and Delacroix was replaced by Daniel Huygens

---

[33] Interview with Petitjean.
[34] Interview with Delacroix.
[35] Interview with Robert.
[36] *Le Soir*, June 13, 2006.
[37] *Le Soir*, November 14, 2008.

as the FNb's president. The other competitor for the position – Charles Petitjean – then left the party entirely and announced he was forming his own. The regional and European elections of June 7, 2009, revealed that the party's electoral support had hemorrhaged since the same elections were held five years earlier: the party won 1.9% in Brussels (a loss of 3.5%), 2.9% in Wallonia (a loss of 5.3%), and 3.6% in the elections for the European Parliament (a loss of 3.9%). Féret's departure thus did little to solve the FNb's chronic problems.

The Dutch Center Democrats

The Dutch Center Democrats, the most significant radical right party in the Netherlands in the 1980s and 1990s, suffered from many of the same pathologies as the FNb. Rather than marching through them formulaically, however, the following case study – like those in the rest of the book – is organized chronologically, and the five internal features of parties I outlined in Chapter 2 emerge from the narrative. While the history of the CD reveals multiple examples of incompetence and criminality, the struggle between moderates and extremists was particularly strong in this case.

"Fascism and Nazism were always marginal in the Netherlands," writes one of the leading historians of the Dutch far right (Van Donselaar 1991: 9). However, the fascist wave of the 1930s did not entirely pass the Netherlands by. As in Wallonia, a political opportunist – Anton Mussert – founded a minor fascist party – the Nationaal Socialistische Beweging (NSB) – which scored some modest electoral successes in the middle of the decade but had faded long before the German occupation. The NSB contained fascist elements, although its exclusion of biological racism placed it closer to Italian fascism than German National Socialism, to whose adjectives Mussert was obviously attracted. The NSB counted 52,000 members at its height in 1935 and won 8% of the votes in the provincial elections of 1935. Only two years later, however, the party managed only 4.2% of the vote in the 1937 parliamentary election, and membership had declined by nearly half before the German invasion (Mudde and Van Holsteyn 2000: 145). However, under Nazi occupation the NSB became the only legal political party and counted 100,000 members.

Yet even before the war had ended, the Dutch government in exile made plans to obliterate all traces of fascism in the Netherlands. Queen Wilhelmina signed the "Resolution Concerning the Dissolution of Treasonous Organizations" on September 17, 1944, which banned not only the NSB but also future organizations that pursued the same goal. This law, combined with instant amnesia regarding collaboration and an "antifascist, repressive climate," largely prevented any regeneration of far right political activity (Van Donselaar 1991: 49). As in Wallonia, and in contrast to Flanders, social organizations intended to aid former collaborators were virtually nonexistent in the Netherlands. The largest of such organizations, the Stichting Oud Politieke Delinquenten (Foundation for Political Delinquents, SOPD), consisted of perhaps a hundred former internees (Mudde 2000: 117). When members of the SOPD tried to form a political party, the Nationaal Europese Sociale Beweging (NESB) in 1951, the Dutch government applied the 1944 resolution and banned it in 1955. Although the NESB counted only somewhere between one hundred and four hundred members, it was clear that while a "coterie of national socialists" like the SOPD was tolerated, "a political party of national socialists was not" (Van Donselaar 1991: 79).

Several fascist organizations operated clandestinely after the banning of the NESB, but the far right landscape was essentially barren for more than a decade. Unlike the situation in France, decolonization in the Netherlands did not follow intense and protracted conflict, and did not result in a wave of disgruntled settlers returning to the mother country from Indonesia (Husbands 1992: 96). In the 1960s, the Boerenpartij (Farmer's Party, BP) sought to harness the discontent of Dutch farmers. Although the BP explicitly distanced itself from fascism, it did attract former NSB members (Mudde 2000: 118). Whether the party can be properly labeled a far right party is still debated (Van Donselaar 1991: 125). What is clear is that the party suffered the same fate as the Poujadist movement to which it was often compared: after peaking at 4.7% of the national vote in the 1967 elections, the party splintered into competing factions and quickly disappeared from the scene (Husbands 1992: 108).

In the 1970s, the only significant far right party in the Netherlands was the Nederlandse Volks-Unie (Dutch People's Union, NVU) founded by Johaan Georg Glimmerveen in 1971. The combination of former NSB members in its ranks (Van Donselaar 1991: 143) and Glimmerveen's rabidly anti-immigrant discourse placed the NVU in the extremist category. For the 1974 municipal elections in The Hague, the NVU distributed an election pamphlet that read, "The Hague must stay white and safe! Away with the Surinamese and Antillianese who parasite on our energy and on our welfare. Help me free our city from the plague of Surinamese and Antillianese" (quoted in Husbands 1992: 110).

Although the NVU counted only about several hundred members at its height and although the party was electorally insignificant (its best result was 0.4% in the national parliamentary election of 1977), the Dutch state took action against it. In 1978, an Amsterdam court ruled that the NVU was a "criminal association" and excluded it from the local election of 1978. A complex set of circumstances led to the repeal of this verdict in 1979 by the Dutch Supreme Court (see Van Donselaar 1991: 165–167), but the NVU was effectively finished by this stage. "By late 1979, with the electoral road effectively blocked, the party and its publications had lapsed overtly into neo-Nazi sympathy, bemoaning the continued imprisonment of Rudolf Hess and openly adopting revisionist positions about the Holocaust" (Husbands 1992: 111).

In December 1979, four former members of the NVU founded the Nationale Centrumpartij (National Center Party, NCP). The adjective "center" was meant to suggest a clean break with the radicalism of the NVU, but the violent proclivities of some of the party's activists led to its immediate demise. Following the very first public meeting of the NCP in February 1980, several of its members raided a church in Amsterdam and attacked the Moroccan immigrants who had sought refuge in it (Voerman and Lucardie 1992: 40). The resulting protest and negative publicity forced the NCP to dissolve itself on March 10, 1980 (Mudde and van Holsteyn 2000: 146).

The next day, Henry Brookman (one of the founders of the NVU) launched the Centrumpartij (Center Party, CP). Brookman was a professor of social science at the Free University in Amsterdam, and the small circle of activists around him was also highly educated. In contrast to Glimmerveen and other activists from the NVU, Brookman was a moderate and sought to distance his new party from extremism. Yet pressure from his employer prevented Brookman from taking a prominent role in the new party, and he drafted Hans Janmaat, who had no connections with the right-wing extremist subculture, to lead the party in his stead.[38] Brookman appeared to have hoped that Janmaat could be controlled. Indeed, Janmaat had a "history of various short-lived and failed professional and political careers" (Mudde 2000: 120), and his reputed membership in both left-wing and right-wing political organizations suggested that his political views were far from fixed, and perhaps pliable. When the CP garnered 0.8% of the vote in the 1982 parliamentary elections, Janmaat took the one seat that the party had won under the extremely

---

[38] Paul Lucardie, personal communication.

proportional electoral system of the Netherlands. The CP may have done significantly better in this election had it been able to field candidates in multiple constituencies, but the lack of any party cadre made this impossible (Ignazi 2003: 164). However, the CP did do surprisingly well in some cities like Rotterdam, where it captured 4.0% of the vote, indicating that there was demand for an anti-immigrant party like the CP in the Netherlands. In the 1984 European elections, during which the party adopted the slogan "Get Foreigners out of Europe," the CP won 2.5% nationwide.

Despite becoming the most successful radical right party in the postwar Netherlands by virtue of its single parliamentary seat and modest showing in a European election, the CP was soon destroyed by factionalism. It became clear that Brookman had miscalculated, as Janmaat proved to be fiercely independent. Personal rivalries and opposition to Janmaat by the CP's extremist holdovers from the NVU led to the expulsion of the party's single parliamentary representative in 1984. Janmaat soon became leader of yet another offshoot of the Center movement, the Centrumdemocraten (Center Democrats, CD), which was founded by his former aides (Mudde and Van Holsteyn 2000: 147).

The self-inflicted loss of its parliamentary representative (and the state subsidies that came with it) magnified the internal divisions within the CP. The party's two moderate leaders were both schoolteachers and, like Brookman, were threatened with unemployment unless they left the CP (Mudde and Van Holsteyn 2000: 147). Their exit, as well as the departure of some moderates who followed Janmaat into the CD, left the CP in dire straits for the 1986 parliamentary elections, in which it won 0.4% and no seats. The party had resorted to creative measures to gather enough signatures to contest the elections; citizens believed that they were signing a petition against rent increases (Lucardie 1998: 113). A Dutch court ordered the CP to compensate these victims of electoral fraud, and the party went bankrupt in May 1986 and was subsequently dissolved. Yet a group of extremists from the NVU succeeded in renaming themselves, and the CP became the CP'86. Starved for candidates, the CP'86 was unable to contest the 1989 parliamentary elections. By the late 1990s, the party had become "an empty vessel, probably containing only the inactive 'party leader' [Martin] Freling who had lost all his former comrades as well as the party's funds, allegedly as a consequence of his drug addiction" (Mudde 2000: 147).

While the CP'86 collapsed over the course of the 1990s, the CD of Janmaat would register some modest electoral successes. The first years were hardly auspicious, however, as the CD won just 0.1% in the 1986 parliamentary elections and Janmaat lost his seat in parliament. The party appeared to be moribund and unable to compete with the CP'86. Three years later, however, Janmaat defied all expectations and returned to parliament as the CD won 0.9% in the 1989 parliamentary elections. But the CD's high point came in the 1994 election year, when it won seventy-seven seats in municipal councils in March and 2.5% of the vote in parliamentary elections in May, which produced three seats. The party was in fact disappointed by its national performance, for public opinion polls conducted by Dutch Gallup suggested that the party would have received 5.5% of the vote had elections been held in November 1993 (Mudde and Van Holsteyn 2000: 156). But despite this erosion of support and despite the fact that the CD was tiny compared with radical right parties elsewhere in Europe at the time, the Social Democratic chief and future prime minister, Wim Kok, labeled the May elections a "black day in Dutch history" (Mudde and Van Holsteyn 1994: 132).

In retrospect, Kok's fears were misplaced. The CD crumbled over the next four years, winning only 0.6% in the 1998 parliamentary elections and thereby losing all three seats. Moreover, the party retained only *two* of its seventy-seven seats in municipal councils. If the CP'86's radicalization doomed its electoral fortunes, the same cannot be said about the CD, as it was offering the same basic platform as successful radical right parties elsewhere in Western Europe. In addition, the highly industrialized area in the south, known as the Randstad, provided a fertile breeding ground for the radical right: the CD polled 7.9%, 9.2%, and 10.2% in Amsterdam, The Hague, and Rotterdam, respectively (Mudde and Van Holsteyn 1994).

The problem was not a lack of voters, but a lack of activists. The conflict between moderates and extremists pulled activists away from the CD. The core of the NVU and the NVU's youth organization went over to the CP'86 after the split. For the first several years of the CD's history, its membership was probably far below 100 (Mudde 2000: 123). The party did claim to have 3,000 members at its highpoint in the early 1990s, but specialists put this number closer to 1,000–1,500 (Van den Brink 1994: 211–212). Moreover, probably only about 100 of these could have been considered active (Mudde 2000: 127). The party never had the organizational resources to field candidates in more than a small percentage of municipal elections. In its best year, 1994, the party contested only about 7% (43 of more than 600) of the races.

If the CD had difficulties recruiting candidates to stand for office, it had even more trouble holding the seats that it did win, particularly after the 1994 municipal elections, in which it won seventy-seven seats. Not only was it unable to fill all of those seats (Lucardie 1998: 115), but the party quickly lost the seats it did occupy. By the end of the year, the party itself reported that it had lost "twenty odd" (Mudde 2000: 126). By May, there were only forty-one CD councilors left. This hemorrhaging of the party on a local level was the result of defections to other parties, expulsions or suspensions by the CD, and resignations from the council.

On closer examination of several CD councilors, this self-destruction becomes easier to understand. Henry Selhourst, who had won a seat in the town of Arnhem, was a notorious drug dealer who collected his signatures to stand for office from drug addicts. He was imprisoned during his term. A CD councilor in the town of Almelo suffered from dementia. Richard van der Plas, a career neo-Nazi who had been caught possessing a gun, drugs, and Nazi propaganda, represented the CD in the town of Purmerend. The majority of the CD councilors were attracted by the modest salaries that the jobs provided, and many either never showed up to meetings or stopped attending after a couple of sessions.

Why was the CD so starved for talent? As already noted, the lack of a nationalist subculture meant that there were no recruitment networks on which to draw. Although most of the small right-wing extremist milieu found its way to the CP'86 and its offshoots, some individuals with violent pasts and openly neo-Nazi sympathies – such as Van der Plas – ended up with the CD. Yge Garman, who had also won a council seat in 1994, was later imprisoned after he was caught on film bragging about committing arson against refugees in the early 1980s (Mudde 2000: 125). Although the CD would periodically expel right-wing extremists, they continued to flock to the party and kept it under a cloud of suspicion.

The second important reason the CD failed to recruit capable members was that the political environment was highly repressive. This did not affect the extremists, who generally do not seem to care about social or economic sanctions. But it did certainly change the calculations of individuals with radical right sympathies who may have stood for office under other circumstances. This repression went far beyond the existence of a cordon sanitaire, which was announced the moment the CD won its parliamentary seat and was enforced by every political party at every political level. It also involved significant pressure from employers, antifascist groups, the media, and the state's internal security services.

Brookman and other educated leaders of the party were given the choice of either continuing their involvement in radical right politics or keeping their jobs. Like other individuals in the party with white-collar jobs, they chose employment over politics. Blue-collar workers who were visible in the Center parties faced pressure as well. Hank Ruitenberg was fired from his job in a Skania automobile factory in Zwolle for being a member of the CP'86.[39] A member of the CD recounts how his former boss reacted to his participation in an extreme right demonstration:

I saw you on television. What were you doing there? I don't want you here any-more. Your future here has finished.... And of course, quite a few members of my family did not know.... All those bald heads and then they think are you a part of this? I have always seen you as a nice guy. Their whole ideal fell apart so to say.[40] (Linden and Klandermans 2006: 198)

Any individual weighing the risks of becoming, or continuing to be, an active member of either the CD or CP'86 would most likely have heard of stories like the ones recounted here. If they were unaware of these, however, they certainly would not have missed the case of Janmaat himself. After losing his seat in parliament, Janmaat exercised his legal right – a right upheld in court – to return to his old teaching job. The school refused to take him back, however, and the court allowed the school to pay Janmaat compensation instead of allowing him to return (Mudde 2000: 124). Janmaat reentered politics in large part because he had nothing else to lose, a calculation that describes the vast majority of the Center Democrats.[41]

It is impossible to determine how many people thought about join-ing the CD but were ultimately dissuaded by the consequences. In-depth interviews with CD politicians conducted by Annette Linden, however, show that they did not take the decision to join the party or stand for office lightly. One member who eventually joined in 1989 described his calculations as follows:

I had thought a long time already. From the very beginning that the CD existed, I wanted to become a member. But I thought, why should I do it.... I have a son who has a job in the security business, I have a son who has a hotel in this town, thus you must consult your children.... They must agree with it.... Once they had a meeting here, and then they have pushed Janmaat's car into the water.... Well, a month later the parents of my daughter-in-law are still being threatened. (Linden and Klandermans 2006: 188)

The consequences of CD membership were not only economic, but social as well. Center Democrats report that their involvement in politics cost

---

[39] Interview with Paul Lucardie, Groningen, October 2006.
[40] The English translations from the Dutch interviews are from Linden and Klandermans.
[41] Interview with Rinke Van den Brink, Amsterdam, October 2006.

them friendships and alienated them from family members. According to one member:

Over time one gets used to the estrangement from family members. In the beginning it really hurts but right now I say they are grown-ups. It's the way it is. But my brother and two sisters have made that choice.... I don't see them anymore.... An Indonesian guy who is born and grown up here with whom I have been on vacation several times felt that he couldn't be friends any more. I had quite a few friends from the business club ... who because of their business couldn't talk to me anymore. In private in a bar or a restaurant yes, but not in public. (Linden and Klandermans 2006: 197)

Another member laments the loss of her best friend:

That has been a great shock to me. I know her since I was five years old. We were friends in everything, in joy and sorrow. She was like a sister to me. And then her husband called that they had taken our address out of their address book and they did not want to have anything to do with me anymore. (Linden and Klandermans 2006: 187–188)

Such stigmatization helps explain why radical right parties operating in highly repressive environments tend to have more couples than one might expect. A typical pattern is that one partner (usually the husband or boyfriend) first crosses the threshold, which then makes life difficult for the other. Feeling isolated, the spouse or partner then joins the party, not necessarily out of political conviction but out of a need to re-create some semblance of a social life. As one middle-aged (female) Center Democrat explained:

I was already isolated, for me the step was not so difficult, of course. Because of my husband's position I was already isolated. For some time already I didn't have many acquaintances and friends. Much people beyond fellow party members and friends you have, I hadn't anyway. The people who got to know me, learn who I am and then don't want me anymore. Well, I have experienced that for so many years already, it hurts, but I don't bother anymore. (Linden and Klandermans, 2006: 187)

Active members of the CD also had good reason to be concerned about their safety. The election of Janmaat to parliament in 1982 resulted in the immediate formation of antifascist committees across the country (Voerman and Lucardie 1992: 41). The core members of this movement were left-liberal activists, anarchists, and veterans of the squatters' movement, and they did not always shy away from violence and intimidation in their battles against the far right. In the most notorious incident, antifascist militants set fire to a hotel in Kedichem in March 1986 where the CD and the CP'86 were meeting to discuss a possible merger. Wil Schuurman, the CD party secretary, lost her leg as a result of jumping from the second story of the burning building. Individuals who agreed to stand for office could also be sure of receiving "visits" from antifascist committees once the party list was deposited at, and made public by, the voting authorities.[42]

The real threat of violence undoubtedly turned away many radical right sympathizers who may have otherwise become active party members. It also meant the CD had immense trouble achieving simple tasks, such as finding places to meet. The CD was never able to get permission to meet in public venues, and private owners, out of either conviction or the fear of violence, were unwilling to rent to the party. In addition, the location of any meeting had to be kept secret for as long as possible to prevent antifascist committees from disrupting it. CD events thus came to rely heavily on stealth. For example, CD members were often told to meet at a rest stop on the highway, and from there they received directions to the party meeting.

The Dutch media also did all it could to damage the party's reputation. In 1994, no less than three undercover journalists gained entrance into the CD and published highly critical pieces about the party, two of which appeared before the 1994 parliamentary elections in weekly magazines (Kooiman 1994; Rensen 1994a; Van Hout 1994). A book entitled *Dancing with the Devil* appeared later in the year (Rensen 1994b). Aside from portraying the CD as a collection of "fascists, criminals, and scum" (Rensen 1994a), the journalists laid bare the party's perpetual organizational chaos and amateurism. Peter Rensen, for example, posed as a homeless person living outside of Hans Janmaat's apartment, which doubled as the CD party office (1994a). Janmaat, who had apparently noticed him before, referred to him as "the kid who lives on the street." When Rensen expressed interest in joining the party but claimed to have no money for the membership fee, he was immediately put to work at administrative tasks. There he overheard – and later recounted – conversations about Hitler's achievements, neo-Nazi films, and violence against foreigners. The publication of this article, combined with the airing a week before the parliamentary elections of a television program that captured a CD politician bragging about committing arson, most likely decreased support for the CD (Mudde and Van Holsteyn 2000: 148).

[42] Interview with Van den Brink.

The hostility of the Dutch media, the willingness of the state to ban extremist parties, and the continuing battles with the CP'86 all contributed to Janmaat's paranoia. Had Janmaat actually created auxiliary groups, such as a youth organization, the party would have received subsidies from the Department of Culture, Health and Welfare (Lucardie 1998: 117). But the leader of the CD feared that such groups would be infiltrated by informers or agents of the internal security service. Janmaat's attempts to create these organizations on paper and collect the subsidies led to continual skirmishes with the state, battles that he always lost. The only people that he truly trusted were his girlfriend (Wil Schuurman) and her son. Some of this undoubtedly is related to Janmaat's character. By all accounts, he could not stand any challenges to his authority, and only "nitwits and nobodies had a chance next to him."[43] But the climate of repression and the physical and financial risks that came along with active membership in the CD meant that Janmaat was likely to be surrounded only by such people in the first place. The CD attracted only those who welcomed confrontation with antifascist activists, those who calculated that the potential financial compensation of a council seat was worth risking their job for, those who participated in criminal activities, and those whose political convictions outweighed all of the negative repercussions. This ended up being a small and motley group who, when given their first real opportunity in the municipal elections of 1994, quickly proved incompetent.

The Sweden Democrats

On May 18–20, 2007, the Sweden Democrats (SD) finally held their annual party conference in Karlskrona. The event had been delayed for more than a month as the party scoured southern Sweden for a venue, receiving dozens of rejections in the process. In mid-April, it appeared that the party had finally secured a hotel in Copenhagen and thus would have taken the extraordinary step of holding the party conference outside of Sweden. But the Danish hotel canceled as well, and it was only the intervention of a liberal politician in Karlskrona who, citing the right to freedom of expression, made a public meeting hall available. About two hundred SD party delegates attended the conference. Forty police were dispatched to protect them from attacks by radical left-wing activists who, in this case, never materialized. But the preceding October in the

---

[43] Interview with Van den Brink.

town of Elsöv, antifascists had overcome the two-person security force protecting the SD meeting, shattering windows and roughing up several party members. The police took no chances in Karlskrona; a 5:1 delegate to police ratio ensured there would be no trouble.[44]

Despite the SD's recent disappointment in Copenhagen, the party secretary, Björn Söder, drew a sharp contrast between the political environment in the neighboring countries during his speech, declaring, "We in Sweden look at Denmark like the citizens of the DDR used to look at West Germany." His remark went over well and was often repeated to me during my subsequent interviews with SD politicians. Yet despite the feeling of living under totalitarian rule, an optimistic mood prevailed in Karlskrona. The leader of the Social Democrats, Mona Sahlin, had recently sparred with SD party leader Jimmie Åkesson on television, marking the first time any notable politician had agreed to a debate with the SD. In the elections of October 2006, the SD had won 2.9% of the vote and 282 seats in local councils, by far its best result to date. The party executive was dominated by young, reasonably well educated men who had no criminal or right-wing extremist history. As the SD's local leader in the town of Lund told me, he expected the party to double its voteshare in every election until it became the largest force in Swedish politics. His optimism, to be sure, far exceeded that of the other SD politicians I spoke with. But most were sure that they would surmount the 4% hurdle for representation in the next parliamentary election.

The Sweden Democrats may very well improve on their modest electoral success. Yet as leading members of the party acknowledge, they are still one of the least successful radical right political parties in Western Europe (although they prefer the term "nationalist" to radical right). They have remained on the margins of Swedish politics for nearly two decades. And there are good reasons to believe that even if they enter the Riksdag in several years, they are unlikely to duplicate the successes of either the Danish People's Party or the Norwegian Progress Party. The legacy of history and the strength of norms against anti-immigrant parties will be very difficult to overcome.

As in Denmark and Norway, interwar fascist parties were marginal forces in Sweden. All three Scandinavian countries lacked the type of conditions that had spawned fascism in other contexts. None of the three had entered the First World War and therefore did not suffer from the national humiliation of defeat. None had unfulfilled territorial

[44] Participant observation by the author.

aspirations. All three were ethnically homogeneous and, most important, had developed stable parliamentary institutions before the fascist wave of the 1920s and the Great Depression. Fascist movements found a particularly infertile environment in Sweden, even compared with Denmark and Norway. After a long series of splits and name changes, the National Socialist Workers Party / Swedish Socialist Assembly (NSAP/SSS) emerged as the largest fascist party, peaking at 0.7% of the vote in the 1936 parliamentary elections.[45] Although one should be wary of trivializing support for fascist ideas in Sweden, the perception of Swedish interwar fascism "as a mishmash of ridiculous NSDAP-look-alikes and Hitler-wannabes constantly fighting each other, never gaining any influence over Swedish politics, and failing spectacularly" is not far from the truth (Berggren 2002: 395).[46]

Given this legacy, it follows that the postwar far right landscape in Sweden consisted of tiny, marginalized associations. The fascist Neo-Swedish Movement (Nysvenska Rörelsen) and the extreme right National League of Sweden (Sveriges Nationella Förbund) survived the end of the war but "were mostly discussion clubs for aging gentlemen" (Widfeldt 2007). The largest of the new parties, the Nordic Realm Party (Nordiska Rikspartiet), has been described as a "gang of loonies" and Hitler admirers (Lindquist 1979: 24). But the Swedish far right landscape changed markedly in the late 1970s and early 1980s with the advent of violent neo-Nazi and skinhead groups (Lööw 1999). Sweden became a major exporter of "white power" music, videos, and other merchandise.[47] The Swedish neo-Nazi scene is numerically much larger than the neo-Nazi presence in Denmark and Norway, and nearly all of the various groups that are part of it stem from either the Bevara Sverige Svenskt ("Keep Sweden Swedish," BSS), described later, or the White Aryan Resistance (VAM). VAM was a paramilitary group modeled on the American white supremacist group the Order. The offshoots of VAM and BSS include the National Socialist Front (NSF), the Swedish Resistance/National Youth (SMR/NU), and Blood and Honour (B&H).

The Sweden Democrats emerged from this right-wing extremist subculture, and that is the primary reason for the party's failure for the first decade and a half of its existence. In 1979, neo-Nazi and violent elements

---

[45] The best scores for the Danish and Norwegian fascist parties were, respectively, 1.8% for the DNSAP in 1939 and 2.2% for the NS in 1933.

[46] Berggren, it should be noted, does not share this view.

[47] "Sweden," Annual Report of the Stephen Roth Institute. http:///www.tau.ac.il/Anti-Semitism/asw2004/sweden.htm.

in Swedish society formed the BSS, whose main activity was distributing racist leaflets and bumper stickers. In 1986, BSS merged with the tiny Swedish Progress Party (Framstegspartiet) to form the Sweden Party, which split a year later.[48] In 1988, members of the BSS tried again and formed the Sweden Democrats.

Anders Klarström was the leader of the party for the first seven years of its history, a period that SD members refer to alternatively as the "circus years" or the "dark years." One member who joined in 1991 found that the party consisted of "people with crazy ideas, Nazi ideas, and even worse."[49] Another joined the SD in 1992 but quit shortly thereafter (rejoining again only in 1997) because "the people there were not my kind; they were very racist and wore bomber jackets and army boots.... We had real weirdos in the party in the 1990s, to be honest."[50] These impressions are consistent with the few existing studies of the SD that cover this period (Larsson and Ekman 2001; Widfeldt 2007). Right-wing extremists and criminals predominated. Klarström himself had been a member of the neo-Nazi Nordiska Rikspartiet and had been convicted of several crimes, including vandalism, theft, and telephone threats. Another of the party founders, Ulf Ranshede, had attacked a fourteen-year-old immigrant and was convicted of inflicting grievous bodily harm. Until 1994, half of the party members had criminal records and a third were directly connected with neo-Nazi organizations (Larsson and Ekman 2001: 225). In 1991, the party won two council seats in the whole of Sweden. The first was in the small village of Dals Ed, where the leader of the local party list could not occupy the seat because of his criminal record. The seat was then occupied by another Sweden Democrat with legal convictions for making threats and dealing in stolen property. The situation initially looked better in the town of Höör, where a nurse with no criminal record named Tina Hallgren Bengtsson took the seat and later became a member of the party executive. But in 1996, Bengtsson left the SD to join the neo-Nazi National Socialist Front. In addition to neo-Nazis, the party counted several former, unrepentant members of the NSAP/SSS (the Swedish Nazi Party) among its ranks.

The Sweden Democrats would remain a barely organized, highly fractionalized collection of racists and petty criminals until 1995, when Mikael Jannson took over and tried to purge the party of these elements.

---

[48] The Swedish Progress Party, founded in 1968, predated its Danish and Norwegian counterparts but never managed to attain any electoral success.

[49] Interview with Poul Svenson (SD), Ystad, May 2007.

[50] Interview with L. J. Hollgren (SD), Malmö, May 2007.

A factory worker whose nine-to-five job prevented him from devoting himself full time to politics, Jannson nevertheless possessed more organizational skills than Klarström and, equally important, no record of extremist or criminal activity. In 1996, Jannson instituted a "uniform ban" at SD functions, a clear challenge to the neo-Nazi skinheads who normally wore military garb. In 1999, the party officially renounced Nazism. Although this certainly marked an ideological shift within the party, the condemnation was also designed to stem the negative treatment of the party in the media following the murder of two policemen and a trade union activist by Swedish neo-Nazis (Rydgren 2006).

It was only in late 2001 that moderates gained the upper hand in the party. In that year, Anders Steen and Tor Paulsson – who had fought Jansson's efforts to steer the party away from the extremist fringe – were expelled and formed the National Democrats (Nationaldemokraterna). Although the split allowed the SD to finally part ways with most of the extremists in its ranks, it weakened the party tremendously in the short run. Many of the most engaged foot soldiers followed Steen and Paulsson. As one Sweden Democrat, who joined the party in 1995 put it, the party lost only "ten to fifteen percent of the cadre [as a result of the split], but the problem was that they were highly motivated and worked very hard for the party."[51] Most of the Stockholm section defected, and the Sweden Democrats have yet to build a meaningful party organization in their capital city. The party was poorly prepared for the 2002 parliamentary elections; it barely made the deadline for submitting its parliamentary lists. According to one report, members were still filling out forms at the post office minutes before they were due and were able to field candidates in only 80 of 289 constituencies.[52] The party received 1.4% of the vote. Its performance was even worse in the 2004 European elections: 1.13%.

In 2005, the twenty-six-year-old Jimmie Åkesson wrested the party leadership from Jansson. Åkesson is part of a small group of educated young men with clean records who met while students at the University of Lund and have effectively taken over the leadership of the party. This group includes Matthias Karlsson, Richard Jomshof, and party secretary Björn Söder. As a result of its 2006 electoral performance and resulting state subsidies, the party currently has twelve full-time paid positions, which allows this group to concentrate full time on politics. These individuals have made a high-stakes wager that the SD will gain parliamentary

---

[51] Interview with Jan-Åke Isaksson (SD), Ystad, May 2007.
[52] Interview with Rikhard Slått, editor in chief of *Expo*, Stockholm, May 2005.

representation – and hence more money and paid positions – in the next election.

The SD has clearly moved from a right-wing extremist party to a radical right one. It is probably true, as many Sweden Democrats allege, that Swedish neo-Nazis detest the party for moving toward the center and no longer seek a place within it. Members of the party openly admit that they import their policy positions from the Danish People's Party and look to it as a model. One cannot therefore claim that the Sweden Democrats have failed because their policies, in relation to those of radical right parties elsewhere, are too extreme. Still, the fact that the SD originated from the right-wing extremist subculture not only precluded electoral success until the final break with extremism, but also continues to plague it. The Swedish media have hours of footage of SD functions from the 1990s (the time before the uniform ban), which it often runs when it covers the party today. As one member put it, it would have been better had the party changed its name in the late 1990s to distance itself further from its past.[53] Most Swedes associate the SD with neo-Nazism and will most likely continue to do so for a number of years.

This association helps explain, and continues to reinforce, the repressive political and social reaction to the SD. "Sweden is not a democracy" was the refrain of my interviews with Sweden Democrats. Söder's remark about eastern Germany encapsulated the general sense of marginalization and intimidation that permeates the party's activists. There is no doubt that being a Sweden Democrat in Sweden is not easy: the costs are high and the benefits few. The net result of the political and social reaction to the party has been to reinforce the essential characteristics of the party cadre since its founding. We are a party, one member succinctly put it, "of people living on the edge."[54]

In terms of political coalition markets, the cordon sanitaire against the SD has been as tight as anywhere in Europe. Even though the party polled a mere 1.4% in 2002, the mainstream parties felt it necessary to announce that there would be no cooperation at any level with the radical right. In 2002, the ruling Social Democrats and opposition Liberals issued a joint press release – formalizing a policy that had been in place for years – pledging to work across party lines to prevent anti-immigrant parties from wielding any power in local councils. The Conservatives also received orders from the national level to never approve any proposal

[53] Interview with Mattias Karlsson (SD), Malmö, May 2007.
[54] Interview with Hollgren.

emanating from the SD. Most of these proposals, like most proposals in municipal politics, are not deeply ideological but concern such things as the location of traffic lights. As one Sweden Democrat complains, "No matter what we propose, the proposals are voted down, and no other parties will utter a word."

On several occasions, political parties have been forced to abdicate power or form uncommon alliances simply to prevent the SD from wielding influence. For example, in 2002 the SD won one seat in the local council in the town of Ystad. The ruling Conservatives were one seat short of a majority but chose to go into opposition rather than cooperate with the single SD councilman. In 2006, the SD won 10 out of 149 seats in the regional council of Skåne. Again, rather than enter into an alliance with the SD, the Conservatives chose to cooperate with the Greens, who in turn agreed to the unlikely coalition because they did not want the Sweden Democrats to become kingmakers.[55]

There has been only one documented attempt by mainstream parties to cooperate with the SD. In the town of Trelleborg, in which the Social Democrats had ruled for decades, two Social Democratic politicians – Egil Ahl and Kjell Nilsson – tried to enter an agreement with the SD, which had become the third-largest party in the council. The local leader of the SD, Per Klarberg, claims he tried to warn them of the consequences: "I said to Egil 'are you aware that collaboration with the Sweden Democrats will shake the window panes all the way up to your party headquarters in Stockholm?"[56] This is exactly what occurred, as the pressure on Nilsson and Ahl became so great that they decided to resign. As another Social Democrat put it, their attempts to cooperate with the SD led to their "political deaths."[57]

The cordon sanitaire is one factor that prevents ambitious political entrepreneurs from joining the party. But an equal, if not greater, deterrent is the credible threat to one's economic livelihood. There have been several high-profile cases of Sweden Democrats who have lost their jobs as a result of their politics. Richard Jomshof, a part-time high school teacher and SD municipal councilor from the town of Karlskrona, was dismissed from his position. He was subsequently fired from two other teaching positions when his activities in the SD became known. Kenneth Sandberg, a member of the SD who worked at an immigration center

[55] Interview with Thomas Lantz (Conservative), Ystad, May 2007.
[56] *Local*, October 19, 2006.
[57] Interview with Anders Rubin (Social Democrat), Malmö, May 2007.

handling applications, was fired for his membership in the party.[58] Kent Ekeroth, a twenty-five-year-old trained economist, was sacked from his position as an intern at the Swedish Embassy in Tel Aviv because of his links to the SD. At the time of this writing, none of the three had found permanent employment.

All of the Sweden Democrats I interviewed were familiar with these cases, and many shared their own fears, or actual experiences, of losing their jobs. Michael Rosenberg, the local leader in the town of Helsingborg and the party's blogmaster, drove a taxi for the elderly. He joined the party in 1996 but refused to stand for local office or to "become too well known" out of fear that he would lose his contract with the city for his services. It was only when he became a regular taxi driver (and thus had no more contracts with the city government) that he became actively engaged with the SD.[59] L. J. Hollgren was working as a salesman in Malmö when the CEO of his company in Stockholm learned of his membership in the SD. He was given the choice of leaving the party or losing his job. He chose to stay with the party but admits that he is one of the few people he knows who decided to place their political principles over their economic livelihood.[60] In the run-up to the elections of 2006, the party had many calls from potential candidates who withdrew because of threats from their employers.

In addition to unemployment, potential members of the SD must weigh the risks to their physical safety and to the safety of their families. Left-wing groups like Antifascist Action Group (AFA) have staged numerous violent protests against the SD. Members of AFA have also gone after individual Sweden Democrats when they encountered them on the street, and vandalized their homes. Most Sweden Democrats who receive any publicity apply for unlisted addresses. Matthias Karlsson installed bulletproof windows in his apartment to protect himself and his family. Hans-Olaf Andersson, the local party leader in Lund who delivers papers for a living, always carries defense spray (a legal product, akin to mace, used to ward off attackers).[61] L. J. Hollgren tries to avoid large groups of people when he goes out. He has no nameplate outside his apartment and takes the morning paper as soon as it arrives to prevent someone from setting fire to it.

The threat of physical violence and vandalism drastically curtail the ability of the Sweden Democrats to meet and interact with the electorate.

---

[58] Interview with Slått.
[59] Interview with Michael Rosenberg (SD), Karlskrona, May 2007.
[60] Interview with Hollgren.
[61] Interview with Hans-Olaf Andersson (SD), Lund, May 2007.

The party's trouble finding a venue for the 2007 congress is a typical experience: private individuals (such as hotel or restaurant owners) will not rent to the SD because of the possibility of vandalism. And although state officials are legally obliged to make public spaces available for every political party, in practice they often ignore this rule or set up insurmountable bureaucratic hurdles when dealing with the radical right. Although theirs is the third-largest party in Helsingborg with 10% of the votes in 2006, the Sweden Democrats were unable to hold a meeting for five months in 2007 because they could not find a place to meet. The local leader of the party looked at thirty potential offices but was denied each time.[62] The party has also been unable to secure an office in Stockholm, which has made it more difficult to establish local roots in the capital. The local chapter in Ystad has not even considered searching for a permanent space: "If we put up an office, I guarantee it will be destroyed by left-wing activists within a week."[63] Landskrona, where the SD won 22% of the vote in 2006, is the only locality to my knowledge with a party office, and finding it was a laborious activity.[64] Throughout the rest of Sweden, members of the party normally meet in one another's homes, if they meet regularly at all. Local leaders are wary of sending mail to all of their members, fearing that "spies" from AFA and other groups have penetrated their organizations.[65] To spread their message to the electorate, the SD relies almost entirely on leaflets, since interventions by the AFA make face-to-face contact with voters problematic. Even if the Sweden Democrats are protected from protestors by the police, "ordinary people won't stop to listen because of the hostile atmosphere."[66] It is thus little wonder that the Sweden Democrats are barely noticeable during election campaigns; even in Landskrona, where they received 22% of the vote, one hardly saw them.[67]

Sweden Democrat politicians claim that the repressive political environment in Sweden "creates a social selection among our cadre."[68] "People know they have to walk over a threshold to become Sweden Democrats," the local leader of Lund explained to me, and very few are willing to make

---

[62] Interview with Rosenberg.
[63] Interview with Svenson.
[64] Interview with Thor Lindblom (SD), Landskrona, May 2007.
[65] Interview with Andersson.
[66] Interview with Karlsson.
[67] Interview with Marko Huttunen (Moderates), Landskrona, May 2007.
[68] Interview with Karlsson.

the sacrifice.[69] "Most don't dare," the longtime party leader in Landskrona, the SD bailiwick, admitted.[70] As in Wallonia and the Netherlands, the vast majority of people who take this step are those who have little to lose. It is obviously not in the party's interests to admit this, but it was a point mentioned numerous times over the course of my interviews. In addition, the Swedish daily *Aftonbladet* published a report in 2007 showing that one-third of SD representatives live on state handouts. The article pointed out that while the SD routinely claims that there are twice as many immigrants in state-funded early retirement program than native Swedes, only 10% of immigrants receive such benefits while 20% of the members of the SD do.[71] As mentioned earlier, the Sweden Democrats whom I spoke with did not hide the social profile of the party cadre. "People in high-paying jobs with large homes and social networks have a lot to lose. The unemployed and retired have a lot less to lose, and they are the people we get."[72]

Although the leaders of the party stress that their elected officials are "honest people" and, as opposed to the situation in the 1990s, "not freaks," they readily acknowledge the problems associated with having few educated members in the party. "Our problem is not votes," one local leader explained, "but getting good people to fill the places we win." By good people, he continued, he meant "people who could get a job anywhere" and people "who could sit down and write an article." He estimated that there were perhaps 20 such individuals among the party's 2,800 members.[73] A party newsletter from 2004 was frank about the problem and readied its members for future organizational turmoil:

As a growing party we must constantly go through a process of cleansing to separate the wheat from the chaff. Put bluntly, this means that a party in its formation stage always attracts a number of individuals with everything but the party's and the country's best [interests] at heart. Such unsuitable people must be sidelined and removed, if it does not happen naturally. In some cases this entails a temporary loss for the party but in the long run such a purging process is necessary if we are one day to have a genuine influence on Swedish politics.[74]

There are a small number of SD politicians with political experience in mainstream political parties. Usually, they join the SD because their

---

[69] Interview with Andersson.
[70] Interview with Lindblom.
[71] *Local*, May 17, 2007.
[72] Interview with Karlsson.
[73] Interview with Andersson.
[74] SD Newsletter, January 13, 2004. Quoted in Rydgren (2006: 118).

prospects within their former parties appear slim. For example, Sten Andersson, the SD leader in Malmö, began his career as a labor organizer. He first joined the Social Democrats and then the Moderates before joining the SD.[75] According to another Moderate politician, Andersson left that party because he did not receive a place on the party list for the 2002 parliamentary elections, primarily because he had taken anti-immigrant positions.[76] Michael Zand, whose parents immigrated to Sweden from Iran in 1986, joined the SD after it became clear that his former party, the Moderates, were about to expel him. Zand, a member of the local council in Halmstad, had received national attention for his proposal that Sweden drastically decrease the number of refugees it accepts. According to Zand, Prime Minister Fredrik Reinfeldt (Moderates) told him to drop this topic. Zand, however, persisted, and the local, and later the national, media began to focus on him. The local party leader, apparently with instructions from Stockholm, put tremendous pressure on Zand to resign and fill his seat with another Moderate politician. In the end, however, Zand kept his seat but defected to the SD.[77]

Aside from a few people like Andersson and Zand, elected representatives from the SD have little to no political experience. And since inner-party training is nearly nonexistent, they have difficulty being effective in local councils. "We don't always look as good as we should," admits the local leader in Helsingbor.[78] There have also been several bizarre incidents involving SD politicians that were harmful to the party's image. In May 2007, for example, an SD member of the Landskrona municipal council was shut out of a meeting after he arrived in a tank top, a military jacket, and underpants.[79] His SD colleagues admit that the offending individual had a strange personality but that he would be given several chances to modify his behavior before they would kick him out of the party.[80]

The underwear-wearing SD councilman made the national news, which was small consolation to a party that compares the Swedish media to that of North Korea. To be sure, the Swedish media has ignored the Sweden Democrats, denounced them as a threat to Swedish democracy, or, in this case, made them appear ridiculous. This strategy, particularly the second component, has become official policy. The Swedish broadcasting

[75] Interview with Rubin.
[76] Interview with Lantz.
[77] Interview with Michael Zand (SD), Karlskrona, May 2007.
[78] Interview with Rosenberg.
[79] *Local*, May 7, 2007.
[80] Interview with Stefan Olsson (SD), Landskrona, May 2007.

corporation adopted a rule in 2002 that whenever the Sweden Democrats were referred to, the fact that they were "xenophobic" would also be mentioned.[81]

The Sweden Democrats may eventually overcome both their history and the multiple hurdles that political parties and civil society have placed in their way. Those hurdles might also become lower if, for example, the Moderates (or another party) were to enter into a local deal with the Swedish radical right. A stunning success in the next election, for example, might spark local politicians to cooperate with the SD in order to hold onto power, as the Social Democrats in Trelleborg once attempted to do. Once broken in one place, the cordon sanitaire would most likely crumble across Sweden and increase the legitimacy of the radical right. The SD would then be in a position to receive more politicians attracted by the proposition of advancing rapidly within the party. In this case it might be able to attract politicians discouraged by the inflexible seniority of mainstream parties: as Michael Zand complained, "The Moderates are really stiff; if you haven't been with them for twenty years, they won't let you climb."[82]

It is more likely, however, that the cordon sanitaire will remain in place and that the SD will remain a marginal party. Even in political conditions that in many ways are favorable to an anti-immigrant message, the party has struggled in the face of a political culture that is highly repressive toward them. Their prospects never looked better as of May 2007; their performance in the 2006 elections and their televised debates in April with the leaders of the Social Democrats and the Moderates gave them unprecedented media attention. A survey conducted by the Swedish Immigration Board found that the percentage of people who "strongly agree" that they could envisage voting for a party like the SD rose from 5.7% in 2006 to 7.3% in 2007.[83] Yet even amid this optimism, life remains extremely difficult for Sweden Democrats. When asked if he ever considered quitting the party, one of the leading figures replied, "Every week."[84] Another likened our interview to a "therapy session" in which he could talk at length about the personal problems that his decision to join the SD had created.[85] Modest electoral performances, such as the 3.3% of the vote and no seats that the party received in the June

[81] Interview with Slått, who worked for the Swedish Broadcasting Corporation in 2002.
[82] Interview with Zand.
[83] *Local*, May 31, 2007.
[84] Interview with Karlsson.
[85] Interview with Andersson.

2009 elections for the European Parliament, are probably not enough to sustain commitments in such a repressive environment. The small group of university students from Lund who are now guiding the party have wagered a great deal on the party entering the Riksdag in the general elections of 2010, and thereby providing a financial lifeline to more SD politicians. Even if they succeed, the struggle over those positions is likely to be fierce and to test the party's unity. Given their dependence on political novices and their history of factionalism, electoral success could do more than anything else to weaken the Sweden Democrats' embryonic organization. As we have already seen in the Wallonian and Dutch cases, it has happened many times before.

Britain

History provided the British radical right with no usable resources and a legacy of neo-Nazism that it has never shed. Oswald Mosley's British Union of Fascists (BUF) was an electoral failure, even if it once claimed a membership of 50,000 in the mid-1930s and was praised by the *Daily Mail*. But the Public Order Act of 1936 effectively destroyed the BUF, and Mosley, along with other active British fascists, was interned in 1940. British fascism was essentially mimetic and unconnected to any nationalist cause capable of mobilizing a larger constituency. The postwar far right in Great Britain shared these characteristics: it was biologically racist, consumed with anti-Semitic conspiracy theories, and profoundly antidemocratic. This milieu has been described as "an absurdity" (Billig 1978: 2) that has produced only "a lengthy list of one-man-and-his dog" political movements (Eatwell 1995: 179). It did succeed in coalescing, however, in 1966 under the umbrella of the National Front (NF). The leader of this organization, John Tyndall, was fond of dressing in Nazi regalia and was clear about his desire to create a National Socialist regime:

We are organizing ourselves on the system of Germany between 1933–45. The average man today is indifferent to politics, but this will change. In the meantime we are recruiting the best types to be trained as leaders and are not after an elusive mass following.... We want to see the whole democratic regime come crashing down ... we shall get power with whatever means are favorable.[86]

The NF did surprisingly well in some local elections in declining urban areas in the mid-1970s. It was best known for its provocative marches

[86] *Guardian*, June 19, 1962.

through immigrant neighborhoods and its propensity for street violence with antifascist protestors. But the organization soon collapsed amid intense infighting based on both personal and ideological differences. The latter conflict pitted overt neo-Nazis against those who sought a more respectable facade for what were still extremist positions. There was no internal debate, for example, about the forced repatriation of immigrants, which was the NF's main policy idea throughout its history.

Tyndall founded the British National Party from the ashes of the NF in 1982. Given his long history in neo-Nazi and paramilitary organizations, it is not surprising that the BNP made no attempt to moderate its image. There was an overwhelming continuity in personnel, and the party devoted itself to disseminating conspiracy theories and pamphlets that denied the Holocaust. The party specifically sought to attract working-class skinheads and other "red-blooded" types willing to spar with antifascist activists, as opposed to individuals from the upper and middle classes who were deemed too cowardly to serve the cause (Goodwin 2007a: 120–121). As is typical of extremist parties, the BNP was concerned with constituency representation – which, according to its members, largely meant marching and fighting with the "reds" – as opposed to electoral competition. As one member notes:

The BNP's growing period during the late 1980s and early 1990s was characterized by many marches, public meetings and rallies.... These events led to recruitment of a steady stream of new people to the party ... such recruits were 'red-blooded' types, *people temperamentally unsuitable for normal political work.* East London was a particular magnet to the 'red-bloods' due to all the political action going on there.... They are attracted by the possibility of street violence with reds, and regard leafleting and canvassing as fit for 'mugs.' (Goodwin 2007a: 121; emphasis mine)

With activists like these, it is not surprising that the BNP was barely visible during elections and fielded only *two* candidates nationally for the general elections of 1987. The party was also unable to escape the factionalism that had characterized the postwar far right (Copsey 2004), and it also faced competition for its tiny electoral constituency from the NF, which continued to exist despite having lost most of its members to the BNP.

Against this background, the BNP's electoral breakthrough in Millwall, a working-class section of London's East End, came as a surprise. A former school bus driver named Derek Beackon became the first-ever BNP council member by winning 33.9% of the vote in a by-election in September 1993. The outcome generated enormous media attention and increased the visibility of the party immensely. Millwall seemed to represent a victory for the "modernizers" in the BNP who wanted to canvass and leaflet rather than march and brawl. This group, as we shall see, also wanted to imitate successful radical right parties elsewhere, particularly the French National Front. Although some of these modernizers had violent pasts, they could be considered moderates in the context of the British far right. They found themselves at odds with the "hard liners," whose biological racism, violent proclivities, and antidemocratic views correspond to my definition of extremists.

Rather than setting the stage for an electoral takeoff, their success in Millwall generated an internal party crisis that set the BNP back for nearly a decade. The BNP victory led to antifascist protests, which in turn "raised the media profile of the BNP's more violent wing, which was only too happy to be provoked" (Eatwell 2004: 67). Some of the hard liners (extremists) physically assaulted modernizers (moderates), driving some activists from the party and creating even deeper internal divisions (Goodwin 2007a: 147). It soon became clear that Beackon was a highly ineffective councilor with only a rudimentary understanding of the British political system and a professed inability to follow council politics (Copsey 2004: 63). Threats from antifascist activists forced him to live in hiding during his tenure. Beackon did stand for election again the next year, and even managed to increase his voteshare, although mobilization by the Labour Party produced a much higher turnout that led to his defeat. Yet Beackon's travails were well publicized in the media and increased the public's perception that BNP members were not only fascist, but incompetent as well.

In the longer run, however, the example of the "Euronationalist" parties on the Continent, particularly the French National Front, was too compelling to ignore. Tony Lecomber wrote:

Le Pen understood back in the early 1980s that any association with past nationalist regimes is the kiss of death. Le Pen devised a whole new suite of nationalist policies that were practicable and had voter appeal.... Nationalists in all these countries, particularly Austria, France, Belgium and Italy, are on the electoral motorway. **It is no coincidence that *all* these nationalists are *modern* nationalists.** (Quoted in Goodwin 2007a: 159; emphasis in the original).

The moderates received a considerable push when Nick Griffin ousted John Tyndall as leader of the BNP in 1999. Although Griffin had formerly embraced Holocaust denial, biological racism, and paramilitarism, he became, by his own admission, a "born-again modernizer" (Goodwin 2007a: 151). In 2002, Griffin urged members of his party to avoid the "three Hs": "Hard talk, Hobbyism, and Hitler." Hard talk referred to crude racist and violent discourse, while hobbyism "referred not just to those who were unwilling to devote considerable time to party activity, but also to the heavy drinkers in the party" (Eatwell 2004: 77). Alcohol consumption had apparently become a drain on party funds. Contacts between the BNP and FN increased substantially, and the former launched an annual Red, White and Blue Festival on the model of the latter's Fête des Bleu–Blanc–Rouge. The BNP also dropped its biological racism in favor of ethnopluralism. In 2001, its monthly newspaper, *The Voice of Freedom*, wrote that "the BNP does not claim that any race is superior to any other, simply that they are different" (quoted in Eatwell 2004: 69). The party also finally changed its stance on immigrant repatriation from forced to voluntary, a move that was designed to appeal to a more moderate anti-immigrant electorate but that encountered significant resistance from the hard liners.

Modernization thus implied a basic switch from the logic of constituency representation to the logic of electoral competition. In addition to moderating its ideology to resemble more successful "Euronationalist" parties on the Continent, the BNP began to focus on organizational issues that would hasten its transformation from, according to its own internal party literature, a "Street Gang to [a] Political Party." Here again, the BNP used the French National Front as a model: it founded a summer school to train its activists and constructed ancillary organizations to link it with broader social groups. Like the early FN, as well as the contemporary German Democratic National Party, the BNP began to focus its efforts on specific localities that it thought might be particularly receptive to its message. In particular, it targeted northern towns like Burnley in which rioting between white and Asian youths had broken out in the summer of 2001. The BNP built an organization from just two paid members in 1999 and brought in activists from outside to help with canvassing and leafleting in advance of local elections (Eatwell 2004: 74). This strategy paid off in 2002, when the party elected its first three city councilors since Millwall. Following similar strategies elsewhere, the BNP elected fifty-two councilors nation-wide in the local elections of May 2006.

Given these events, it is not surprising that several scholars posit a causal relationship between the BNP's modernization and its electoral upswing since 2002 (Eatwell 2004; Goodwin 2007a). Yet these same scholars also predicted that both modernization and electoral success would precipitate a conflict between moderates and extremists. Electoral success brought a wave of new moderate recruits, many of whom had

little interest in violent activism or neo-Nazism. Indeed, Goodwin's interviews with BNP activists suggest that many needed to overcome their
belief that the party was dominated by extremists before joining:

Basically I felt the same way as most people feel about the party when they hear
the BNP; they think Nazi's and thugs, criminal elements, nasty people really. So I
didn't have a good view of the party before I joined.

When I went to my first meeting I was wondering; 'Am I gonna be the only person
there who wasn't a rough-type skinhead?' I had long hair at the time ...

I went to a meeting in Leeds. At the time I listened to a gentleman called John
Tyndall ... but as I sat down again after that meeting I had a little think to myself
and thought maybe that's just a little bit too, I wouldn't say extreme, but a little
bit too strong, bit full-on ... I left it. (Goodwin 2007a: 268–270)

Despite these apprehensions, a significant number of activists who did
not identify themselves as hard liners joined the party. Yet they soon
found out that it was unwilling to break with its extremist past. Goodwin
(2007a: 271–272) describes the experience of Dean, an eighteen-year-
old who joined the BNP in 2003 and became a local organizer quickly
thereafter. Buoyed by Griffin's attempt to "bring the party into the mainstream," Dean advocated dropping the party's whites-only membership
policy in favor of an "open" membership regime along the lines of the
French National Front. He explained:

This all-white membership is all good and well if you're a quasi-Nazi political
party, but if you're trying to move into the political mainstream and trying to get
rid of that extremist image, surely what you need to do is try and accept that, at
the end of the day, there are ... numerous people of different racial groups [who]
can also be part of what, we see in effect, as our Britain.

Yet the party disappointed Dean not only by sticking to its whites-only
policy, but also by failing to discipline the hard liners. "You know, they're
good activists," said Dean of the hard liners, "but the only problem is
that they get a few beers down them and their real views come out." He
was particularly incensed by the party's toleration of a local activist in
his area who openly admired Nazism and had admitted to throwing two
petrol bombs into a mosque. After three years of activism, Dean left the
BNP in 2006.

A year later, the BNP was engulfed in its most significant factional war
to date. The split of 2007 pitted moderates against extremists and led to
an exodus of the former. In late 2007, a blog called enoughisenoughnick.
blogspot.com appeared that criticized Griffin for tolerating extremists

within the party. The bloggers focused on two BNP members in general: Mark Collet, the director of publicity, who had praised Nazism and made racist statements in a documentary film titled *Young, Nazi and Proud*; and Dave Hannam, the BNP deputy treasurer, who had been convicted in 2000 for the production and dissemination of hateful materials. Griffin hired a South African security firm to discover the source of the leak, which turned out to be the BNP's group development officer, Sadie Graham, and its head of administration, Ken Smith. Both Graham and Smith were expelled from the party, along with seven other senior party officials.

More purges followed in early 2008 when Colin Auty, the candidate of the modernizers, challenged Griffin for the BNP leadership. At least sixty activists were expelled during this round. Although Graham encouraged current BNP activists to work within the party to topple Griffin, she founded the organization Voice for Change, which seeks to support "Independent Nationalists" in local and by-elections. This split is reminiscent of the one following Millwall, during which "modernizers" were chased from the party and the BNP suffered several years of dismal electoral returns as a result. The splitters also appear to include the young, competent wing of the party that is skilled with the news media and able to project a reasonably respectable image on camera. The loss of activists like Dean is something that the BNP can scarcely afford. We have seen how the party's negative reputation already makes recruitment quite difficult. Legal prohibitions against membership for some professional groups – such as police and prison officers –and de facto prohibitions for others – such as doctors, nurses, and teachers – limit recruitment further.[87] One BNP organizer claimed that he "gets emails from professors, doctors, and barristers saying that they support us, but that they can't join." These are not the types of people who generally "thrive on all the attacks and physical confrontation," though he added that such experiences only stiffened his own resolve.[88]

Like highly stigmatized parties elsewhere, the BNP keeps its membership list secret. An article published in the left-leaning newspaper the *Guardian*, the fruits of a seven-month undercover operation by the journalist Ian Cobain, revealed that many members use pseudonyms, that their email addresses are encrypted to shield their identities from other members, and that they use clandestine rendezvous points to conduct

[87] Doctors, nurses, and teachers cannot allow their political beliefs to compromise their professional conduct. Doing so would be grounds for dismissal.
[88] Interview with Robert Bailey (BNP), London, June 2009.

party business.[89] Few reveal their professions to the party. More is known about individuals who work openly for the BNP, such as its twenty-eight regional or branch organizers. Of these, the BBC found that eleven had criminal histories and/or ties to football hooliganism. Antifascist organizations have documented the incompetence and/or criminal backgrounds of the BNP's elected councilors, although these are clearly biased sources.[90]

Given this secrecy, the publication of the BNP's entire membership by a disgruntled former member on November 17, 2008, will perhaps be even more damaging than the split of 2007. The names, addresses, and telephone numbers of approximately 13,500 people who were either BNP members, former BNP members, or people who had expressed interest in joining the party, were uploaded onto the Internet on November 17, 2008. Individuals on the list immediately reported receiving threatening phone calls and email threats, and those who worked in the public sector feared for their jobs. The media immediately focused on the handful of policemen and university-educated professionals whose jobs were listed. Yet in fact a very small percentage of BNP members provided any employment details. According to Nigel Farage, the leader of United Kingdom Independence Party (UKIP), a Euroskeptic party that has flirted with xenophobia, "It says it all about the BNP that so many of those on their database seem to be worried about being revealed as members. Who would join a party where membership is a social and professional embarrassment?"[91]

Despite its success in the June 2009 European elections (6.3% of the national vote and two seats in the European Parliament) and rising latent support for the party (John and Margetts 2009), organizational and recruitment problems will prevent the party from becoming anything more than a political irritant. The 2010 general election demonstrated yet again the BNP's propensity for self-destruction. The campaign began with publicity director Mark Collett being arrested on suspicion of threatening to kill Griffin and ended with the closure of the party's Web site by its own manager, who accused Griffin and James Downson, the BNP's election fund-raiser, of being "pathetic, desperate and incompetent."[92] The night before the election, the BNP's London organizer, Bob Bailey, was caught on camera throwing punches and kicks at teenagers. All but two

[89] *Guardian*, December 21, 2006.
[90] See, e.g., www.hopenothate.org.uk.
[91] *BBC News*, November 19, 2008.
[92] *Guardian*, May 14, 2010.

of the twenty-eight BNP councilors standing for reelection were beaten, and the party lost all of its twelve councilors in its supposed stronghold of Barking and Dagenham in east London.

Conclusion

Looking across the four radical right parties covered in this chapter, we see striking similarities in the microlevel processes that led to the failure of each. Activists from all four parties complained about the quality of their personnel. They told the same types of stories about losing jobs and friends as a result of their activism. They developed similar tactics for avoiding, albeit often unsuccessfully, antifascist activists. Some openly regretted their decision to work on behalf of a radical right party, while many others strongly implied that, if they could turn back the clock, they would choose differently. Dealing with a hostile external world was difficult enough: when party meetings devolved into fistfights, even the most committed activists withdrew from the inner-party fray. The ethnographic evidence also demonstrated that the link between repressive environments and activists with lower SES that we documented in Chapter 2 is not simply a correlation: the incentive structure in all four cases clearly selected for individuals who were less sensitive to the "social and professional embarrassment" of active membership.

The four cases also demonstrate that the process of radical right party building is highly path dependent. Lacking postwar nationalist subcultures, the far right consisted only of the so-called lunatic fringe. Yet this extremist fringe proved difficult, if not impossible, to replace when moderates tried to substitute the logic of constituency representation for the logic of electoral competition. The parties' reputations also proved very sticky and self-reinforcing: modernization did not lead to any decrease in social stigma, and endless media footage of past street battles and racist epithets attracted a new generation of extremists. This led to more factionalism and precluded any hope of increasing the party's legitimacy. Political entrepreneurs in these four countries may have learned from their counterparts elsewhere, but the history of both their country and their party prevented them from following more successful models.

4

Nationalist Subcultures and the Radical Right

Radical right activists in Flanders, France, and Austria often place their movements in historical perspective. As one Vlaams Belang (VB) activist put it, "We have been fighting for our identity for five generations." Members of the French National Front consider themselves part of a "two-centuries-old galaxy" of extreme right counterrevolution, Bonapartism, and the integral nationalism of Action Française (LaFont 2006). The Austrian Freedom Party is rooted in a political subculture whose adherence to nationalism, rather than to Catholicism or Socialism, has placed it at odds with the two other major subsocieties (or *lager*) since the founding of the Austrian Republic.

Yet such historical and ideological continuities on their own cannot explain the electoral success of the VB, FN, and FPÖ. The issues that have traditionally been important for the Flemish, French, and Austrian far right are today irrelevant for the vast majority of these parties' voters. When asked to identify the most important reason for voting for the party, only 4% of the VB's electorate in 1999 cited Flemish nationalism, as opposed to 27% who mentioned immigration (Swyngedouw and Van Craen 2002). Pan-Germanism has long since become a losing issue among the Austrian electorate, and it is highly doubtful that more than a tiny percentage of FN voters have heard of Charles Maurras, the founder of Action Française. More generally, the presence of a significant far right movement at some point in history cannot explain the success of contemporary radical right parties, as the German case illustrates. Any causal argument involving historical legacies must specify both the historical juncture that created them and the mechanism linking them to contemporary outcomes.

In all three cases, the critical juncture was the immediate aftermath of a war: the Second World War in the Flemish and Austrian cases, and the Algerian War in the French one.[1] The far right had clearly been on the losing side of the Second World War in all three places, but only in the first two was it able to reconstitute itself as a relevant political actor. In France, as in Germany, the far right was decimated by war and defeat, and had the FN been constructed solely from the remnants of Vichy it would never have amounted to more than a historical footnote. The Algerian War provided the far right with a new mobilizing issue and, more importantly, with a new reservoir of activists. This chapter will chronicle how defeat and nationalist grievances became fused in a way that allowed the far right to extend beyond a hard core of unreconstructed fascists in all three cases.

The causal mechanism is continuity of personnel rather than simply continuity of ideology. The leaders and activists in both the FPÖ and the VB, particularly in the 1980s, had long been involved in far right politics. To a large extent this was because neither party was really new: the FPÖ's transformation from a liberal party in the 1970s to a radical right one under Haider is similar to the trajectories of parties in Denmark, Norway, and Switzerland. The VB split from the Flemish interest party, Volksunie, and first brought along the right wing of that party before decimating its ranks entirely. But what differentiates Austria and Flanders from the cases treated in Chapter 5 is that these political parties existed alongside strong nationalist subcultures, which facilitated the recruitment of leaders and activists. France again was somewhat different, in that the FN *was* a new party and because the nationalist subculture on which it drew was more fractionalized and less integrated with the rest of French society. Yet this subculture produced activists that were fiercely loyal to Le Pen and willing to invest their energy in a political movement that was electorally irrelevant for more than a decade. When the FN suddenly became visible, it drew upon these preexisting networks to construct its party organization. In sum, the networks from which the parties in this chapter recruited their activists were both much larger and far less marginalized than those that served as the foundations for the "parties of poor souls" that we encountered in the preceding chapter.

In addition to useful historical legacies, the radical right in Austria, Flanders, and France benefited from a permissive political environment

---

[1] The Second World War also marks the critical juncture in the Italian case, analyzed in Chapter 7.

during critical stages in party building. Because a strong cordon sanitaire has existed in France and Belgium for nearly two decades, it is easy to forget that this was not always the case; mainstream parties adopted a common policy toward the radical right only after several years of keeping their options open, by which point both the FN and the VB had effectively consolidated themselves in the party system. Similarly, although the FPÖ complained it was the victim of a cordon sanitaire for more than a decade, it was only the Social Democratic Party of Austria (SPÖ) that ruled out cooperation with the radical right, and the FPÖ was left out of governing coalitions only at the national level. In all three cases, the combination of open coalition markets and a lack of social stigmatization brought more moderates, as well as many opportunists, into the party.

Without the examples of the failed radical right parties from the preceding chapter in mind, the growth and electoral persistence of the Vlaams Blok (and its successor party, the Vlaams Belang), the Austrian Freedom Party, and the French National Front seem almost natural and mundane. Indeed, aside from a few examples of factionalism and incompetence that stymied their progress, the story of their electoral consolidation is hardly puzzling and, particularly since it has been covered at length elsewhere, is not the focus of this chapter. Rather, the goal here is to demonstrate how the historical legacies (the means) and the reaction to the radical right (the opportunity) had similar consequences in the three cases.

Historical Legacies

Flanders

The Vlaamse Beweging (Flemish Movement) dates from the latter half of the nineteenth century. When the Belgian state was founded in 1830, French became the official and only language of public affairs, and the Dutch-speaking majority found itself politically and economically subordinate to the Francophone minority. The small Flemish middle class pushed for greater language rights for Dutch speakers in the military, the schools, and the courts in the nineteenth and early twentieth centuries. The introduction of universal suffrage in 1919 gave this movement a political voice in the form of the Frontpartij (Front Party), a party founded by Flemish veterans of the First World War who resented the exclusive use of French in the military. To this day, tens of thousands of Flemish nationalists take part in an annual pilgrimage to the Izjer Tower in Diksmude to commemorate the death of Flemish soldiers in the war, many of whom were said to have perished because orders were given solely in French. The Front Party campaigned for linguistic reform and enjoyed moderate success in the interwar years, gaining a handful of parliamentary seats in the elections of 1919, 1921, and 1925. Although the Belgian state responded to Flemish demands by introducing new language laws, these laws were slowly and inconsistently implemented and thus failed to satisfy Flemish nationalist groups (Capoccia 2005: 134). However, the Front Party was never able to fully mobilize this discontent and faded after its defeat in the 1932 parliamentary election.

The Flemish Movement did not produce a genuine far right organization until the foundation of the authoritarian and Nazi-financed Vlaams Nationaal Verbond (Flemish National Union, VNV) in 1933. The VNV brought together the myriad Flemish organizations, including the deteriorating Front Party, and agitated for the reunification of Flanders and the Netherlands in what would be a fascist state. The party received 13.5% of the vote in Flanders and Brussels in the 1936 elections and 15% in 1939. In contrast to the Francophone Rexists, whom we encountered in the preceding chapter, the VNV not only had consolidated itself but was expanding its voter base and membership before the war. It is thus not surprising that a substantial minority of the Flemish population collaborated with the Nazis after the VNV had offered its full cooperation with the German occupiers. The VNV successfully recruited Flemish elites and was deeply rooted in Flemish society. As of 1944, the VNV still had ten thousand paying members and controlled half of all cities in Flanders.

The purge of collaborators following the war nearly destroyed the Flemish Movement and the Flemish far right. In the long term, however, the pattern of postwar justice in Belgium provided Flemish nationalists with both a narrative of victimization and a geographic concentration in the city of Antwerp, as many collaborators were legally required to leave their native villages. Those Flemish collaborators who were not executed or imprisoned lost their civil rights, and these so-called *incivieken* (those unworthy of citizenship) still numbered 150,000 in 1954 (Gijsels 1992: 41). Many of them could find work only as traveling salesmen, peddling soap, pencils, cigars, and the like to other former VNV supporters and sympathizers. Their routes came to constitute informal networks of *incivieken*. Several more formal self-aid organizations also sprang up in the immediate postwar years to help those who were widely viewed as the victims of postwar justice (Vos 1992: 34). The Sint-Maartensfonds (SMF), for example, was founded in 1953 to provide material and moral help to soldiers who had volunteered to fight on the eastern front, and to

their families. In sum, postwar repression strengthened the "lager mental-
ity" of former collaborators and produced dense social networks.

Although the resistance movement initially insisted on severe punishment, several factors pushed Flemish society toward moderation and
even sympathy for former collaborators. Repression, it was generally
agreed, should not be allowed to impede postwar economic reconstruc-
tion (De Witte and Klandermans 2000: 175). A significant group within
the Flemish center-right had links with those who had cooperated with
the Germans on ideological or pro-Flemish grounds. The latter two categories were well represented within the Catholic Party (CVP), which
also integrated many former collaborators (Gijsels and Velpen 1994: 23).
A majority of the CVP office holders supported softening the repression
against collaborators (Van Doorslaer 2003). Moreover, within Flemish
society in general, collaborators were often viewed as well-meaning, if
politically misguided, patriots whose alliance with Nazi Germany was
driven by their desire for Flemish independence. The collaborators were
presented as victims of resistance and of the (anti-Flemish) Belgian state.

In Belgium, as elsewhere in Western Europe, the onset of the Cold
War created a new set of enemies: communism, rather than fascism, was
considered the primary danger. In this climate, political regimes sought
above all to achieve national unity against the communist threat; repression of collaborators quickly gave way to forgiveness and accommoda-
tion, and the uncompromising anticommunism of the far right came to
be seen as a virtue of sorts. In 1949, several radical Flemish nationalist
organizations were founded, including the antirepression party Vlaamse
Concentratie (Flemish Concentration, VC) and the direct action group
Vlaamse Militanten Orde (Order of Flemish Militants, VMO), whose initial purpose was to protect the VC from leftist attacks and would later
develop into a paramilitary organization. The state also did not prevent
the proliferation of Flemish nationalist newspapers or journals; the best
known of these, *'t Pallieterke*, began as a satirical weekly newspaper but
quickly became a focal point for extreme right and antirepression views
(Vos 1992; Vanvaeck 1987). But the true political regeneration of Flemish
nationalism occurred when the Catholic Volksunie (People's Union, VU)
was formed in anticipation of the 1954 electoral campaign. The VU initially drew its leaders from nationalist circles that had not collaborated
with the Nazis, but nevertheless soon became the party of the "blacks"
(former collaborators). There were former VNV politicians within its
party executive, and although most founders and party workers did not
have a political past, most were related to former collaborators (Seberechts

1992). The VU pushed for a complete amnesty and framed the postwar repression of collaborators as yet another example of Francophone domination. Like its predecessors, the VU pressed for cultural and political autonomy and eventual independence. The party won a modest 6% of the vote in Flanders in 1961 but would more than triple this result within a decade.

The Flemish nationalist subculture, and particularly its far right wing, also flourished in the 1960s and 1970s. Nationalist-minded youth and student organizations transmitted the ideas and rituals of the Flemish Movement to what would become the next generation of Flemish militants.[2] The intellectual organization Were Di drew on the ideology of the French New Right, which we will encounter later in this chapter, and the direct action group Voorpost carried on in the tradition of the VMO. Along with the formal and informal networks of formal collaborators, the far right of the Flemish nationalist movement constituted a distinct subculture, or a "parallel circuit," in Belgian politics and society (Seberechts 1992).

Due to its revisionist readings of the Second World War, its demands for immediate independence for Flanders, and its flirtations with paramilitarism, the far right was hardly viewed positively by many within the broader Flemish Movement. Nevertheless, the far right was not marginalized and was treated as a legitimate political actor. As Gijsels and Velpen (1994: 58) note, "Amnesty always constituted the cement between the extreme right and a non-negligible party of the 'respectable' right [the Volksunie]." In a gesture to its right wing, the VU filled two of its first Senate seats with former collaborators. Even as the VMO radicalized and amnesty became a less pressing – albeit still important – theme for the Volksunie, the party continued to lend legitimacy to the far right. For example, Volksunie politicians attended a ceremony in honor of Staf de Clercq, cofounder of the fascist VNV. Members of the Volksunie also attended the funeral of Wim Maes, one of the cofounders of the VMO. Thus, while links between the VU and the VMO were formally

---

[2] These organizations include the Vlaams-nationalistische Jeugdverbond (VNJ), which was founded in 1961; the Algemeen Vlaams Nationaal Jeugdverbond (AVNJ), which split from the VNJ in 1971 to pursue a more radical course; the Katholiek Vlaams Hoogstudentenverbond (KVHV), which was transformed into a Flemish nationalist organization in the 1970s, and its more radical offshoot, the Nationalistische Studentenverbond (NSV), which dates from 1976, and the Nationalistisch JongStudentenVerbond, founded in 1981. For more on these groups, see Vos (1992: 39) and Gijsels and Velpen (1994: 101–103).

severed in 1963, informal contacts persisted. Again, this is hardly surprising because the Volksunie contained many far right activists within its ranks. Moreover, the party's attitude toward the far right was not out of step with Flemish elite opinion. For example, the Flemish newspaper of record, *De Standaard*, published an editorial following the death of Maes, describing him as "a good man" and as a "son of the people, sensitive, and sincere" (Gijsels and Velpen 1994: 59).

Although the VU tried to hold its centrist and far right elements together, intra-party tension became more intense following the radicalization of the Flemish Movement in the late 1960s and early 1970s. The 1960s witnessed remarkable economic development in Belgium. This growth, however, was concentrated in Flanders and led to the rapid expansion of the Flemish middle class. With the industrial economy of Wallonia in decline, Flemish leaders pushed hard for regional autonomy and sparked a conflict that threatened to tear apart the Belgian state, eventually leading to a split within the Belgian political party structure. The VU was a prime beneficiary of these developments, winning a record 18.8% of the Flemish vote in the 1971 parliamentary elections and thereby becoming the third-largest party in Flanders. Yet internal party conflict erupted in 1977 when the VU leadership signed the so-called Egmont Pact, which called for the federalization of Belgium. The right wing of the VU viewed the pact as too great a compromise and rebelled against the party leadership. While the story is too complicated to present here, the result of the VU's signing the Egmont Pact was the departure of several prominent leaders, a backlash from the party's base, and the eventual foundation of the Vlaams Blok in May 1979.

The Flemish nationalist organizations provided the VB with a ready-made rank and file and organizational network. The majority of the early members came from the Volksunie, and the new party adopted the same organizational structures as the VU.[3] About a third of the VB candidates for the 1985 parliamentary elections were members of Voorpost (Gijsels and Velpen 1994: 100). The local branches of Voorpost, Were Di, and the VMO doubled as local party branches of the VB in the early years of the party's history.[4] The members of these organizations provided a stream of highly committed activists who volunteered their time and allowed the party to mount permanent electoral campaigns. Numbering somewhere between two and three thousand, these "political soldiers" did the "dirty

---

[3] Interview with Gerolf Annemans, VB, Brussels, February 2007.
[4] Interview with Bob Hulstaert, VB, Antwerp, February 2007; see also Mudde (2000: 87).

work" of campaigning, stuffing tens of thousands of mailboxes with campaign material and postering the city of Antwerp.[5] The following path to activism within the VB is representative of the historical continuity within the Flemish far right and is therefore worth quoting at length:

My grandfather was with the VNV. He was a teacher and pro-Flemish. And before that, certain branches of the family had also been pro-Flemish, not outspokenly so, but there was a reflex, at least. After the war, my grandfather spent several years in prison, particularly because he was a teacher, I think, because people felt greater resentment when the collaborator was an educator. My grandmother also did some time. So I more or less grew up in the Flemish Movement. My parents took us along to the bigger activities (the IJzer pilgrimage, song festivals). When I was 6, I became a member of the VNJ. It's an ideological youth movement, and many children of Flemish nationalists are members. You are given certain values and a particular vision: the pan-Dutch and right-wing view in general. When I was 16, I joined the VNJ leaders' corps, and at 20 I became active within the Language Action Committee (TAK), of which my father was also an active member.... In my region, the TAK actions were performed together with *Voorpost*, because the viewpoints of both organizations overlapped. At a certain point, X asked me to become a member of *Voorpost*. I agreed, because ideologically I backed *Voorpost*, and because I had already participated before.... It's assumed that someone from my background knows what *Voorpost* is about. In fact, not much has changed.... I recently became a member of the *Vlaams Blok*. (Quoted in De Witte 2006: 133)

This trajectory is typical for VB elites. As one expert notes, "Nearly all of the VB's founders, officers, and elected representatives were former members of one or more of these [nationalist] organizations or were trained by them" (Swyngedouw 1998: 61). In his study of the party, Gijsels (1992) provides a short biography of fifty-eight minor politicians with the party, fifty of whom were at the time members either of the provincial parliament or of city councils (the remaining eight were active within the party). Of these fifty-eight politicians, all but six had been a member of at least one of the aforementioned Flemish nationalist organizations. The founder and first chairman of the Vlaams Blok was Karl Dillen, a Flemish nationalist who had bolted from the VU in 1970 as the party moderated its demands. Dillen was active in many Flemish nationalist organizations and was the leader of Were Di for several years. Filip Dewinter and Frank Vanhecke (the current party leader) were leaders of the Nationalistische Studentenvereniging (Nationalist Student Movement, NSV). The two were also the founding fathers of the Vlaams Blok-Jongeren (Vlaams Blok

---

[5] Interview with Filip De Man, VB, Brussels, February 2007.

Youth, VBJ). Gerolf Annemans, who along with Dewinter and Vanhecke has constituted the VB's leading trio since the late 1980s, was a member of the Catholic Flanders University Union (KVHV). Of the eighteen VB parliamentarians elected to the Federal Assembly in 1991, all but one had been active in Flemish nationalist organizations.

The existence of a motivated, ideologically coherent, and politically experienced cohort allowed the party to contest a number of constituencies in the early period of its history. Since the Flemish nationalist movement cut across class lines, there were also a significant number of educated personnel in the Vlaams Blok from the beginning. As the NSV began to produce more party cadres, and as the party's local success in Antwerp began to attract more members (again, predominantly from Flemish nationalist organizations), the VB was able to contest more and more constituencies in local elections (see Art 2008). The presence of radical Flemish nationalist movements in the universities also meant that the educational level of the party leadership gradually rose. The party organizes extensive training sessions for their local personnel through the Association of Vlaams Belang Mandates in which fledgling councilors learn the basic procedures of communal politics. The party's youth organization (Vlaams Belang Jongeren, Flemish Interest Youth, VBJ), founded by Dewinter, also trains future politicians and maintains recruitment networks (Hooghe, Stolle, and Stouthuysen 2004).

The Vlaams Belang has never suffered from factionalism or defections to the same degree as some other radical right parties. It is no secret that loyalty is demanded from party members and is a requirement for receiving a prime place on the national, provincial, or local lists (which are all decided by the party leadership). But a more important reason for the coherence of the VB is that its members have been socialized within the same nationalist subculture and share a deep commitment to it. As the leader of a rival Flemish nationalist party put it, "You can only understand why a brilliant young lawyer like Gerolf Annemans put all his efforts into a tiny party like the Vlaams Blok in the early 1980s if you recognize that he is a product of the Movement."[6]

Although there are undoubtedly extremists within the Vlaams Belang, the party tries to keep them at arm's length and periodically distances itself from them. In 2001, for example, after the VB's vice president, Roeland Raes, cast doubt on the scale of the Holocaust in an interview with Dutch television, the Blok's leadership called an emergency meeting to "distance

[6] Interview with Bart De Wever, N-VA, Brussels, February 2007.

itself totally" from him, and Raes was forced to resign his post.[7] At the local level, VB politicians screen possible candidates for local lists for connections to extremist groups and eliminate those who might damage the party, even at the risk of not filling the list. As one parliamentarian puts it, "We prefer having five good candidates than five good ones and five lunatics."[8] The party has also tried to avoid any connection with Holocaust denial in reaching out to Jewish voters in Antwerp. Although some of its leaders have extremist pasts, the VB is controlled by moderates – many of whom are highly educated – who realize the importance of cutting a respectable image. In sum, the size and depth of the Flemish nationalist subculture allow the VB to pick and choose those elites who are most likely to help the party and not, as in the case of neighboring Wallonia, to depend on a small pool of "poor souls."

Austria's "Third Lager"

The origins of the Austrian Freedom Party lie in the pan-Germanist subsociety (or *Lager*) that along with the Socialist and Catholic subsocieties formed the central lines of cleavage in Austrian politics from the 1880s until at least the 1980s (Pelinka 1998). Although this so-called third lager has historically comprised both German nationalists and liberals, the former group has always been stronger. During the First Austrian Republic (1918–1938), an entity that ordinary Austrians often referred to as "the state no one wanted," the third lager was characterized by its intense anti-Semitism, desire for union with Germany, and embrace of fascism. It should be noted, however, that both of these elements could be found in the other two subsocieties as well. Turn-of-the-century Vienna under Mayor Karl Lueger, founder of the Christian Socialist Party (the forerunner of the Austrian People's Party ÖVP) was the birthplace of political anti-Semitism, and the Socialists routinely made anti-Semitic appeals too. *Anschluss* with Germany was popular among many Socialists. During the 1930s, when conflict between Catholics and Socialists brought Austria to the brink of civil war, the former created a dictatorship that was loosely modeled on the Italian example and has been called *Austrofascism*. It was not only members of the third lager who became Nazis and supported the Third Reich. Postwar Austrian historiography aside, the Anschluss was very popular with ordinary Austrians and most supported the Third Reich until the very end of the war. Membership in the Nazi Party in

[7] *Guardian*, 9 March 2001.
[8] Interview with Luc Sevenhans, VB, Brussels, February 2007.

Austria was above the German average, and Austrians played a central role in the Holocaust.

Yet the Allied powers treated Austria as a victim, rather than a perpetrator, at the end of the Second World War. They put the three antifascist parties (the SPÖ, ÖVP, and the Communist KPÖ, which would fade into irrelevance after 1947) in charge of denazification. The three parties formed special commissions to decide who had been a "big Nazi" and who had only been a *Mitläufer* (a fellow traveler). This established a pattern whereby former Nazis sought the protection of a particular party and the parties developed their own clientele of former Nazis (Pelinka 1998: 19). The Socialists, who lacked an educated party cadre, were especially eager to reintegrate Nazi professionals into their ranks. The ÖVP, for its part, reached out to former Wehrmacht soldiers. Still, the two major parties were unable to absorb most of the members of the pan-German camp after the general amnesty of 1947 reinstituted the franchise for 500,000 former Nazis. In 1949, two Salzburg journalists, Viktor Reimann and Herbert Kraus, founded the League of Independents (Verband der Unabhängigen, VdU) to gather their votes and, ostensibly, to refound Austrian liberalism. Although the party was an electoral success, winning 11.7% in the 1949 national parliamentary elections, it never developed a coherent ideology. As it increasingly became the party of choice for former Nazis, it began to embrace pan-Germanism. In 1955, the former Nazi minister of agriculture Anton Reinthaller founded the Austrian Freedom Party, and most VdU supporters simply switched their allegiance. Kraus, however, chose to resign and accused the FPÖ of trying "to create a new political platform for the once tumbled greats of the National Socialist regime" (Riedlsperger 1989: 260). Although in absolute numbers more Nazis had joined the two larger parties, they formed a larger percentage of FPÖ members (Höbelt 2003: 10). After Reinthaller's death in 1958, the former SS officer Friedrich Peter became the leader of the FPÖ, which further solidified its image as the party of former Nazis. Particularly in this early period, FPÖ politicians and publications failed to clearly distance themselves from National Socialism (Bailer and Neugebauer 1994: 359).

The third lager was sustained by several other political and voluntary associations in the postwar era. The Ring Freiheitlicher Studenten (Circle of Liberal Students, RFS) dates from only 1950 but traces its lineage back to the nationalist student groups of the nineteenth century that took a decidedly illiberal and anti-Semitic turn in the interwar period. The RFS nurtured close relationships with the student dueling fraternities

(*Burschenschaften*) that preserved this ideology (Gärtner 1989: 283). The RFS won between 25% and 30% of the vote in Austrian University elections from the mid-1950s to the mid-1970s and served as a training ground for many of the FPÖ's leading politicians. The strength of the RFS in the universities reflected the fact that the pan-Germanist camp was composed primarily of the middle and upper middle class. Indeed, many of the leading FPÖ politicians pursued careers in law (Norbert Steger and Norbert Gugenbauer), academia (Friedhelm Frischenschlager and Jörg Haider), or business administration (Höbelt 2003: 34).

The Austrian Gymnastics Federation (Österreichischer Turnerbund, ÖTB) counted 70,000 members in 1994. Although most of its members are purely interested in sports, the ÖTB has a long history as a pan-German organization charged with fostering national pride. Its official publication, the *Bundesturnzeitung*, regularly printed pan-German and Nazi apologist statements up until the early 1990s (Bailer and Neugebauer 1994: 199–201). The ÖTB has since moderated its ideology and tried to defend itself from charges of right-wing extremism. In 1996, the organization created ten guidelines; the fifth states that "the ÖTB stands by the democratic republic of Austria, the constitution, and human rights," while the sixth identifies the ÖTB as a democratic organization. Yet elements of the ÖTB's *völkisch* ideology remain. Its fourth guideline is that "the ÖTB wants to educate its members to be conscious of their homeland, people, and state," and the seventh states that the organization "stands for the preservation, cultivation and promotion of German folklore."[9] Although the ÖTB claims to be nonpartisan, it has always been closely associated with the third lager and the FPÖ.

The veterans' organizations (*Kameradschaftsbünde*) that are important fixtures in most Austrian villages and towns have historically been carriers of what Anton Pelinka calls a "soft right-wing extremism" (Pelinka 1994: 312). Members include veterans of the Second World War, reserves of the Austrian Bundeswehr (Austria's national army), and other individuals who identify with the military. Although there are certainly gradations of historical revisionism (with the organization Kameradschaft IV being the most extreme), most members of Austrian veterans' organizations still defend the position that they (or their fathers and grandfathers) were "just fulfilling their duty" during the Second World War and deny any complicity in the Holocaust. This view was not held solely by the third lager, and both the ÖVP and SPÖ courted the Kameradschaftsbünde

---

9 http://www.oetb.at/leitbild/leitbild.htm (accessed on December 27, 2007).

around election time. It is fair to say, however, that the FPÖ has always tried to attract this constituency, and some of Haider's most controversial remarks about the Nazi past were directed toward it.

In sum, the third lager has existed since before the founding of the First Austrian Republic in 1918, and some of its core ideas have found expression in the other two political camps. Although one historian writes that "the FPÖ was treated by the major parties as if it were the Nazi Party incarnate," it is difficult to argue that the party was really ostracized at all (Riedlsperger 1989: 263). The FPÖ was often a coalition partner on the state or local level: it cooperated openly with the SPÖ in the state of Salzburg and with the ÖVP in Vorarlberg (Höbelt 2003: 11). Although it was shut out of national-level politics in the 1950s and 1960s, the Socialists in particular cultivated ties with the FPÖ. The pivotal figure in this relationship was Bruno Kreisky, who served as chancellor of Austria from 1970 to 1983. The son of a Jewish clothing manufacturer, Kreisky emigrated to Sweden in 1938 and observed how the Swedish Social Democrats had been able to split the bourgeois parties and create hegemony. By strengthening the FPÖ to the detriment of the mainstream conservative party (ÖVP), Kreisky sought to secure permanent absolute majorities for the SPÖ; it was a policy of harnessing the far right in order to divide and conquer conservatives, which would later be echoed by French Socialists faced with a burgeoning National Front. To this end, despite the fact that the two parties were on opposite ends of the ideological spectrum, the SPÖ made substantial contributions to the FPÖ's election campaign fund in 1963. Kreisky also cultivated personal ties with the FPÖ's leadership, and particularly with Friedrich Peter. This strategy bore fruit in 1970, when Kreisky led the SPÖ to its first postwar victory in national parliamentary elections and formed a minority government with the toleration of the FPÖ. In what was widely attributed as a gesture to the FPÖ, Kreisky appointed four former members of the Nazi Party to his eleven-member cabinet. The ÖVP too began formal cooperation with the FPÖ at the regional level, launching the so-called Graz model (which was later repeated in Klagenfurt) in 1979. In 1983, the FPÖ's integration was seemingly completed when it formed, for the first time, a national coalition government (referred to as the "small coalition" to distinguish it from the more common large coalitions between the two major parties) with the SPÖ.

The liberalization of the FPÖ over the past several decades, beginning under Friedrich Peter, had made the small coalition possible. Peter had calculated that the FPÖ would need to shed its nationalist elements and nostalgia for the Nazi past, and model itself on the German Free Democratic Party in order to win a measure of power at the national level. A new cadre of FPÖ leaders, all of whom had their roots firmly within the third lager, thus embraced economic liberalism and formed the so-called Attersee Circle. When the FPÖ was admitted to the Liberal International in 1979, it appeared that the transformation of the party from a bastion for former Nazis to a modern liberal party was complete. Or, put another way, the minority political tradition within the third lager had apparently triumphed over the previously predominant illiberal one.

Yet appearances were deceiving. The liberalization of the party touched a portion of the FPÖ elite but had little effect on the nationalist (pan-German) base. Norbert Steger, a founder of the Attersee Circle, FPÖ party chairman from 1980 to 1986, and vice-chancellor from 1983 to 1986, never won the loyalty of the party rank and file. When the FPÖ suffered a string of losses in local and state elections, and when polls showed the party running around 2% nationally, animosity toward Steger and the liberal leadership mounted. A rebellion was building, and representatives from the nationalist camp sought to find a challenger to Steger at the 1986 party congress in Innsbruck.

That challenger was Jörg Haider. He was born in 1950 to two unrepentant National Socialists. His father, Robert, was a shoemaker who had left Austria in 1934 to join the Austrian Legion, a group of Nazi exiles in Germany. He served in the war and, after reacquiring his civil rights with the amnesty of 1957, became a member first of the VdU and later of the FPÖ. Haider's mother, Dorothea, was a schoolteacher who was banned from teaching until several years after the war. As a high school student in Upper Austria, Haider was a member of the dueling fraternity Albia. His first notable political achievement was winning, at the age of sixteen, a speech contest sponsored by the ÖTB. As a student of law at the University of Vienna, he joined the fraternity Silvania and was simultaneously the leader of the Circle of Liberal Youth (RFJ; the FPÖ's youth wing) from 1971 to 1975. Haider was, in short, a product of the third lager.

Haider had left his native Upper Austria for the province of Carinthia in 1976. This was significant because long-standing ethnic tensions between Germans and Slovenes had made Carinthia more nationalistic than the rest of Austria and a bastion for the FPÖ. The confrontation between Haider and Steger at the Innsbruck party congress amounted to a battle between the nationalist, non-Viennese wing of the party and the liberals concentrated in the capital. Haider beat Steger 59.5% to 40.5%

and would serve as chairman of the FPÖ from 1986 to 2000. Chancellor Franz Vranitzky (SPÖ) responded to Innsbruck by announcing the end of the small coalition and calling for new elections; cooperation with a renationalized FPÖ was no longer possible. The FPÖ surpassed anyone's prediction by winning 9.6% of the vote in the November 1986 elections. The next fourteen years would witness a nearly unbroken string of electoral victories for Haider's FPÖ.

Although there are multiple reasons for the FPÖ's success, that a culture of far right nationalism was deeply rooted in Austrian society and that the party had already amassed an organization of nearly 37,000 members as of 1986 (Luther 2006a) were necessary conditions for its growth and electoral persistence. FPÖ politicians were experienced, educated, and, with respect to their counterparts in the parties we surveyed in Chapter 3, moderate.

Algérie Française and the Front National

Because the French far right is as old as the First Republic, finding precursors to the Front National is an easy exercise. The theme of decadence, for example, has a long lineage, dating at least from the humiliation of the Franco-Prussian War. Religious anti-Semitism is older still, but anti-Semitism in the service of political ends dates from around the late nineteenth century. The publication of Edouard Drumont's best-selling *La France Juive* in 1886, which blamed Jews for unemployment, the Dreyfus trial of 1898, which generated the proto-fascist Action Française of Charles Maurras, and the invective heaped on France's first Jewish premier, Leon Blum, in the 1930s all anticipated the murderous anti-Semitism of collaboration. The Vichy regime experimented with many other older extreme right ideas as well, including Catholic corporatism, despotism, and ultranationalism. Yet the FN was not born from the ashes of Vichy, and although former collaborators and veterans from Action Française and the extreme right leagues of the 1930s would eventually join its ranks, the key figures in the movement were those who, like Jean-Marie Le Pen, came of political age after the liberation of France.

The French Fourth Republic (1946–1958) did not survive the trauma of decolonization. The first Indochina War (1946–1954), which ended in France's humiliating defeat at Dien Bien Phu, magnified political divisions in the National Assembly and in French society more generally. At the poles of the debate over decolonization were the Communists, who decried French involvement in Indochina as *la sale guerre* (the dirty war), and the Nationalists, who sought to preserve French grandeur and fend off the Communist challenge, both at home and abroad. Many in the French military, charged with defending the empire, found themselves in ideological proximity to the far right. Some of the most highly motivated young army officers joined Jeune Nation, an extreme right organization founded in 1950 that was virulently anticommunist, antimodernist, xenophobic, and in favor of preserving the empire (Milza 1987: 296). Many of those who volunteered to fight in Indochina, particularly those who became *paras* (parachutists), would become disenchanted by the Fourth Republic's inability to conduct the war and would later turn against the regime. The young Jean-Marie Le Pen, who volunteered for the French Foreign Legion and arrived in Vietnam shortly after Dien Bien Phu, is the best-known representative of this group.

I returned from Indochina with a concrete revelation about the Communist enemy, its terrible methods, the pitiless manner of liquidating its adversaries, its techniques of psychological warfare, its destruction of man from within.... The Indochina humiliation and the first murderous encounters in the Algerian war decided my political engagement. (Le Pen 1984: 39; quoted in Simmons 1996: 14)

Pierre Poujade, the populist we encountered in the opening paragraph of this book, initially had nothing to do with the battles over decolonization. Poujade was a stationery salesman, and his party, the Union de Défense des Commerçants et Artisans (Union for the Defense of Tradesmen and Artisans, UDCA), began as a protest movement of shopkeepers and other members of the petty bourgeoisie against the tax collection policies of the Fourth Republic. The UDCA unexpectedly won 11.6% of the vote and fifty-two seats in the National Assembly in the 1956 parliamentary elections. The location of the UDCA on the left–right spectrum and its relation to fascism have been debated in the literature (Hoffman 1956; Milza 1987; Algazy 1989), and there is not sufficient space here to recapitulate those arguments. What is clear, however, is that Poujade made ever more frequent appeals to the proponents of Algérie Française, especially in 1957 and 1958 (Milza 1987: 305). Le Pen joined the movement and became the youngest deputy in the National Assembly, winning a seat for the UDCA at the age of twenty-eight.

As the crisis in Algeria heated up, the battle for Algérie Française took the place of Poujadism as the key terrain for the French far right. As Shields (2007: 93) notes, Algeria "provided a unifying focus for activism and a recruiting ground expanded beyond the narrow circuit of Pétainists, Vichy nostalgics, and residual fascists toward army veterans, serving soldiers, colonial settlers, and those who saw the defence of the French Union as a patriotic imperative." Critically, the cause of Algérie Française brought together collaborators and resisters, thereby attenuating a major rift on the French right. Le Pen fought in Algeria, and he would retain the network he forged there throughout his political career. Initially, the military and the *pieds-noirs* welcomed General de Gaulle's return to power in 1958 and the demise of the hated Fourth Republic. But although de Gaulle initially vowed to keep Algeria French, with a path to victory in Algeria becoming more and more unlikely, he switched his position and called a referendum on Algerian independence, which three-quarters of the French electorate supported. The proponents of Algérie Française and the *pieds-noirs*, however, felt betrayed by the general and many would never reconcile themselves with the mainstream right. Some French soldiers and settlers vowed to keep up the fight and formed the clandestine Organisation de l'Armée Secrète (OAS), which committed numerous violent acts and attempted on multiple occasions to kill de Gaulle. At the beginning of the 1960s, it appeared that the combination of de Gaulle's decisive action on Algeria, his creation of the Fifth Republic, and the violence of the OAS had completely marginalized the far right.

The presidential campaign of Jean-Louis Tixier-Vignancour in 1965 confirmed this assessment. Tixier-Vignancour (or "TV," as his supporters called him) had been an adjunct secretary for information during Vichy and a defense attorney for two generals who had joined the OAS. It was Le Pen, however, who had handpicked Tixier-Vignancour as the presidential candidate for the French far right and formed the "Committee TV" to coordinate his campaign. Tixier-Vignancour appealed directly to the *pieds-noirs* by advocating the abrogation of the Evian Accords that had ended the war in Algeria. He drew the bulk of his support from these repatriated French Algerians, who were concentrated in the south of France (Chiroux 1974). A SOFRES poll found that 65% of his supporters voted for Tixier-Vignancour because of his role in defending French Algeria (Shields 2007: 132). Despite considerable attention from the press and a peripatetic electoral campaign that crisscrossed France, Tixier-Vignancour won a meager 5.3% of the vote, confirming the electoral irrelevance of the far right. Yet if the election was a major disappointment and convinced members of the far right that parliamentary activity was in vain, the Committee TV left an important legacy: it would form the core of the Front National when the party was founded in 1972.[10]

---

[10] Interview with Jean-Pierre Reveau, Paris, May 2007.

In the late 1960s, the French far right took an extraparliamentary turn. Groups like Ordre Nouveau and its precursor, Occident, fought leftists in the street, hoping to bring down the Fifth Republic and replace it with an authoritarian regime. Although these extremists had little sympathy for politicians like Le Pen, the success of the Italian Social Movement – which won 8% in the 1972 parliamentary elections – convinced them that contesting elections should be part of their overall strategy. Their idea was to outwardly project as moderate an image as possible without giving up their revolutionary goals. The leaders of Ordre Nouveau turned to Le Pen, who had been running a recording studio specializing in patriotic songs since the failed "TV" campaign, to be the first president of the new party.

From the beginning, there was a certain tension between veterans of the extraparliamentary movement who viewed party politics as a regrettable necessity on the way toward an authoritarian state and those like Le Pen who were committed to parliamentary democracy. The Front National's disappointing performance in the 1973 legislative elections (1.3% overall) led to an open rift between the two groups. Members of Ordre Nouveau wanted to abandon the electoral path and return to its extraparliamentary roots. After Ordre Nouveau was banned in 1973, its partisans founded an organization called "Faire Front" in opposition to Le Pen's party. But Le Pen brought the matter to the courts and ultimately won the rights to use the "Front" label (Camus 1998: 21). In November 1974, former militants from Ordre Nouveau founded the Parti des Forces Nouvelles (PFN), which, despite its members' hostility toward party politics, contested elections against the FN throughout the 1970s. This bitter division on the far right rendered both parties marginal.

Although one might imagine that, given its history, the PFN was the more radical of the two parties, the FN also possessed its share of extremists during the 1970s. Locked in a fratricidal conflict with the PFN, the FN accepted recruits from any source. The wing around Francois Duprat, who was actively involved in Holocaust denial, was relatively strong. In March 1978, however, Duprat was killed by a car bomb, an event that immediately weakened the extremist wing of the FN. Le Pen then moved quickly to eliminate Duprat's followers from the party (Milza 1987: 346). This proved to be an important turning point, for the resulting schism "allowed Le Pen to temper the ideological strands of his party and to fashion a new identity for the FN" (Ivaldi 1998: 46).

This period of electoral insignificance and competition with the PFN came to be known, according to the party's own lore, as the "traverse through the desert," and it was primarily the partisans of Algérie Française that stuck with Le Pen during the 1970s and early 1980s. As one specialist notes, "One can speak of an Algerian war generation inside the FN: there is a large number of former officers and soldiers ... who served between 1950 and 1962 among the party cadre" (Camus 1998: 111). Much like the participants of the "Long March" of the Chinese Communist Party, those who traversed the desert with Le Pen continue to occupy leading roles in the party. For example, in 1998 seventeen of the forty members of the Political Bureau (the party's executive committee) were directly linked to the Committee TV, the OAS, or other movements against Algerian independence.[11] Eleven were members of the Committee TV, meaning that more than one-quarter of the FN's party elite can be traced to a period of political engagement that occurred thirty-three years before. As of 2007, a direct link to Algeria appeared to be almost a requirement for membership in the Executive Bureau – a group of nine members formed to stand above the Political Bureau. In addition to Le Pen and his daughter Marine, the Political Bureau included Roger Holeindre, Alain Jamet, and Jean-Pierre Reveau, all of whom served with Le Pen in Algeria and participated in the Committee TV. Martine Lehideux was also involved in the Committee TV and aided Algerian settlers in the early 1960s.[12] The mother of Louis Aliot was repatriated from Algeria. Jean-Claude Martinez was not directly tied to Algeria, but taught in Morocco. Bruno Gollnisch is the only member of the Executive Bureau without direct ties to the former colonials.

The former partisans of Algérie Francaise still form a loyal core around Le Pen. As Roger Holeindre once put it, "In the Front National, one keeps one's mouth shut. We have one leader and we know it" (Birenbaum 1992). Bruno Mégret lashed out at this old guard after his rift with Le Pen in 1998:

They are people without stature.... They accompanied Le Pen during his traverse of the desert when he was nothing but an individual ... These are not politicians, but revanchists who want to avenge their past defeats from Vichy, Indochina, Algeria, or elsewhere. (Quoted in Dély 1999: 92–93)

Although this assessment may have been correct, Mégret was wrong to downplay the influence of this cohort. A combination of their shared experiences, ties to their leader, and friendships with one another meant

---

[11] This figure was arrived at during interviews with Martine Lehideux and Jean-Pierre Reveau, and through my own research.

[12] Interview with Martine Lehideux, Paris, May 2007.

that the FN would not be plagued by the types of interpersonal conflicts that destroyed other radical right parties in their formative stages.

The Algerian connection is also strong at lower levels of the party. According to a study in the southeastern province of Isère in 1992, one-quarter of FN members had lived in Algeria (Ivaldi 1994). Daniel Bizeul, who conducted ethnographic work on the FN from 1996 to 1999, esti-mates that between a third and a half of the FN members over fifty that he associated with had come from Algeria (Bizeul 2003). A survey con-ducted by Ysmal and Birenbaum of 1,002 FN delegates to the 1990 party convention found that 60% had joined the nationalist movement, which for most meant Algérie Française, before the founding of the FN in 1972 (Lafont 2006: 92).

The available evidence suggests that the Algerian issue matters for FN voters as well. Veugelers (2005) concludes that "the ex-colonials from Algeria show a much stronger tendency to vote for far-right parties and politicians." During the 1984 European elections, for example, support for the FN was strongest in areas where former colonials from Algeria were resettled. The town of Carmoux in the department of Bouches-du-Rhône, which has the highest percentage of *pieds-noirs* in France, cast 32.8% of its votes for the FN (Marcus 1995: 57).

Summarizing the three cases, it is clear that the foundations for radical right party building were much stronger in France, Austria, and Flanders than they were in the Netherlands, Britain, Sweden, and Wallonia. Radical right parties in the former group drew their initial activists from national-ist subcultures that were large, organized, and embedded in their societies, and not from the small, balkanized, and marginalized extremist networks that typify the latter. But these indigenous resources were not enough to guarantee success. For example, although the FN contained a core of expe-rienced and loyal veterans from Algérie Française, it would have taken a prophet to predict that it would ever even match the electoral tallies of the failed campaign of Tixier-Vignancour. In order for the FN to reach a national audience and attract new followers, mainstream parties needed to provide it with an opening. It is the reaction to the radical right, first in France, and then in Austria and Belgium, to which we now turn.

Reacting to the Radical Right

France

In February 1978, Jean-Pierre Stirbois announced his candidacy for the National Assembly in the second district of Eure-et-Loir. Stirbois, along with his wife, Marie, was a veteran of various far right movements, including the Committee TV. The district contained the town of Dreux, which had attracted a large number of immigrants during its period of industrial expansion in the 1960s but was suffering from rising unemployment. Stirbois's slogan in the 1978 elections was "A million people out of work are a million immigrants too many" (Bréchon and Mitra 1992: 72). Although he would gain only 2% of the votes, Stirbois set about building a local organization and contested every election possible. He hammered away at the themes of immigration, unemployment, and crime. Four years later, Stirbois registered his first success by winning 12.6% of the vote in the 1982 cantonal elections. His wife, a candidate in a neighboring canton, won 9.5%. Although these were at the time the best results ever for the FN, they attracted relatively little notice.

A year later, however, the FN would be thrust upon the national stage as a result of the municipal elections of 1983. In March, the RPR (the Gaullist party) took the unprecedented step of forming a joint ticket with the FN. The RPR–FN slate, which pledged to "reverse the flow of immigrants," won 31% in the first round, while the left won 40% (Marcus 1995: 53). The local head of the UDF, the other main center-right party that had won 18% in the first round, decided to support the RPR–FN ticket in return for getting some of his own candidates on the new list (Gaspard 1995: 125–126). The second round delivered a razor-thin victory to the left, but the united right challenged the result. The Administrative Tribunal of Orléans found enough discrepancies in the registration lists to void the results, and new elections were scheduled for September (Gaspard 1995: 128). This time, the RPR decided to form an electoral list with the UDF rather than with the FN. But Stirbois captured 16.7% in the first round, and to ensure a rightist victory the RPR and the UDF formed a joint ticket for the second round. With 55.3% of the vote, the right won and three members of the FN entered the municipal council.

The cooperation of local rightist leaders with the far right produced a variety of reactions from the national leadership. In January 1983, after the first RPR–FN slate was announced, RPR leader Jacques Chirac denounced the deal: "I have personally requested that this slate not be granted the official approval of the RPR. I repeat, I have personally made this demand. In my eyes those people have a congenital defect: they are racists." The RPR's local leader, however, claims that the national party approved of the cooperation: "Look, before taking a decision like this, we obviously got a green light from the national leadership" (Gaspard 1995: 129). The signals were apparently clearer in September. The national leader of the UDF, Jean-Claude Gaudin, sent a telegram wishing the joint list in Dreux success.[13] One Giscardian (UDF) deputy urged the citizens of Dreux to back the rightist alliance: "If I were a Dreux voter, I would not abstain. To do so would make oneself an objective ally of the communists and socialists."[14] After the elections, Philippe Séguin downplayed the significance of the electoral alliance, describing it as "more silly than wicked."[15] Chirac also changed his tune slightly. Quoting Raymond Aron, Chirac argued that "four National Front members on the opposition list in Dreux is not the same as four communists in the cabinet."[16] By early 1984, the leader of the RPR's group in the National Assembly, Claude Labbé, openly approved local-level cooperation: "Le Pen exists, it is one of today's political realities. We have to take into account a political formation that exists to work together, to act in concert with them, and not say 'I do not recognize you.'"[17]

The mainstream right's courtship of the FN continued for the next five years. Since many politicians on the right believed that the FN would suffer the flash-party fate of the Poujadists, they believed the party to be a useful short-term tool in the struggle against the left. In addition to creating electoral pacts, as in Dreux, the FN and the mainstream right entered into stand-down deals, meaning that either party would defer to the candidate with the best chance of beating the leftist opposition. In the 1988 legislative elections, for example, the FN and the UDF negotiated an explicit stand-down deal in the province of Bouches-du-Rhône (Marcus 1995: 145). In several of the newly formed regional councils, such as in that of Provence-Alpes-Côte d'Azur, in which the majority comprised twenty-five FN, twenty-three UDF, seventeen RPR, and seven councilors from other parties, the FN governed in coalition (Marcus 1995: 140). Although Charles Pasqua (RPR) had ruled out deals with the FN before the first round of the 1988 legislative elections, the RPR changed its strategy in the second round and entered into a stand-down deal with the FN in Marseilles, with both parties withdrawing eight candidates (Simmons 1996: 93).

After the 1988 legislative elections, the examples of local cooperation with the FN became rarer as the mainstream right began to institute a

---

[13] *Le Figaro*, September 7, 1983 (quoted in Marcus 1995).
[14] *Le Monde*, September 7, 1983.
[15] *L'Express*, September 30, 1983.
[16] *Le Monde*, September 20, 1983.
[17] *Le Monde*, February 16, 1984.

cordon sanitaire. Yet one continues to find examples of it into the 1990s. In fourteen of the twenty-two regional assemblies in the early 1990s, conservatives relied on the votes of FN councilors to form majorities (Schain 1999: 11). A similar situation still prevailed in five regions after the 1998 elections (Shields 2007: 278). When one adds to this ledger the recurring debates within the RPR and the UDF over the wisdom of continuing the cordon sanitaire, it is clear that, although the FN faced a much less favorable political opportunity structure after 1988, it was not marginalized to the same degree as some other radical right parties like the German Republicans or the Sweden Democrats.

While the right viewed the FN as a tool in its battle with its major political rival, the Socialists appeared to have made a similar calculation. As one Socialist close to President François Mitterrand put it in 1994, "Without Le Pen, the left would not have been able to remain in power for ten years. Mitterrand is a fine tactician, a champion. It's customary, you know, to divide your adversaries. If you are on the left, you can't help but approve." For Mitterrand, the differences between the FN and the mainstream right were minor – "the extreme right is the right," he once told the historian Benjamin Stora, making the FN nothing more than "a force like all the others" (Faux, Legrand, and Perez 1994: 27–28). Jean-Christophe Cambedelis, a Socialist deputy who criticized this strategy and attacked the FN noted:

The President and many Socialist leaders believed that in the final analysis there was no such thing as the extreme Right. The extreme Right is part of the Right as a whole; the mainstream Right is within the extreme Right. That is to say that, at root, Le Pen is nothing more than the most visible expression of a set of political ideas which have always been present on the French Right, which has always been conservative, xenophobic, and nationalist, and therefore one shouldn't wage a specific campaign against the National Front. (Marcus 1995: 153)

Although the left never entered into any electoral deals with the FN, Mitterrand helped the extreme right at two junctures. First, in May 1982, Le Pen wrote a letter to Mitterrand complaining that France's state television was not covering the FN's party congress. Given that the FN had won a mere 0.2% of the votes in the 1981 legislative elections, the lack of media attention was not surprising. Mitterrand, however, responded in a letter dated June 22 that "it is regrettable that the congress of a political party is ignored by Radio-Television.... The incident that you referred to will not be repeated" (Faux et al. 1994). One week later, Le Pen appeared on the daily news program of the channel. Over the next several months, the leader of the FN made other television appearances, and this newfound media exposure was undoubtedly a factor in the party's electoral breakthrough in the 1983 municipal elections. After Le Pen appeared on the TV program *L'heure de Vérité* – which Le Pen himself describes as "the hour that changed everything" (Shields 2007: 196) – the FN's central office received sacks of letters from people who wanted to join the party. Combing through them, Stirbois and Jean-François Touzé identified potential local leaders in municipalities throughout France, many of whom they successfully recruited. "From those letters," claims Touzé, "we were able to add several thousand members in a matter of months."[18]

Mitterrand's second gift to the FN was the shift from first-past-the-post to proportional representation in the 1986 legislative elections. To be sure, proportional representation had been on Mitterrand's agenda since he had taken power in 1981. His major goal was to protect his own party, which had been declining in the polls, from a massive defeat by changing the rules of the game. However, the timing of the decision has fueled speculation that the president also sought to strengthen the FN in the process. According to Pascal Perrineau, it was only after the FN showed strength in municipal and European elections that Mitterrand decided to institute proportional representation (Faux et al. 1994: 29). Mitterrand himself once stated that he considered a victory for the RPR a greater danger than the election of some FN candidates to the National Assembly (Favier and Martin-Roland 1990: 308–309).

The sudden shift in the political environment led to an influx of a new type of activist: the opportunist. Before its electoral breakthrough in 1983, the FN was composed of a hard core of loyalists around Le Pen. The party recruited from a far right milieu that was larger than most others in Western Europe, and the purge of extraparliamentary extremists and Holocaust denialists in 1978 constituted an important step in party building. But had the FN never been able to reach beyond this small reservoir of activists, it is unlikely that it would have achieved the enormous success it did. The commitment of the party cadre was not in question. However, its ability to appeal to a broader electorate was dubious. As one member remembered:

There was absolutely no political hope, absolutely no hope of being elected. There were a lot of people who were socially a little strange, who were a little crazy, who were a little original, people who just weren't at ease in society, who didn't have balanced personalities, therefore it was necessarily a fringe movement. (Quoted in DeClair 1999: 152)

---

[18] Interview with Jean-François Touzé, Paris, May 2007.

According to another, "With no elected officials, no audience, [the FN] serves no purpose. I waited for a real party" (DeClair 1999: 65).

That moment came after Dreux and before the European elections of 1984. Dreux had shown that elected office for radical right candidates was a real possibility, as the mainstream right was willing to enter into coalitions with the FN. Le Pen, sensing that his party had just become a potential option for opportunists, embarked on an intense recruitment effort among what he referred to as "notables" – people who were well known in their local communities and may have held political office for another party. The European elections, which were held under proportional representation, provided an auspicious beginning for this strategy. Of the eighty-one FN candidates, only fifty-nine had been members of the party. The other twenty-two were new recruits who owed their place on the FN's electoral list to their ability to augment the respectability of the party (Birenbaum 1992: 13). These *elites-vitrines* (showcase elites) included such figures as Jean d'Orgeix, an Olympic medalist in equestrianism; Marguerite de MacMahon, the duchess of Magenta; Count Olivier d'Ormesson, already a member of the European Parliament (from the UDF) and mayor of the town of Ormesson-sur-Marne; Bruno Gollnisch, professor of Japanese language and civilization at the University of Lyon; Jean Marie Le Chevallier, a high-profile defector from the mainstream right; and many others.

Le Pen continued to employ this strategy during the cantonal elections of 1985. Since the party's organization was embryonic in many places, Le Pen reached out to local notables, particularly former politicians from the mainstream right (Birenbaum and François 1989: 86; Ivaldi 1998: 48–49). One of these was Bruno Mégret, whose mobility within the RPR had not been rapid enough to fulfill his ambitions. According to his colleague Yvan Blot, Mégret was "fed up" with his former party: "The RPR is highly structured and hierarchic: he quickly found himself marginalized" (Dély 1999: 39). Mégret initially formed his own party, the CAR, but after it won less than 2% in the 1985 cantonal elections, he shifted to the FN and brought the rest of his small party along with him (Dély 1999: 42).

This was significant, for Mégret was the most prominent representative of the Nouvelle Droite (New Right) to join the FN, and his defection from the mainstream to the radical right led a number of other intellectuals to follow his lead. The New Right was responsible for developing the ethnopluralist doctrine that, as we have seen, many radical right parties adopted in the 1980s and 1990s. Primarily an intellectual group, it looked to the Italian communist Antonio Gramsci as a model for action, if not for ideology, and sought to achieve cultural hegemony as a condition for achieving political power. It thus set out to win the war of ideas with the left and fought its enemies in the opinion pages of French newspapers rather than in the streets or at the ballot box. The think tank GRECE (Groupement de Recherche et d'Études pour la Civilisation Européenne), founded by Alain De Benoist in 1968, became synonymous with the New Right. It attracted doctors, lawyers, academics, and other highly educated professionals.

Although most members of the group agreed with the strategy of achieving cultural hegemony, some wanted to take a more direct route to political power. Yvan Blot and Jean-Yves Le Gallou, both of whom had just graduated from the prestigious ENA, founded the Club d'Horloge in 1974. The young Bruno Mégret was recruited to join the intellectual group, as were other high-level functionaries in the state administration (Dély 1999: 21). Particularly after the left came to power in 1981, the Club d'Horloge served as a meeting ground for members of the far right and the mainstream right: politicians such as Raymond Barre and Alain Juppé took part in some of the club's events (Dély 1999: 36–37). In the early 1980s, the FN successfully established links with the Club d'Horloge as part of its overall strategy of acquiring legitimacy (Ivaldi 1998: 47). Several of the Orlogers, including Blot, Le Gallou, and Mégret, would become members of the FN's Political Bureau in the 1980s.

Like the European elections, the legislative elections of 1986 were held under a system of proportional representation and the FN was poised to win many seats in the National Assembly. Le Pen continued to recruit among the notables, but his task had become significantly easier since the FN had shown such strength in 1983 and 1984. A good place on the list ensured a seat in the National Assembly and, as the mainstream parties' response to the FN suggested, there were no real downsides to joining the FN in the form of social stigma or exclusion. Since the FN was nearly certain to win parliamentary seats, Le Pen was anxious to find candidates who would represent the party well and be up to the task not only of campaigning but of governing:

I joined the Front because the president, Jean-Marie Le Pen, needed, in view of the legislative elections of March 1986, professionals – people having abilities of a sufficiently high caliber. And he did not want to have people in the assembly who weren't up to the task of dealing with the problems they would face in the National Assembly. In addition, he didn't want to have representatives who weren't able, at least, to discuss at an equal level with other political parties. (DeClair 1999: 66)

Le Pen succeeded in attracting another round of opportunists to the party. These included figures like Pascal Arrighi, a partisan of Algérie Française and former president of the University of Toulon; François Bachelot, a radiologist and former member of the RPR; and Jean-Claude Martinez, a professor of law and political science. The press began to refer to this new FN cohort as the "moderns," which demonstrated that Le Pen's attempt to sanitize the party's image was working (Birenbaum 1992: 76). According to one of these opportunists:

A Martinez, a Mégret, or a Bachelot, they created problems of conscience for a lot of people who knew them because they were politically active: Mégret in the RPR, Martinez at the Faculté, and Bachelot in politics. Some people who knew them followed them. They also had an impact on the rank and file of the party. They [the rank and file] were able to say "we have intellectuals in the party and not just skinheads." That was psychologically important for the rank and file. That was the strategy. (DeClair 1999: 67)

In sum, the infusion of opportunists, and particularly members of the New Right, had a number of important effects on party development. Although these opportunists were not all as moderate as their media image suggested (Birenbaum 1992: 97–103), and even though most of these "showcase elites" would never become very powerful within the party, the instant infusion of elites who could not be labeled extremists moved the FN farther away from its extraparliamentary roots and its extremist image. As Mégret and the Orlogers increased their power within the party, they also helped to temper the crude xenophobia of many Frontists and replace it with the more sophisticated discourse of ethnopluralism that would appeal to a much wider swath of the electorate. In other words, they were important in shifting the Front away from a logic of constituency representation to a logic of electoral competition. The new opportunists were also instrumental in founding the General Delegation (Délegation Générale), which served within the party both as a think tank and as a body to coordinate the ideological formation of the rank and file (Ivaldi 1998: 50).

In Chapter 2, we noted that the overall SES of the FN's candidates for the 2007 parliamentary elections was quite high. But since the data provided only a snapshot of the FN's socioeconomic profile, one could argue that many managers and professionals joined the FN precisely because it was successful, and therefore that patterns of activist recruitment are endogenous to electoral success. However, Ysmal's data on FN candidates for office in the mid-1980s make it clear that the FN attracted individuals

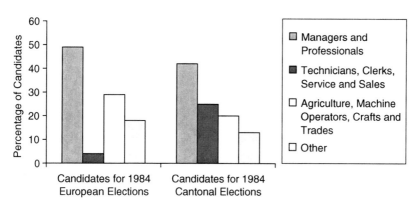

FIGURE 4.1. Candidates for the Front National in 1984.
From Ysmal (1984) (data recoded by author).

with high SES from the moment that the political environment became permissive. The socioeconomic profile of FN candidates, according to the ISCO-88 coding scheme, is presented in Figure 4.1. Ysmal also found that while FN candidates come from all sectors of society, its elected office holders overwhelmingly hail from the ranks of the liberal professions and senior executives: 72% of the FN's representatives in the National Assembly between 1986 and 1988 belonged to one of these categories. These data are consistent with the results of Birenbaum's (1992) survey of 1,004 delegates to the FN's party convention in Nice in 1990. Only 7% of the delegates did not possess a diploma, the same percentage that held a doctorate (Birenbaum 1992: 354). In sum, the available data strongly support the argument that open coalition markets and the lack of social sanctions for radical right activists allowed individuals with high SES to join the FN in the 1980s.

As I have argued, the influx of the opportunists benefited the FN in many ways. Yet as I noted in Chapter 2, attracting opportunists carries risks as well as rewards. Although Le Pen managed it for more than a decade, Mégret's challenge to his authority led to the party's largest split to date. After Le Pen took several steps to clip his wings in 1997 and 1998, Mégret broke from the party in January 1999 and founded the Mouvement National Républicain (MNR) in October of that year, bringing with him the Nouvelle Droite wing of the party and many others as well. In fact, the defections were massive: the FN lost 140 of its 275 regional councilors, 52 of the 120 central committee members, and 14 of the 44 members of the political bureau (Shields 2007: 279).

With the party organization in shambles, the media reporting gleefully on the breakup, and the existence of another radical right competitor, the FN posted its worst showing since 1984 in the 1999 European elections: 5.7%. Here is a clear example of how factionalism leads to poor electoral performance.

Yet it was the FN, rather than the MNR, that would survive the split and regain its strength within a matter of years. As the MNR quickly faded into oblivion, the 2002 presidential election demonstrated Le Pen's resiliency. Although often described as an "earthquake," Le Pen's first-round performance of 16.9% was not dramatically higher than his 15% in 1995. What was different was that the balkanization of the French left allowed Le Pen to move into second place in front of the Socialist candidate, Lionel Jospin, and face Chirac in the second round. Although the result was a foregone conclusion (Le Pen won only 17.8% of the vote), the resurgence of the radical right, confirmed in the 2004 regional elections when the FN gained 15%, led mainstream politicians to co-opt the Front's message in a manner reminiscent of the mid-1980s. There were, of course, other issues – terrorism, debates about headscarves, and riots in the suburbs, to name a few – that increased the salience of the FN's basic position on law and order, immigration, and national identity. Even absent Le Pen, it was not inconceivable that a politician like Nicolas Sarkozy would adopt positions and discourses that were essentially similar to those of the radical right and that even Sarkozy's rival in the 2007 presidential elections, the Socialist candidate, Ségolène Royal, would stress issues of law and order. Yet the conventional wisdom that Sarkozy sought to win the election by courting traditional FN voters is nevertheless correct. For the first time ever, Le Pen faced a viable candidate in the first round who had succeeded in building a hard-line reputation on crime and national identity (Ivaldi 2008). His 10.44% in the first round was his worst performance since winning only 0.75% in 1974.

In a conversation at the FN party headquarters in May 2007, Le Pen appeared uncharacteristically at a loss about how to react to Sarkozy.[19] It remains to be seen whether his daughter Marine will consolidate power or whether his departure will spur a leadership crisis that ultimately destroys the party he built. Whatever the outcome, the rise of the FN has profoundly shaped French politics in the past several decades, even though it has never acquired power at the national level. The decision

[19] Informal conversation with Le Pen, St. Cloud, May 2007.

by the extremists of Ordre Nouveau to provide an electoral cloak for their extraparliamentary activities had the unintended consequence of eventually producing one of the largest and best-organized radical right parties in Western Europe. As I have argued here, the permissive reaction to the Front when it first achieved national visibility was a critical factor in its success. Let us now turn to Austria, where the dynamics were quite similar.

Austria

We have already seen how the far right – as both a social force and an organized political party – was stronger in postwar Austria than anywhere in Western Europe, with the possible exception of Italy. When looking at the factors that contributed to the rise of the Austrian Freedom Party under Haider, the electoral success of the Austrian radical right appears to be overdetermined. The gradual erosion of the subsocieties produced a reservoir of floating voters that the FPÖ, as a populist party, was well positioned to capture. The grand coalition between the Social Democratic Party of Austria and the Austrian People's Party that governed Austria from 1986 to 2000 allowed Haider to market himself as the only opposition (aside from the left-libertarian Greens) in the country. Many Austrians, particularly those who were left out of the patronage system reserved for the Reds (SPÖ) and the Blacks (ÖVP), found Haider's anti-system message appealing. A string of scandals in the 1980s exposed corruption in the governments of mainstream parties, and the system itself seemed unable to deal with new problems resulting from a postindustrial economy. The collapse of the Iron Curtain brought a wave of new immigrants and asylum seekers, and the percentage of foreign-born residents increased dramatically between the late 1980s and 1990s. The FPÖ's first sustained foray into anti-immigrant politics in the Viennese elections of 1991 with the slogan "Vienna must not become Chicago" was an enormous success. The party won 22.5% of the vote in an area of the country in which it had historically been weak. Haider often received the support of Austria's most powerful newspaper, the tabloid *Kronen Zeitung*, which claims a readership of nearly 40% of the population. The Austrian media as a whole was captivated with Haider for more than a decade; he received far more attention than any other Austrian politician. Finally, Haider was an excellent orator and tireless campaigner, and the rise of the FPÖ was due in no small part to his charisma.

Yet had the FPÖ faced significant political or social repression, it would have been difficult for it to capitalize on these favorable conditions.

Instead, Haider's FPÖ was even less ostracized than the party was in the 1950s and 1960s, despite Vranitzky's policy of *Ausgrenzung* (the German expression for the cordon sanitaire). It is true that the SPÖ ruled out a coalition with the FPÖ at the national level from the moment Haider seized control of the party and that this policy resulted in a grand coalition with the ÖVP from 1986 to 1999. However, *Ausgrenzung* really did not occur at the local or state level. Social Democrats continued to cooperate with their FPÖ counterparts to pass legislation in communal and state parliaments. Kreisky had made the FPÖ *salonfähig* (respectable), and Vranitzky's change of course did not alter long-standing attitudes and patterns of behavior.

While the SPÖ's policy of marginalization was far from complete, the ÖVP's was practically nonexistent. From the 1986 elections to the formation of the ÖVP–FPÖ government in February 2000, the ÖVP never ruled out a national coalition with the FPÖ. Indeed, ÖVP leaders occasionally played the "Haider card," the threat to leave the Grand Coalition and side with the FPÖ, in order to extract concessions from the SPÖ. It was also ÖVP politicians who helped Haider become the governor of the state of Carinthia in 1989 after the FPÖ gained 35% to the ÖVP's 21% (the SPÖ led with 46%). By handing Haider governmental responsibility and endowing him with the substantial media attention that provincial governors receive, the ÖVP both legitimated the FPÖ and helped Haider consolidate his power in Carinthia.

Radical right politicians in Austria did not risk significant financial, social, or physical harm as a result of their politics. There were no sustained protests against the FPÖ until February 2000, and even then they were confined largely to Vienna. There have been no cases, to my knowledge, of FPÖ politicians losing their jobs as a result of their political activities. Members of the FPÖ were treated, in short, like politicians from any other party.

The lack of stigmatization and the promise of mandates in local or regional parliaments during the FPÖ's years of nearly constant electoral growth from 1986 to 1999 brought a wave of new recruits – opportunists – into the party. These so-called *Quereinsteiger* (literally, one who enters diagonally) were similar to the notables that the FN attracted, although they were more likely to be complete political amateurs. This group of opportunists included Olympic skiers, talk-show hosts, and business tycoons, and they were given excellent places on party lists to widen the party's appeal among voters. As one specialist notes, "These outsiders belonged to the realm of image or media politics ... they created a splash when their candidacy was first announced. In the optimum case, they helped to build up or sustain momentum during the crucial phase of the campaign" (Höbelt 2003: 155). Although the influence of some of these individuals proved fleeting, most were fiercely loyal to Haider. So too were another category of *Quereinsteiger* that the Austrian media often lampooned as the *Buberlpartie* (the boy gang). Some of these were young men that Haider recruited to the party through chance meetings along campaign stops or because they had some personal connection to him, for example as his tennis partner, bodyguard, or helicopter pilot. These individuals often served as Haider's *deputees*, or "enforcers" (Heinisch 2002: 96).

This was part and parcel of Haider's move to consolidate power and to make advancement within the party dependent on him. As Luther notes, Haider was the first leader of the FPÖ who, because of his political strength, "could not only fully exploit his statutory competencies, but also formally and de facto expand them" (Luther 2006a: 369). Haider determined the places on the party lists and replaced potential enemies in the party hierarchy with *Quereinsteiger* or loyalists from the *Burschenschaft* milieu. The FPÖ's Presidium, the organization responsible for the day-to-day management of the party's affairs, became a dumping ground for these new recruits (Heinisch 2002: 94–95). Changes in the party statutes in 1992 and 1995 effectively liberated Haider from the FPÖ's traditional party organization (Luther 1997). For example, whereas previously the party's executive committee (*Bundesparteiführung*) consisted mostly of nonelected party officials, after 1992 the number of ex officio members (whose electoral fortunes were directly tied to Haider) increased dramatically (Heinisch 2002: 94; Luther 2006a: 369).

Haider forced out dozens of FPÖ politicians who challenged his authority. He himself was honest about his intolerance of inner-party dissonance in an interview with the magazine *Basta* in June 1991: "He who strays from the political line must go. One needs to show toughness" (Bailer and Neugebauer 1994: 382). Haider frequently turned on both his former benefactors and his protégées to consolidate his power. But after isolating potential rivals, he sometimes allowed them back into the fold. He proved a master at controlling different tendencies within the party, and there was remarkably little deviation from Haider's line between 1986 and 2000.

Haider also decreased factionalism by eliminating most of the extremist and liberal elements from the FPÖ in the early 1990s. Haider had at first welcomed the former group by appointing the extremist Andreas Mölzer

editor in chief of the *Kärntner Nachrichten* (the party's newspaper) in
1985. In 1992, Haider put Mölzer in charge of the FPÖ's party academy
(Freiheitliche Akademie) and made him his personal *Grundsatzreferent*,
a sort of ideological adviser and strategist. This caused a major controversy within the party as Mölzer warned of the *Umvolkung* – a Nazi
term loosely translated as "population supplantation" – of the German
people through immigration. This was too much for the liberals, most of
whom had stayed on after Steger's departure, who were already incensed
by Haider's praising of the unemployment policies of the Third Reich in
the Carinthian parliament and his launching of a national referendum
("Austria First") against immigration. Heide Schmidt, a minor television
personality and one of the first *Quereinsteiger* to become a leading figure
in the FPÖ, announced her defection and her subsequent formation of the
Liberal Forum (LiF) in February 1993. Although Schmidt was relatively
well known, she was unable to bring along many FPÖ heavyweights with
her; those who did so left in part because their chances for reelection were
marginal (Höbelt 2003: 96). The LiF did succeed in crossing the threshold
for representation in the 1994 and 1995 elections, but has failed to do so
since then. The party was confined largely to Vienna and never succeeded
in building a grassroots organization. The departure of the liberal wing
of the party thus did not prove electorally costly to Haider and eliminated one source of division within the party. Haider then moved against
the extremists he had previously courted. As the FPÖ extended its voter
base, the die-hard pan-German camp was becoming a liability. Austrian
national identity, weak through the 1950s and 1960s, had become much
stronger by the 1980s and 1990s, and Haider accordingly converted from
a pan-German nationalist into an Austrian patriot. To take one example,
he maneuvered the pan-Germanist Krimhild Trattnig out of power in
Carinthia, and thus distanced the FPÖ from the extremist group around
her (Heinisch 2002: 99).

To tighten his control further, Haider forced FPÖ officials to sign the
"Contract of Democracy" (*Demokratievertrag*) in 1998, in which they
disclosed their financial situation and renounced certain financial pension
benefits for holding public office (Heinisch 2002: 101). This followed
on the heels of a well-publicized financial scandal within the party in
which a former FPÖ official embezzled a large sum of money and fled
to Brazil. The *Demokratievertrag* was obviously intended to salvage the
FPÖ's anticorruption image, but by including passages about party loyalty (which Haider by and large defined) it bound individuals even more
closely to the party's leader.

Although the appearance of *Quereinsteiger* combined with Haider's purges led to a changeover in the FPÖ party elite, or what Kurt Richard Luther has referred to as a "permanent revolution" (Luther 1997), the FPÖ's party membership did not increase in line with its rising electoral success. Indeed, party membership increased only 40% between 1986 and 2000 (36,683 to 51,296), a period in which the FPÖ's voteshare increased by 180% (Luther 2006b). In part, this modest increase was an artifact of the already high membership rate for a party that hitherto had gained about 5% of the vote. But the party was also selective in its recruitment. One of the goals was to increase the percentage of white-collar workers within the party; indeed, Haider spoke often of the need to recruit yuppies. Although we have extremely limited data on the FPÖ's party membership, internal party statistics from Upper Austria – the province that counted one-fourth of all party members as of 2003 – suggest that Haider might have achieved his goal. The percentage of white-collar workers within the party increased from 16% in 1986 to 22% in 1998, while the percentage of blue-collar workers held steady at 25% and 24%, respectively (Höbelt 2003: 157). Thus, while the FPÖ attracted a primarily working-class voter base in the 1990s, the party attracted a new crop of educated professionals. This was certainly apparent at the top of the party, where young university graduates such as Karl-Heinz Grasser, Herbert Scheibner, Peter Westenthaler, and Susanne Riess-Passer became part of Haider's inner circle.

Between 1986 and 1999, Haider turned a liberal party garnering around 5% of the vote into a radical right one capturing more than five times that number. Yet his success in winning votes in opposition was not to be reproduced in government. Immediately after the formation of the ÖVP–FPÖ coalition in February 2000, the fourteen other member states of the European Union placed diplomatic sanctions on Austria to announce their displeasure (Howard 2000; Markovits 2002). Both domestic and international observers argued at the time that the sanctions were ill conceived and would produce a nationalist backlash, which they proceeded to do as the popularity of the ÖVP–FPÖ government soared. The "EU-fourteen" were forced by the spring of 2000 to find a face-saving escape from the situation and appointed a three-man commission to investigate Austria's internal politics. These "wise men" produced a report in September 2000 that, while criticizing the FPÖ for populist and xenophobic tendencies, concluded that neither Austria's minorities nor its democracy were at risk. The sanctions were quietly lifted. Yet although they were generally viewed as a failure, the sanctions did prevent Haider from taking a cabinet position in the new government and led him to step down as party leader in May 2000 in the hope of ending them. Although still governor of Carinthia, Haider claimed that he would become a "simple party member" and allow his appointed team of politicians (which included Riess-Passer as vice-chancellor and party leader, Grasser as minister of finance, and Scheibner as secretary of defense) to work without his interference. No one expected his retreat from national politics to be permanent, and the so-called simple party member continued to determine the FPÖ's policies behind the scenes.

As in the French case, the recruitment of opportunists had long-term costs as well as benefits. The first "black and blue" coalition (the colors of the ÖVP and FPÖ, respectively) revealed the inexperience of several FPÖ ministers and the costs of favoring loyalty over competence (Luther 2003: 140). There were no less than four FPÖ ministers of transportation. Elisabeth Sickl, the widely ridiculed minister of social affairs, was replaced after only eight months in office by Herbert Haupt. Since the social affairs portfolio included the women's ministry, headlines across Austria read, "Man Sworn in as Minister for Women." In all, half of all FPÖ ministers resigned or were forced out during the less than two years of the first ÖVP–FPÖ coalition (Heinisch 2003: 115).

Yet there were several FPÖ ministers whose popularity and competence offset the weaknesses of their colleagues. Vice-Chancellor Riess-Passer and Finance Minister Grasser in particular scored high in numerous likeability polls and acquired a reputation for seriousness (Luther 2003: 140). The media began to portray them as the acceptable face of the FPÖ, and Grasser even became the most popular politician in Austria for a period in 2001. The FPÖ leaders had always assumed that their participation in government would cost them at the ballot box, yet Riess-Passer and Grasser's performance helped the party to remain between 23% and 25% in the public opinion polls until the autumn of 2001.

By this point, Haider had apparently tired of being merely the governor of Carinthia and wanted to reenter national politics. He attempted to seize control of the party from Riess-Passer but was rebuffed. He responded with a seemingly unending critique of the coalition that he himself had formed, which culminated in his rallying the party base against the party leadership, finally resulting in the resignations of Riess-Passer, Grasser, and several other members of the FPÖ's governing team. Because Wolfgang Schüssel (the ÖVP chancellor), like Vranitzky in 1986, refused to cooperate with the leaders of the FPÖ's revolt, new elections were called for November 24, 2002.

The election campaign revealed the extent of the FPÖ's inner-party turmoil. Haider initially intended to head the FPÖ's party list, but a wave of resignations within his own party and unmistakable signs of voter disenchantment with the FPÖ persuaded him to withdraw rather than suffer his first major electoral defeat. His claim that he feared assassination was widely derided in the press. The task of leading the FPÖ to certain defeat eventually fell to the uncharismatic Herbert Haupt, after another candidate, Matthias Reichhold, had initially accepted but later declined it. With the party bitterly divided, the FPÖ captured only 10% of the vote, its worst performance since 1986. The ÖVP, by contrast, was the election's big winner, improving upon its 2000 result by more than fifteen percentage points. Schüssel then formed another coalition with the enervated FPÖ.

The magnitude of the FPÖ's electoral defeat only exacerbated the infighting. A rift opened between those who wanted to maximize votes by returning to populism and xenophobia, and those who wanted to remain in the government. This time, Haider found himself in the latter camp and pitted against former allies Ewald Stadler, Andreas Mölzer, and Heinz-Christian Strache. After several years of turmoil, Haider left the FPÖ in April 2005 to found the Alliance for the Future of Austria (BZÖ). He brought along with him the FPÖ cabinet ministers, the majority of the FPÖ representatives in the National Council, and virtually the entire FPÖ organization in Carinthia (Luther 2007: 239). The BZÖ thus became the first party in Austria to hold ministerial positions without winning an election.

The BZÖ looked moribund in 2006, when it mustered only 4.1% of the vote in the national parliamentary elections. But its future looked significantly brighter after Haider led the party to a surprising 10.7% in the parliamentary elections of September 2008. Yet just two weeks after this stunning return to national politics, Haider was killed in a car crash. The BZÖ's party executive elected Stefan Petzner to succeed Haider as party leader, but then quickly dislodged him from this post after he suggested that he and Haider had had an intimate relationship.[20] Since the BZÖ was held together by loyalty to Haider, it seems unlikely that the party can persist without him.

---

[20] Haider's sexual orientation had been an open secret in Austrian politics for at least a decade. However, since neither the media nor his political adversaries normally mentioned it, much of the Austrian public was surprised by Petzner's remarks and the revelations that followed.

The FPÖ, on the other hand, is currently stronger than it has been for close to a decade. Although its voteshare in national and state elections initially plummeted after 2001, the party retained its organizational strength. As of 2004, the FPÖ reported 44,959 members, down less than 10% from its highpoint of 51,259 in 1999 (Luther 2006b: 34). Returning to anti-immigrant themes, the FPÖ under party leader Strache won a surprising 14.8% in the Viennese state elections of October 2005. It repeated this strategy in the 2006 national parliamentary elections with slogans such as "Austria First," "Prosperity Instead of Migration," and "At Home Instead of Islam" (*Daham statt Islam*) and improved slightly upon its 2002 score (before the split) with 11% (Luther 2007: 239). Two years later, the FPÖ more than doubled this score by capturing 22.5% in the national parliamentary elections of 2008. Together, the BZÖ and FPÖ won nearly a third of the vote, putting to rest both the claim that the Austrian radical right had been "tamed" by its experience in government and the claim that the FPÖ could not prosper without its former charismatic leader.

Flanders

Belgium is the birthplace of the term "cordon sanitaire," and no political party has ever formed a coalition with the Vlaams Belang at any political level. This policy, however, has not prevented the radical right from increasing its voteshare in nearly every election. Should one infer from the Belgian case, as many observers have, that marginalizing the radical right is a counterproductive strategy? Before reaching this conclusion, it is necessary to examine the evolution of the cordon sanitaire. Although it is generally perceived to be one of the tightest in Europe, it has always had cracks.

When the Vlaams Blok was founded in 1979, the party was not labeled a radical right party, but rather a conservative separatist party that strove for the independence of Flanders. In 1981, the then-president of the Volksunie Vic Anciaux attempted to reattach the Vlaams Blok to his party. Anciaux was convinced that cooperation among the different Flemish nationalist forces would hasten the federalization of the country. It was not until May 1989, nearly a year after the VB's breakthrough in the Antwerp municipal elections, that every party represented in parliament signed an agreement not to work with it. Yet for the next several years, "the political parties displayed all the stability of a weathervane with respect to the VB" (Swyngedouw 1998: 72). Only a month after signing the initial agreement, the Volksunie (VU), the Liberals (PVV), and the Christian Democrats (CVP) abrogated it, leaving only the Greens and the

Social Democrats. According to Mudde (2000: 89), the non-left parties "resumed their ambivalent stance towards the VB: a great deal of anti-VB rhetoric together with conciliatory gestures whenever it proved opportune." The situation changed after the VB's success in the 1991 federal elections (sometimes referred to as Black Sunday) as thousands of politicians from across the political spectrum signed onto a new cordon over the next several years (Damen 2001). It thus took several years for the cordon to become tight, and it became so only after the VB had already scored victories on the local, regional, and national levels. Furthermore, politicians from mainstream parties have publicly debated the utility of the cordon since its creation, and many have argued for its abrogation (Van den Brink 1996: Erk 2005).

On November 9, 2004, a Belgian court of cassation found the Vlaams Blok to be in breach of the 1981 law against racism and xenophobia. This ruling forced it to change its name and its party program in order to continue to receive public funding as a political party. On November 14, the former members of the Blok launched a new political party, the Vlaams Belang (Flemish Interest). Although the Belgian court did not ban the Vlaams Blok, its ruling represents one of the highest-profile actions against contemporary radical right parties in Western Europe. Yet there are good reasons to believe that this ruling has acted as a blessing in disguise for the VB. As Professor Lieven De Winter put it in an interview with *Le Soir*, the court's actions did little to damage the legitimacy of the party: "One Fleming in four has already voted for the Blok. The psychological threshold has already passed. For Flemish voters, a vote for the Blok is already seen as a legitimate option."[21] The ruling in fact allowed the party "to erase some of its more extremist features, which is probably something it wanted to do anyway for a long time."[22] The most significant change in the party's statute concerns immigration. Whereas the Vlaams Blok called for the repatriation of all immigrants, the Vlaams Belang would repatriate only those "who reject, deny, or combat our culture and certain European values such as separation of Church and state, liberty of expression, and equality between men and women" (quoted in Erk 2005: 495).

Moreover, by forcing the Vlaams Belang to moderate its program and rhetoric, the court ruling also jeopardizes the continuation of the cordon sanitaire (Erk 2005: 497). The editor in chief of the daily *De Morgen*

[21] *Le Soir*, November 9, 2004.
[22] *Financial Times*, December 7, 2004.

argued that changes in the Vlaams Belang's party statutes would erode the formal grounds for continuing the cordon policy, an opinion shared by many other Flemish politicians and observers.[23] Yet the cordon broke neither in the 2006 municipal elections nor in the 2007 parliamentary elections, in which the VB won 12% of the vote nationally and remained the second-largest party in Flanders.

In sum, neither the cordon nor the 2004 court verdict appears to have fundamentally damaged the VB's fortunes. This suggests that such measures appear to be effective only early in a radical right party's development: once it has created strong party organization and a voter base, repression appears to be counterproductive.

Still, given the existence of the cordon sanitaire, one might imagine that Vlaams Belang members face a high degree of stigma in their social and economic relations. Yet my in-depth interviews with VB politicians at different levels of government unearthed no evidence for this view. This was surprising because, even if social sanctions did not exist, the party has long adopted a narrative of victimization and I thoroughly expected VB politicians to complain about how antifascist activists, left-leaning teachers, and politically correct employers were making their lives miserable. Yet every politician I spoke with noted that the social climate was actually very good and getting better each day. A recent university graduate, and currently an associate at the VB's political research center, had absolutely no problems at the university and claimed that many students of law, engineering, and information technology were also open Vlaams Belang supporters.[24] Another parliamentarian, who joined the party in the mid-1990s, claimed that he did so in large part because the social acceptance of the Vlaams Blok was increasing.[25] Bruno Valkeniers, one of the founders of the National Student Movement, the former president of the committee of the Flemish Song Festival, and a successful businessman, joined the party in 2006. He won a seat on the Antwerp city council – so his political affiliation is now highly visible – and reports no negative repercussions from his decision. In fact, Valkeniers reports that his friends and business colleagues overwhelmingly supported his decision to join the VB, and many wondered why it had taken him so long to do so.[26]

[23] *De Morgen*, November 10, 2004.
[24] Interview with Steven Utsi, Brussels, February 12, 2007.
[25] Interview with Bert Schoofs, member of Federal Parliament (VB), Brussels, February 15, 2007.
[26] Interview with Bruno Valkeniers, member of Antwerp city council (VB), Antwerp, February 19, 2007.

Some party members report a shift, though not a net loss, in their friends and business connections. Hugo Coveliers, a lawyer and head of a small party (VLOTT) that cooperates with the VB, claims that his politics lost him one client, yet gained him many more.[27] His comments echo those of Ghislaine Peleman, a former schoolteacher who joined the party in the mid-1990s. She recalls that while "some of her colleagues didn't speak with her anymore, others became very friendly again."[28] In this social climate, organizing party functions is relatively unproblematic. My interviewees all reported that antifascist activities appeared to have been on the wane over the past several years and that their meetings were no longer disrupted. Indeed, Peleman reports that the only problem in her locality is "finding a large enough meeting place for all our members."[29]

Since all of my respondents perceived a change in the level of stigmatization of the Vlaams Belang, it would be plausible to guess that members of the party had faced a hostile social climate during the early years. Again, however, I found little evidence for this. Hugo Verhelst, a former member of the Volksunie who joined the Vlaams Blok in the late 1970s, stated that it was "easier to go the Vlaams Blok than stay in the Volksunie" because he "met all his old friends from his former party who had made a similar step."[30] Luc Sevenhans, a dockworker in the port of Antwerp who also shifted from the Volksunie to the Vlaams Blok a decade later, was kicked out of the Socialist trade union but was allowed to join the liberal one. His superiors were supportive of his political affiliation.[31]

In fact, none of the interviewees could recall stories of economic or social hardship from anyone they knew in the party. The only widely reported negative repercussion of membership in the Vlaams Belang was the loss of trade union membership. In 2006 alone, more than three hundred people were ejected from the unions because they stood for office on VB electoral lists. The large number of expulsions suggests that this policy does not serve as a deterrent to publicizing one's VB party affiliation. Moreover, the liberal union allowed these expellees to join.

In sum, the idea that VB members are "social pariahs" is false. Flemish society is polarized between opponents and supporters of the party, but

[27] Interview with Hugo Coveliers, member of Antwerp city council (VLOTT), Antwerp, February 20, 2007.

[28] Interview with Ghislaine Peleman, VB party member in Schoten, Antwerp, February 19, 2007.

[29] Interview with Peleman.

[30] Interview with Hugo Verhelst, Antwerp, February 19, 2007..

[31] Interview with Luc Sevenhans, member of Federal Parliament (VB), Brussels, February 15, 2007.

VB members are hardly the types of marginalized, stigmatized outsiders that their counterparts are in other countries. This is not surprising given that the Flemish Movement – even its most radical elements – was always perceived to be legitimate by a large sector of the population.

Conclusion

This chapter has demonstrated that radical right parties in Austria, Flanders, and France possessed both the means and the opportunity for electoral persistence. They all drew from large nationalist subcultures to build a genuine rank and file. Although they did not entirely avoid factionalism and charges of incompetence – and we have seen how these experiences led to a temporary cratering of electoral support for the Austrian Freedom Party and the French National Front – these parties were far more unified and professional than those we encountered in Chapter 3.

In terms of legitimacy, it is true that Haider, Le Pen, and Dewinter all made, at one time or another, statements that only right-wing extremists could condone. Each also cultivated relationships with members of that milieu. Yet at the same time, they also acted to limit the influence of Holocaust denialists and biological racists, and made concerted efforts to recruit individuals for the specific purpose of enhancing the respectability of their parties. The response of mainstream actors contributed considerably to the latter goal. Indeed, it would have been impossible for Schüssel to have formed a government with the FPÖ had not enough members of his own party considered the radical right a respectable alternative to the SPÖ. Similarly, politicians in Flanders would not have questioned the continuation of the cordon sanitaire had the Vlaams Belang been viewed in the same way as the British National Party or the German National Party. The perceived respectability of the Front National is probably currently the lowest of the three cases, but even here we need to remember that the situation was quite different in the 1980s and 1990s.

We have thus far had little to say about the ideological flexibility of the three parties, other than to note that they all seized upon anti-immigration themes to maximize their electoral performance when the issue became politically salient in the 1980s. Such a move, however, did not represent a profound departure from their founding ideologies. As Dewinter once put it, "How can a party resist the Francification of Brussels without resisting its Morocconization?" (quoted in Hossay 2002: 176). The ethnic essentialism that underpinned the FPÖ's pan-Germanism was entirely consistent with its turn to ethnopluralism, even as the party embraced a specifically Austrian national identity. The FN drew not only on France's counterrevolutionary tradition, but also on the hostility of the *pieds-noir* community toward Maghrebins that was tangible long before the breakthrough in Dreux. In states with strong nationalist subcultures, anti-immigrant messages were grafted onto long-standing nationalist ideologies. This was not the case for parties that drew neither from nationalist subcultures nor from small extremist networks, and it is to them that we now turn.

5

Party Transformation and Flash Parties

Up to this point, we have analyzed radical right parties that have been either doubly cursed or doubly blessed: Chapter 3 looked at parties that had neither the means nor the opportunity for party building, while Chapter 4 turned to parties that possessed both. This ordering brought differences in historical legacies and reactions to the radical right into sharp relief, but left open the question of whether both variables were truly determinative of success and failure. This chapter demonstrates that opportunity is not enough. None of the five radical right parties it covers – the Danish People's Party, the Norwegian Progress Party, the Swiss People's Party, New Democracy, and the List Pim Fortuyn – faced either cordons sanitaires or social sanctions. Yet while the first three successful cases emerged through a process of party transformation and thus possessed some indigenous resources, the latter two failures were constructed hastily and from scratch.

Since the parties discussed in this chapter had no connection to previous far right organizations, they were not as plagued by extremist activists as were radical right parties elsewhere. And since the social environment was not repressive, they also succeeded in recruiting educated activists. The major problem each faced was how to create competent and coherent parties. Both New Democracy (ND) and the List Pim Fortuyn (LPF) failed to build any semblance of a party organization; the latter in particular demonstrates the problems that politically inexperienced and opportunistic activists bring. Political entrepreneurs in the Danish People's Party (DF), the Norwegian Progress Party (FrP), and the Swiss People's Party (SVP) suffered through these problems as well but had more time to deal with them. The organizational choices they made were critical for the development of their parties. Yet while leadership certainly mattered in these cases, their job was made much easier by the fact that a party organization already existed. This chapter looks first at these three successful cases before turning to the two flash parties that failed to consolidate initial successes and ended in failure.

Party Transformation

Since the DF, FrP, and SVP began their lives as very different types of parties, it is tempting to draw a distinction between them and the other radical right parties covered in this book. Indeed, there is a general perception that they represent a milder form of nativism than parties like the Front National. Although the results of the expert survey I presented in Chapter 1 suggest that this difference is not so severe, perhaps these data are inaccurate or perhaps these parties have softened their tone in the years since the surveys were conducted in order to appeal to a wider swath of the electorate.

Events in the past five years suggest otherwise. For several weeks in February 2006, Denmark was the focus of some unwelcome international attention. Following the publication of a series of cartoons depicting the prophet Muhammad in the newspaper *Jyllands-Posten*, which many Muslims found blasphemous, crowds across the Middle East burned Danish Prime Minister Anders Fogh Rasmussen in effigy. During this so-called cartoon controversy, the international media began to take serious notice of the Danish People's Party and discovered that it had been taking strident positions against the Islamic community in Denmark for years. In 2000, for example, the DF European parliamentarian Mogens Camre wrote that Islam "is not only a religion but a fascist political ideology mixed with a religious fanaticism of the Middle Ages, an insult against the human rights and all other conditions necessary for creating a developed society" (quoted in Rydgren 2004b: 485). In September 2005, the Web site of DF parliamentarian Louise Frevert alleged that young Muslim men believed they were entitled to rape Danish women and assault Danish citizens. During the height of the controversy, DF party leader Pia Kjaersgaard wrote that the Islamic religious community in Denmark consisted of "pathetic and lying men with worrying, suspect views on democracy and women ... they are the enemy inside. The Trojan horse in Denmark. A kind of Islamic mafia."[1] Even after the

---

[1] *International Herald Tribune*, February 12, 2006.

crisis subsided, DF politicians continued the offensive. In April 2007, Søren Krarup (DF) provoked an uproar in parliament by stating, "The [Muslim] veil is a totalitarian symbol that can be compared to the symbols we know from the Nazi swastika and from communism."[2] He later elaborated on this comparison, arguing that Islam, like communism and Nazism, is totalitarian because it provides a single solution for all of life's problems. Each ideology possesses, according to Krarup, its own holy book: the Koran, *Das Kapital*, and *Mein Kampf*.[3]

In September 2007, Switzerland became the next small European country to draw international headlines for a controversial cartoon. The image in question appeared in the SVP's election brochure, which the party mass-mailed to Swiss households, and on billboards across the country. Three white sheep could be seen kicking a black sheep off of the Swiss national flag "to create security," according to the caption underneath. As part of the campaign, the SVP ran a short film on its Web site titled *Heaven or Hell*. The first two parts of the film, which portray "hell," include scenes of Muslim women in headscarves, Muslim men sitting on street corners, and youths with dark complexions mugging old ladies and assaulting women. "Heaven" is replete with images of churches, mountains, goats, experiments in laboratories, high-speed trains, and women walking together at night.[4] During the campaign, the SVP pledged to create a new law that would allow the state to deport an entire foreign family if one of its children committed a serious crime. It also promised an initiative to ban the construction of minarets, which has since been passed into law. Despite widespread condemnation of its campaign – the president of Switzerland called the sheep poster "disgusting," "unacceptable" and "dangerous" – the SVP won 29% of the vote.

As in Denmark, the radical right had been leading a charged debate over immigration for a long time. In 1992, the Zurich branch of the SVP launched a referendum "Against Illegal Immigration" and distributed a poster of a swarthy man tearing up the Swiss flag (Skenderovic 2007a: 174). During the general election campaign in 2003, the SVP's ads accused "certain ethnic groups" of criminal activity, and one of its posters displayed a black face with the caption "The Swiss are becoming Negroes."[5] The United Nations High Commissioner for Refugees, based

---

[2] Agence France Presse, April 19, 2007.
[3] Interview with Søren Krarup (DF), Copenhagen, May 2007.
[4] *New York Times*, October 8, 2007.
[5] *Financial Times*, October 21, 2003; October 25, 2003.

in Geneva, criticized the party for inciting hatred of foreigners following the election.[6]

Norway's radical right party has yet to receive the international introduction of its Danish and Swiss counterparts. Its members also regularly distance themselves from these types of parties, and claim that theirs is devoted to individual freedom and is in no way anti-immigrant or racist. After he was compared to Le Pen in the 1997 election campaign, for example, Karl I. Hagen responded angrily, "Le Pen is a disgusting and real racist of whom I really disapprove. His ideological attitudes are far, far from what the Progress Party stands for."[7] Yet over the course of the 1990s, the FrP developed an ethnopluralist doctrine, which marked a decisive turn away from neoliberalism and toward anti-immigration and welfare chauvinism. During the 1999 election campaign, two FrP politicians – Øystein Hedstrøm and Vidar Kleppe – held open meetings on immigration, which the press dubbed "immigration shows." Hedstrøm explained that he had "studied integration policies all over Europe" and concluded that "where Christians and Muslims, Jews and Arabs, and other different cultures live together, life is characterized by murder, drugs, and other types of crime."[8] Kleppe asserted that "he had nothing against immigrants" but added that "you cannot deny that they bring some negative aspects to Norway. It can be drugs, crime, and oppression of women. I do not want us to ruin our nation with this."[9] In 2005, one of the FrP's election brochures featured a photo of a man wearing a ski mask and brandishing a shotgun next to the quote "The perpetrator is of foreign origin … !" The brochure explained that "for the FrP a stricter immigration policy and a stricter crime policy is about safety … Safety for people to walk the streets without fear of being raped or robbed."[10]

These messages clearly appeal to FrP voters. In the 1989 and 1993 parliamentary elections, the average position of a Progress Party voter on immigration was already much more restrictive than that of a voter from any other party (Bjørklund and Andersen 2002: 123). In 1993, 43% of FrP voters believed that immigration was the most important issue in the election, compared with only 7% of conservative voters (Aardal 1994). In the 1995 local elections, in which the FrP captured 12.1% of the vote,

---

[6] *Independent*, December 11, 2003.
[7] *Aftenposten*, September 15, 1997.
[8] *Dagsavisen*, June 27, 1999 (quoted in Hagelund 2003: 58).
[9] *Dagsavisen*, July 27, 1999 (quoted in Hagelund 2003: 58).
[10] *Aftenposten*, August 16, 2005.

93% of those who regarded immigration as the most important issue voted for the party. "There is little doubt," concluded two specialists, "that immigration is the core issue that distinguishes Progress Party voters from other non-socialist voters" (Andersen and Bjørklund 2000: 212).

In short, although the FrP may in fact represent a slightly less intense form of nativism than radical right parties elsewhere, the DF and SVP do not. Moreover, anti-immigration has been central to the electoral success of all three parties. The major difference between them and unsuccessful radical right parties lies not in their ideology, but in their internal organization.

Denmark: From the Progress Party to the Danish People's Party

Denmark, like the rest of Scandinavia, lacked a strong far right subculture both before and after the Second World War. The fascist National-Socialist Worker's Party (Danmarks Nationalsocialistiske Arbejder Parti, DNSAP) failed to cross the 2% threshold in either the 1935 or 1939 elections and counted only four thousand members on the eve of the German occupation (Ignazi 2003: 140). Unlike the situation in Norway, the Nazis allowed the existing government in Denmark to remain in power, but the DNSAP mustered only 2.3% of the vote in the 1943 elections. Nazi sympathizers were purged after the war, and no significant far right parties emerged. As one specialist notes, "The successor movements could be characterized as lunatic fringes and were more of a laughing stock than a cause for concern. Electorally, they were miniscule. Organisationally, they were nowhere near strong enough to mobilise resources that could lead to unrest" (Widfeldt 2000).

The history of the Danish Progress Party (FRPd) began with a nationally televised interview in January 1971 with Mogens Glistrup, a prominent tax lawyer. Glistrup argued that present-day tax evaders were as heroic as resisters against Nazi occupation and proudly admitted that he had paid no tax on his income of more than 1 million Danish kroner. A series of hikes in the income tax in the 1960s and 1970s to finance the welfare state had indeed created favorable conditions for a tax revolt (Kitschelt 1995: 129). Drawing on this popular discontent, Glistrup founded the FRPd in 1972 and captured 15.9% of the vote in the "earthquake" election of 1973. Along with a massive increase in taxes, the FRPd benefited from another important event: the European Community referendum of 1972. Although Denmark, in contrast to Norway, voted for EC membership, a flurry of grassroots organizing against membership had mobilized voters and politicized Danish nationalism (Andersen and Bjørklund 2000: 129). The FRPd was one of the only parties to position itself against EC membership, along with the small Danish Communist Party and the newly formed Center Democrats, and cashed in with Euroskeptic voters as a result (Kitschelt 1995: 131).

Glistrup provided a marked contrast to the serious figures that populated the Danish political establishment. His proposal that Denmark's entire military force be disbanded and replaced with an answering service that played the message "We surrender" in Russian in the case of a Soviet attack was a typical example of his provocative and outlandish rhetoric (Kitschelt 1995: 131). As a self-proclaimed warrior against established political parties, Glistrup always conceived of the FRPd as a movement or, less charitably, as his own personal vehicle. But the very success of the Progress Party attracted political entrepreneurs who wanted to create a conventional party organization and seek compromise with mainstream political forces. This led to an inner-party battle between the so-called fundamentalists, represented by Glistrup, and the pragmatists, lead by Pia Kjaersgaard (Widfeldt 2000: 489). A national party organization was built over the protestations of the party's founder, and the pragmatists gained control of the party when Glistrup was imprisoned in 1983 for tax fraud. Kjaersgaard took Glistrup's seat in parliament and began building her own power base. By the time he returned to politics in 1987, Glistrup found that he was no longer in control of the FRPd and founded his own party, the oddly named Cosy Party (Trivelspartiet), in 1990. The move proved to be a disaster, as the Cosy Party failed to win any seats and quickly disappeared.

Despite Glistrup's exit, the party he founded continued to suffer from a number of organizational problems. For example, although the national committee of the FRPd had the right to interfere in candidate selection at the local level, in practice it never did (Pederson and Ringsmosse 2005). The predictable result was that the FRPd became populated by candidates who had never been vetted. Such candidates often had personal motives for seeking election and possessed little loyalty to the Progress Party. Not surprisingly, the FRPd was unable to enforce parliamentary discipline throughout its years in parliament. Kjaersgaard tried repeatedly to bring order to what was a raucous collection of individuals, but as one former FRPd member and now DF parliamentarian remembers, "it was like tilting at windmills."[11]

---

[11] Interview with Birthe Skaarup (DF), Copenhagen, May 2007.

Kjaersgaard and three other members of parliament from the Progress Party founded the Danish People's Party in 1995. The inner-party squabbles between fundamentalists and pragmatists in the FRPd had contributed to a steady erosion of electoral support and precipitated a leadership crisis in the summer of 1995. The chaotic annual party congress, in which disgruntled delegates burst balloons and "village idiots ranted from the podium," marked the final straw.[12] Kjaersgaard was able to take nearly one-third of Progress Party members with her, including about one-third of the FRPd's local city councilors.[13] Within several years, the DF had replaced the FRPd as Denmark's major radical right party.

Kjaersgaard resolved that the DF would never resemble the Progress Party. She became its undisputed leader and created a number of mechanisms to ensure that her position would not be challenged. For instance, the public display of inner-party disagreements by a DF politician results first in a written warning and second in expulsion (Pederson and Ringsmosse 2005). This policy was clearly stated by Kjaersgaard in an article in the party newspaper titled "Top-Steering? Yes – of Course":

The order is clear. If a member of the party criticizes another member or the party in public, he or she will get a written warning. If the criticism is repeated, exclusion will be an issue. This is the way it has always been in the Danish People's Party, and this is the way it will stay as long as I am chairman.... *The Progress Party anarchism will never be allowed to find its way into the People's Party.* (Quoted in Pederson and Ringsmosse 2005: emphasis mine)

As several members of the party put it, "top-steering" has a positive connotation within the party. "In a large firm," one parliamentarian notes, "you need a chief: here we have a leader."[14] There are no discernible factions within the DF, and members of the party always vote as a block in parliament.

Kjaersgaard centralized the process of candidate selection before the 1998 elections. Potential candidates must belong to the party for at least six months and submit an application packet (containing a cover letter, statement of purpose, CV, and criminal background check from the local police) to a regional nominating committee. Finalists are interviewed, and the regional nominating committee sends a list of recommendations to party members for approval. Since two members of the national party

[12] Interview with Skaarup.
[13] Interview with Hans-Peter Skibby (DF), Copenhagen, May 2007.
[14] Interview with Jørn Dohrmann (DF), Copenhagen, May 2007.

always sit on the nominating committees, the preferences of the central leadership are always expressed. In the words of DF parliamentarian Poul Lindholm Nielsen, this entire vetting procedure allows the DF to avoid the "soldiers of fortune" and "village fools" whose candidacies would hurt the party (Pederson and Ringsmosse 2005). Another DF parliamentarian notes that, unlike the situation in the Progress Party, "you can't come straight from the street into the Danish People's Party lists."[15]

Although the new party refused to allow many members of the Progress Party to join, the culture of infighting persisted for several years. Between 1998 and 2001, three of the DF's thirteen parliamentarians left the party because they took issue with "top-steering." But since 2001, only one member of the DF's parliamentary group (twenty-two members from 2001 to 2005, twenty-four from 2005) has split from the party. Defections are also apparently very rare on the local level. None of my interviewees could recall a single example of a member of the local council leaving the DF while in office. Council members are normally well trained by the party and take courses that cover the following practical tasks: making a budget, constructing a Web site, distributing party literature, public speaking, and forming relationships with the local media.[16]

Not only has the DF protected itself from the sorts of individualists and opportunists that dominated the Progress Party; it has prevented extremists from infiltrating its ranks. In contrast to that in Sweden, the right-wing extremist milieu in Denmark is numerically small. Only the Dansk Front, the Danish National Socialist Party (DNSP), and the Danish Forum are worth mentioning. The former two groups are violent neo-Nazi organizations, while the third is the extremist youth wing of the Danish Association. In 1999, nineteen members of the DF were excluded because they had links with the Danish Forum (Bjørklund and Andersen 2002: 112). In 2006, the party's central committee immediately expelled eight local branch chairmen and one local council member after an undercover journalist from *Ekstrabladet* exposed their deviation from the party's line. The journalist posed as a potential DF member and asked if his links with the Dansk Front and the DNSP prevented him from joining the party. Nine out of the eleven local politicians he questioned answered that his right-wing extremist past would not be a problem, so long as he kept quiet about it. Although most of these local politicians had probably never heard of either the Dansk Front or the DNSP (the

---

[15] Interview with Tina Peterson (DF), Copenhagen, May 2007.
[16] Interview with Peterson.

journalist did not identify them as right-wing extremist organizations), they were ejected from the party without debate. As Peter Skaarup, the DF's deputy party leader, explained, "There is simply no place for this sort of thing in the Danish People's Party. Racist, extreme, and undemocratic views run counter to everything that is Danish and therefore also [to] the Danish People's Party."[17]

But that the DF has the luxury of excluding or banishing certain individuals from the party is in large part a result of developments that preceded its founding. Although the Progress Party would never equal its 15.9% in the 1973 elections, it had survived in the Danish system for nearly two decades and possessed a hard core of loyal voters. When Kjaersgaard founded the Danish People's Party, she stated that the DF would promote the same policies as the Progress Party. Thus, while the FRPd had already begun to shift with its increased emphasis on immigration in the late 1980s and early 1990s, Kjaersgaard was able to bring an existing organization along with her. As of May 2007, thirteen out of the DF's twenty-three members of parliament had been members of the Progress Party. In addition to Kjaersgaard, the second- and third-most-powerful members of the party, Kristian Thulesen Dahl and Peter Skaarup, are also FRPd veterans. The leaders of the DF were not political novices, but disgruntled splitters from the Progress Party who succeeded in creating a more organized and professional party.

The Progress Party, for its part, plunged in the polls after the departure of Kjaersgaard's group. It managed to win only 2.4% of the vote in the 1998 election, and two years later the party's four parliamentarians resigned after Glistrup was readmitted. Glistrup's anti-immigrant discourse in the 2001 election campaign made the DF seem moderate by comparison, as did the statement by another Progress Party politician that Somali refugees be repatriated by being parachuted from an airplane. The Progress Party polled a mere 0.4% in the 2001 elections, effectively dying at the age of twenty-eight years.

Rydgren (2004b) writes that "the political environment has put practically no constraints on the Danish People's Party." Since 2001, any semblance of a cordon sanitaire has ceased to exist as minority governments have been openly reliant on the cooperation of the DF. As Pederson and Ringsmosse (2005: 5) argue, "In a parliamentary system that rarely sees a majority government this is as close a party can come to incumbency without actually getting into the ministerial offices."

[17] *BBC Monitoring Europe*, August 21, 2006.

In retrospect, the nonexistence of a cordon sanitaire against the radical right in Denmark is hardly surprising. Although the Progress Party was treated with derision and suspicion, given its lack of internal party discipline, mainstream parties counted on its votes to form governments in both 1982 and 1987 (Bjørklund and Andersen 2002: 127). Although neither the Conservatives nor Liberals promised to cooperate with the Progress Party before the 1994 parliamentary elections, Kjaersgaard had done much to make it more acceptable to both parties (Svåsund 1998). Upon founding the DF, she made it a central goal to become a permanent coalition partner for either the Liberals or the Conservatives. After the 1997 municipal elections, the DF counted eight vice-mayors, which indicated that the party was not at all marginalized at the municipal level (Karpantschof 2002). Although the Danish prime minister, and leader of the Social Democrats, Poul Nyrup Rasmussen, tried to discredit the DF in 1999 by stating, "You'll never be house-trained," the Danish media and DF politicians immediately noted the large degree of cooperation between the DF and other parties at the local level.[18] Liberal leader Anders Fogh Rasmussen destroyed any trace of the cordon in 1999 when he wrote in the DF party journal (*Dansk Folkeblad*) that cooperation might be an option (Rydgren 2004b). This willingness to enter a coalition with the DF was signaled several times before and during the 2001 national parliamentary elections (Givens 2005: 148).

Along with Danish political parties, the Danish print media has contributed to a permissive political environment for the DF. Søren Krarup, whose views on Islam I quoted at the beginning of this chapter, authored more than two hundred articles in the widely read tabloid *Ekstrabladet*. The same paper also ran a series of provocative stories about the cost of foreigners to the Danish taxpayer and has generally disseminated anti-immigrant opinions that are very close to those of the DF (Togeby 1997). DF politicians themselves note that relations with the print media have been quite good, particularly with the mass circulation tabloids. One gushes that "they are very sweet; they print all my letters."[19]

Danish civil society has not stigmatized or protested against the DF. According to one specialist, there has been virtually no protest activity against the party and its members are fully accepted socially.[20] This assessment is shared by DF politicians. None of the ten DF members of

---

[18] Interview with Morten Messerschmidt (DF), Copenhagen, May 2005.
[19] Interview with Mia Falkenberg (DF), Copenhagen, May 2007.
[20] Interview with Rene Karpantschof, former civic activist, Copenhagen, May 2005.

parliament I interviewed (out of a total of twenty-three) claimed that they suffered as a result of their political affiliation.[21] None reported any pressure from their employers. Were a DF politician to lose his or her job as a result of party membership, one parliamentarian predicts that "there would be a public outrage, and even our political opponents would protest."[22] According to another, he never faced a hostile social environment even though many of his friends and classmates disagreed with his political views: "One could have a political debate and then go play football after."[23] In sum, I found virtually no evidence that DF party activists and politicians faced any of the social shunning that members of the radical right encountered elsewhere in Western Europe. Nor have protests disrupted the movement at all. Indeed, since they have become a de facto party of government, the DF is as "normal as anyone else."

Since the costs of joining the DF are no greater than with any other political party, recruitment has, by all accounts, been relatively easy. The case of Morton Messerschmidt is illustrative. Messerschmidt answered an advertisement in a local newspaper in 1997 to become a member of the DF. He built up the party's youth organization in his home constituency of northern Zeeland before running a parliamentary campaign in 2001. At the age of twenty-four, Messerschmidt, then a law student, was elected to parliament in the 2005 elections. Such a rapid rise would hardly have been possible in another political party.[24]

Messerschmidt is only the youngest member of what is a strong cohort of young professionals. If the DF voters are overwhelmingly less educated, this is not the case for party activists. In the 2005 parliamentary elections, the DF fielded a total of eighty-six candidates. Of these, thirty-nine either had a university degree or were studying to get one.[25] Of the sixteen candidates born after 1970, twelve either were students or had an advanced degree, a strong indication that the average level of education for DF party activists will only increase. The DF has built a national youth organization, from which younger candidates are drawn and which will provide a trained cadre in the future.[26]

---

[21] Several claimed that they had heard about "bad experiences," such as harassing phone calls and physical assaults, but were unable to offer any specifics.

[22] Interview with Martin Henriksen (DF), Copenhagen, May 2007.

[23] Interview with Messerschmidt.

[24] Interview with Messerschmidt.

[25] The educational backgrounds (self-reported) of the candidates for the 2005 parliamentary elections can be found at http://www.danskfolkeparti.dk/sw/frontend/show.asp?parent=1834.

[26] Interview with Karina Pedersen, University of Copenhagen, May 2005.

The Norwegian Progress Party

The origins of the Norwegian Progress Party are very similar to those of the Danish Progress Party. The 1972 EU referendum produced turbulence in the Norwegian political system that allowed for the creation of a new party. It was a dog kennel owner and right-wing political activist named Anders Lange who seized the moment, founding the cumbersomely named Anders Lange's Party for a Strong Reduction in Taxes, Duties, and Public Intervention. The referendum demonstrated that voters had entirely different preferences than political elites, and there was a strong surge of anti-establishment sentiment (Svåsund 1998; Andersen and Bjørklund 2000). As a longtime critic of the government and a political outsider, Lange was able to profit from this auspicious political moment and captured 5% of the vote in the 1973 parliamentary elections.

Anders Lange died suddenly in 1974, and it is probably fair to say that his death allowed the party to develop in a direction that would lead to success two decades later. Lange distrusted all political parties and specifically fashioned his own party as a one-man show without any organizational support. Several members of the party who originally supported Lange, including Karl I. Hagen, split with Lange over this issue, forming the Reform Party in 1973. After Lange's death, however, Hagen and others rejoined the party, changing its name to the Progress Party in 1977.

Hagen was a party builder, and his tireless efforts at creating a national party organization would pay off in the late 1980s. Up until the municipal elections of 1987, however, the FrP was a marginal player in Norwegian politics, winning only 1.9%, 4.5%, and 3.7% in the parliamentary elections of 1977, 1981, and 1985, respectively. The breakthrough came when a sudden increase in asylum seekers in the middle to late 1980s turned immigration into a salient political issue. The FrP presented itself as the only party against immigration and argued that the money spent on asylum seekers should be spent on welfare policies for Norwegians.[27] As in Austria, the turn toward nativism created some internal division, and several liberal FrP parliamentarians broke from the party in 1994 and tried – without any success – to organize their own political movement. This was a conflict not between moderates and extremists within the radical right camp, but rather between individuals who were unwilling to politicize immigration for electoral gain and those who were. This type of split, as the Austrian case also illustrates, can be beneficial to radical right

[27] Tor Bjørklund, personal communication.

parties, as it increases internal coherence by eliminating activists who are opposed to one of the party's defining messages.

By the mid-1990s, the party had moved away from neoliberalism and positioned itself as the defender of the welfare state, and of benefits to the elderly in particular. Members of the FrP concede that the party has retracted its neoliberalism and recognized that attachment to the welfare state is so deep in Norway that any attempt to roll it back would be self-defeating.[28] Whether the FrP's defense of the welfare state is a cause or consequence of the party's base of support among the traditional working class is uncertain. What is clear, however, is that the FrP has attracted the same type of voters that in the past voted for the Social Democrats. It is currently the only party in Norway in which unskilled workers are overrepresented (Bjørklund 2007).

The proletariatization of the FrP is not surprising, for the party has always viewed the Norwegian Labour Party as a model. It is no coincidence that the FrP opened its party headquarters directly next to those of the Labour Party in Youngstorget in Oslo, the historical and symbolic heart of the Norwegian labor movement. In the 1997 parliamentary election campaign, the banner hanging from the Labour Party's headquarters read, "Sick and Elderly First," while that of the FrP's read, "Elderly and Sick First." Indeed, Hagen often described the FrP as the twenty-first-century manifestation of the Labour Party.

But it is the FrP's imitation of the organizational features of the Labour Party, or at least the Labour Party in its historical heyday, rather than its imitation of Labour's ideology that is salient. Hagen wanted the FrP to become a mass party with a strong party organization, and he crisscrossed the country in the late 1970s and early 1980s building local party organizations.[29] A youth wing of the party was constructed and would become a key recruiting ground for activists and candidates later on. By the municipal elections of 1987, the FrP had established local organizations across the country. In 1975, the party contested seats in only 11.7% of Norwegian municipalities. The percentage jumped to 21.1% in 1979, 34.7% in 1983, and 40.4% in 1987, all during a period when the party was stagnating in national parliamentary elections. The FrP was thus well on its way to establishing a strong organization *before* its electoral breakthrough.

If Hagen assembled the FrP's party organization, Geir Mo is widely credited with having rejuvenated it in the 1990s. After the inner-party

---

[28] This point emerged in multiple interviews with FrP members of parliament.
[29] Interview with Ulf Leirstein (FrP), Oslo, May 2006.

turmoil of 1994, Hagen tapped Mo as general secretary to lead an organizational renewal and to improve professionalism within the FrP. One of the central tools that Mo latched onto was intra-party political education. Most political parties in Norway, including the FrP, conduct a series of government-subsidized seminars for both party members and the general public. Topics range from the thematic, such as globalization or the European Union, to the practical, such as committee work in local parliaments. Mo expanded this program rapidly, viewing it as a primary means of both training and recruiting new party members. By all accounts, including those of rival politicians and journalists, the Progress Party's political education system has become by far the most developed in Norway, enrolling three to four thousand people every year. The party leadership sends clear signals that any aspiring FrP politician must enroll in these courses, which Mo describes as "basic training" for the party cadre.[30] Although the courses are not technically mandatory, it is well known within the party that the higher places on local party lists are reserved for those who have taken them.[31] Veterans of the party do most of the teaching for free, and the FrP receives public funding from the state to cover administrative costs. One of the most significant consequences of this education program is that FrP members elected to local councils know the ins and outs of the political process before taking office.

The FrP's focus on organization cuts against broader trends. Indeed, while other Norwegian political parties, and parties across Western Europe for that matter, discontinued their party newspapers in the 1980s and 1990s, the FrP not only maintained but also expanded its own.[32] Also in contrast to other parties in Norway, the FrP has expanded its membership in the past decade. The party had approximately 10,000 members in 1995 (Svåsund 1998). By the end of 2000, it had 15,174 members. After the successful municipal elections of 2003, the party swelled to 22,420 members before dropping slightly to 21,744 by May 2006.[33]

The FrP's organizational strength derives not only from its recruitment and training, but also from its ability to exclude disruptive and extremist activists. In the early years of the party, the central committee resorted to measures like party banishment and the dissolution of local organizations very infrequently because the FrP had enough trouble attracting

---

[30] Interview with Geir Mo, general secretary of the FrP, Oslo, May 2006.
[31] Interview with Ronald Roske, political adviser of the FrP, Oslo, May 2006.
[32] Interview with Roske.
[33] Figures provided by Roske.

members. Since the 1990s, however, much like the Danish People's Party the FrP's central committee has wielded more control. In late 2000, Hagen accused members of the party's Oslo branch, particularly the local leader, Dag Danielsen, of trying to unseat him as party leader. The conflict became public when Hagen, during a television interview, said that a "cancerous tumor" had to be removed from the Oslo branch.[34] The party's central committee eventually suspended Danielson and sixteen other members of the party for disloyalty. This purge was widely viewed as an attempt to increase the FrP's chances of becoming a coalition partner, for the Oslo branch contained some of the more extreme elements in the party.[35] To prevent future intra-party disagreements from becoming public, the FrP adopted a new party statute in April 2001 referred to as "resignation by action." If any party member attempted to damage the party in public, including attacking its leaders, the party would interpret that act as a resignation and immediately expel the member without any formal procedures (Heidar and Saglie 2003: 225). The similarity with Pia Kjaersgaard's edict on "top-steering" is unmistakable.

The party of Anders Lange was a self-declared pariah in Norwegian politics, in contrast to the state of the FrP today. Hagen's long-term strategy was to overcome the party's marginalization and to enter into national-level coalitions with other parties, particularly with the conservatives. Until the late 1990s, cooperation with other parties on the national level was a nonissue, as mainstream parties were easily able to exclude the FrP.

Yet there was never any national-level directive by either the Conservatives or the Social Democrats forbidding cooperation with the FrP on the local level. In fact, it has been at the local level where the party has entered into coalitions with almost every political party in Norway. Most cities and towns have both a mayor and a deputy mayor who are elected by a simple majority of the members of the local council. Since the FrP does not enjoy an absolute majority in any local council, the party needs the votes of other parties to win either post. The FrP won its first mayorship in the town of Os, a suburb of Bergen, in 1999. Before that, however, an FrP politician was appointed mayor of Oslo following a scandal, an occurrence that received a great deal of media coverage and raised the profile of the party significantly. Although the FrP would not capture a significant degree of local power until 1999 (Table 5.1), the party had long held a number of deputy mayoralties,

---

[34] *Nordic Business Report*, November 29, 2000.
[35] *Dagens Noeringsliv*, November 28, 2000.

TABLE 5.1. *Local Election Results for the Norwegian Progress Party*

Year	Percentage	Local and Regional Councilors
1987	12.3	–
1991	7.0	568
1995	12.1	805
1999	13.5	1,109
2003	16.4	1,796

indicating that other parties had cooperated with the FrP since at least the late 1980s. Indeed, several of the current members of the FrP faction in parliament began their political careers as deputy mayors in town councils.

The uneasy combination of cooperation of mainstream parties with the FrP on the local level and a cordon sanitaire on the national level sent a mixed signal to voters, as representatives of other parties readily admit. Although the national leadership of the Labour Party disapproved of local cooperation with the FrP and regularly denounced the party as extremist, it did not forbid its local party organizations from working with it. As of 2006, there were seven communities in which the Labour Party held the office of mayor and the Progress Party held that of deputy mayor, and one town in which the situation was reversed. As one political adviser from Labour acknowledges, this pattern of local cooperation and national stigmatization is "confusing" to voters and dramatically weakens the perception of the strength of the national party leadership's policy of cordon sanitaire against the FrP.[36]

Success at the local level has also translated into incumbency advantages. In a study of the 2003 municipal elections, Bjørklund and Saglie (2004) found that the FrP gained votes across the country, but more so in municipalities where it held the posts of mayor or deputy mayor. These authors concluded that "these kinds of positions may improve the party's image. In opposition, the party may be labeled 'irresponsible' and 'extremist'. In office, the party appear [*sic*] as a more responsible and acceptable alternative" (16).

The local level also served as a recruitment and training arena for aspiring politicians. As one longtime member of the party reports, it was a "very big deal" within the party when the FrP entered into its first municipal-level coalitions following the 1987 local elections. It not

---

[36] Interview with Ingrid Sagranden, political adviser (Labour), Oslo, May 2006.

only improved the image of the party, but immediately attracted political entrepreneurs who sought to attain positions and drive policy. These were not primarily those who wanted to "scream and yell," as in the old days of the party, but people who wanted to "achieve something."[37]

If a cordon never existed at the local level, it was essentially broken at the national level after 2001. The government of Kjell Bondevik (Christian Democrat) from 2001 to 2006 required the votes of the FrP to pass several budgets. At the Conservative Party congress in May 2006, the party adopted a resolution that all non-Socialist parties should attempt to work together. This marked a major turning point for the Conservatives, for the subject of possible national-level cooperation with the FrP had been bitterly debated since the late 1990s.[38] With the major Norwegian business organization and even several trade unions calling for cooperation with the FrP, the national-level cordon sanitaire no longer exists.

Over the course of the 1990s, the applicants for positions in the party became both greater in number and better educated. Although the FrP's voters are not as educated as those of any other party, this is hardly true of the FrP's political staff and candidates for office. The party currently employs eighteen full-time political advisers, all of whom have university degrees.[39] The party's most recent advertisement for one of these positions received 150 applications, including bids from graduates of such institutions as Harvard and the London School of Economics.[40] "The FrP," according to the liberal journalist Gudleiv Forr, "is becoming a career for young people."[41] Although General Secretary Mo welcomes the fact that "people now see the Progress Party as a way to make a career, as a way up in society," he concedes that the increasing attractiveness of the party is not solely positive, as it has also made the FrP a magnet for opportunists. This is a problem, however, that many radical right parties across Western Europe do not, but would perhaps like to, have. The dramatic increase in highly educated and politically ambitious individuals within the FrP has only improved the level of professionalism within the party and its reputation among the electorate. The so-called wild days of the 1970s and 1980s are over, and one parliamentarian who joined the (youth wing) of the party in 1980 jokes that the "party is so professional

---

[37] Interview with Morten Hoglund (FrP), Oslo, May 2006.
[38] Interview with Christian Angell, political adviser (Conservative), Oslo, May 2006.
[39] Interview with Ketil Solvik-Olsen (FrP), Oslo, May 2006.
[40] Interview with Mo.
[41] Interview with Gudleiv Forr, editor of *Dagbladet*, Oslo, May 2006.

that I am sometimes scared – it's so much like a business, the loose atmosphere is gone."[42]

The relationship between the Progress Party and the media has changed dramatically over the past several years. Throughout the 1980s and 1990s, the national print media, including both *Dagbladet* and *VG*, was universally critical of the FrP.[43] However, more recently, members of the party have perceived a softening of media criticism, with several members even describing the current relationship between the FrP and the media as "good." Also important to note is that local newspapers, in contrast to national ones, varied in their relationship to the FrP very early on in the party's history. Several current members of parliament from the Progress Party described their local newspaper as "friendly" and "cooperative." Although the relationship between the print media and the FrP remains to be thoroughly researched, it is clear that the party did not face the same degree of media stigmatization as other radical right parties in Western Europe and that the relationship has improved, at least since the FrP began supporting the Conservative government in 2001.

Although the FrP did not have access to a mass circulation tabloid as the Progress Party had in Denmark, television provided an ideal forum for Hagen to increase the profile of the party. After the privatization of Norwegian state television in 1990, the new station "TV2" began to run political debate shows that were ideal for a politician like Hagen. In contrast to some other European countries, in Norway the leader of a radical right party was a regular presence on television, and the fact that other politicians never refused to share the stage with him meant that he was treated and perceived as normal.[44]

The reaction of Norwegian civil society to the rise of the radical right can be summed up briefly: there was none to speak of. The only protest activities against the FrP that I uncovered were those organized by left-liberal youths on May 1, 2006, when the Progress Party insisted on holding May 1 demonstrations on Youngstorget.[45] There is also no evidence of social sanctioning against Progress Party members of the type that occurred in Germany, the Netherlands, or Sweden. If early activists in the party were sometimes a bit eccentric, they also included "respectable" members of the local community, the same people who joined the

[42] Interview with Hoglund.
[43] Interview with Forr.
[44] Interview with Forr.
[45] Interview with Tor Bjørklund, Oslo, May 2006.

Rotary Club and other civic associations.[46] With the increasing success of and rising professionalism within the party, the FrP and its members are no longer viewed as a "wild gang" but as normal and legitimate political actors.

The Swiss People's Party

In the mid-1990s, two scholars described the development of the radical right in Switzerland as the "History of a Divided Family" (Gentile and Kriesi 1998). This fractionalization was in part a product of the country's extreme federalism, which militates against national parties and privileges cantonal ones, and its system of direct democracy, which gives small parties the opportunity to gain exposure through the launching of referenda. But history played a role as well. Unlike Austria, Switzerland had no far right subculture that could form the basis for a radical right party, even though the relatively early appearance of anti-immigrant parties, their strength in cantonal elections, and the near success of several referenda directed against immigrants indicated that there was high demand for one.

By the turn of the twenty-first century, the Swiss radical right was no longer divided. The Schweizerische Volkspartei (Swiss People's Party, SVP) had transformed itself from a party of farmers and shopkeepers to one that resembled closely other radical right parties in Western Europe. The 29% of the vote it won in the 2007 federal elections was the largest percentage ever captured by *any* Swiss political party. The SVP's success derived in large part from its stance on immigration, its vigorous defense of Swiss independence from outside forces (such as the European Union), and the appeal of its media-savvy leader, Christoph Blocher. But the ability of the SVP to consistently harness the demand for radical right ideas, where other parties had failed, derived from two related sources. First, the SVP (like the Freedom Party in Austria and the Progress parties in Denmark and Norway) became radicalized and homogenized while leaving its party organization more or less intact. Second, the SVP had been a party of government since 1929 and was guaranteed one seat in the government's seven-member cabinet under the "Magic Formula" of 1959.[47]

---

[46] Interview with Solvik-Olsen.

[47] Under this system, the government was composed of two members from the Radical Party, two from the CVP, two from the SPS, and one from the SVP. The "Magic Formula" was modified to reflect the growing electoral strength of the SVP, which gained a seat at the expense of the CVP.

It thus maintained the legitimacy of a governing party, even as it co-opted the rhetoric of the various *Überfremdung* (over-foreignization) parties and hailed populist invective against the political establishment. No other party in Europe has migrated toward the radical right to the extent of the SVP while remaining a part of a coalition government (Mazzoleni 2003: 103).

The contemporary success of the Swiss radical right contrasts with the general weakness of Swiss fascist movements in the 1930s. The strongest of these movements, the National Front, began at the University of Zürich in 1930. Over the next several years, the combined influence of Austrian and German National Socialism and the economic crisis led to the proliferation of other Fronts in Switzerland, but the National Front – which was concentrated in the German-speaking areas – remained by far the largest. In 1933, it won 27% of the vote in cantonal elections in Schaffhausen and 10 out of 125 mandates in elections for the Zürich municipal council. It counted about ten thousand members at the height of its power in 1935 (Glaus 1969). Yet the party overreached in that same year by forcing a referendum on a constitutional amendment that would have reordered the Swiss state along fascist lines. An antifascist backlash and a growing perception that the Front was a foreign import hastened its collapse. By 1938, the Front's membership had dropped to a fraction of its former size, and it had lost all of its seats. Because the country maintained its neutrality and independence, there was no defeated Quisling regime that could have formed the basis for a strong far right political movement.

Yet while Switzerland lacked a far right subculture after the war, immigration became politically salient earlier there than in other countries in Western Europe. Switzerland had relied heavily on immigrant labor since the late nineteenth century. Unlike most other Western European countries, its economy was not decimated by the Second World War and expanded rapidly immediately after it. The country thus began recruiting immigrant workers to meet the needs of the labor market a decade before Germany adopted a similar policy. The percentage of immigrants in the population increased from 6.1% in 1950 to 9.3% in 1960 to 15.9 % by 1970 (Skenderovic 2007a: 160, 162). Even when economic downturns in the 1970s led to more restrictive immigration policies, the percentage of residents lacking citizenship remained high because of Switzerland's restrictive citizenship laws. This, combined with a new wave of immigration in the 1980s, pushed the foreign population to 19.3% by 2000 and 20.3% by 2005 (Skenderovic 2007a: 162).

The first anti-immigrant party in Switzerland was the Nationale Aktion gegen die Überfremdung von Volk und Heimat (National Action against Over-foreignization of People and Homeland, NA), founded by James Schwarzenbach in the canton of Zürich in 1961. By 1964, it had attracted only 180 members and its electoral gains were miniscule, although Schwarzenbach did succeed in winning a seat in the Zürich cantonal parliament (Mazzoleni 2003: 16). The party split in 1971, with Schwarzenbach leaving it to found the Schweizerische Republikanische Bewegung (Swiss Republican Movement, SRB). The third member of the so-called Movement against Over-foreignization (Überfremdungsbewegung) was Vigilance, founded in 1964 and based in Geneva. The fourth, the Eidgenössisch-Demokratische Union (Swiss Democratic Union, EDU), was founded in 1975 to fight foreign influence and promote Christian values. Despite some isolated success in local and cantonal elections, all of these parties remained fringe movements and were plagued by internal dissension and chronic infighting (Gentile and Kriesi: 1998). None of them ever possessed much in the way of organization, although there were small networks of activists in some regions. Vigilance, for example, counted about a thousand members, of whom perhaps one hundred were active, in Geneva at its height in 1986 (Mazzoleni 2003: 19).

Although small and divided, the parties of the so-called over-foreignization movement were not without influence in Swiss politics. Through referenda, they managed to make immigration a continuously visible issue. The NA launched the first of these, the so-called Schwarzenbach Initiative, in 1969 to limit the proportion of foreign workers (primarily Italian and Spanish) in Switzerland. In practice, this would have required deporting one-third of the foreign population back to their country of origin (Skenderovic 2007a: 172). When the issue was put to a referendum in 1970 after an intense public debate over immigration, 46% of Swiss approved it. Although the initiative was defeated, the high turnout (74.7%) and the relatively large number of votes for such a restrictive measure demonstrated the strength of anti-immigrant sentiment in Switzerland. Over the next several decades, the NA and similar groups would force a number of similar initiatives that won the support of between 30% and 50% of the voters (Mazzoleni 2003: 51).

In the 1980s and 1990s, two other radical right parties led to a further fractionalization of the Swiss radical right party landscape. Inspired by the Lega Nord in Italy, the Lega di Ticinesi (League of Ticino, LDT) dates from 1991 and did quite well in the Italian-speaking canton of Ticino but, as a regionalist party, had no appeal outside of it. More threatening to the established political parties was the Autopartei der Schweiz (Swiss Automobilist Party, APS) founded in 1985 in the heat of an intense debate over highways and as a reaction to what it called the "ozone hysteria" of the ecological movement. The APS soon branched out from its core issue and adopted an antiestablishment and xenophobic rhetoric, calling for "Turks, Tamils, and Togolese" to be thrown out of the country (Niggli and Frischknecht 1998: 486). Many former members of the smaller over-foreignization parties joined the APS: in Geneva, the shift from Vigilance to the APS was dramatic (Niggli and Frischknecht 1998: 491). The 1991 federal parliamentary elections proved to be the high-water mark for the APS, which won 5.1% of the vote after surviving a leadership struggle in 1990. The other anti-immigrant parties polled another 5.8% between them. But just as the APS drew activists and voters from the older anti-immigrant parties, the rise of the SVP would have similarly damaging consequences for it. The party, which changed its name to the Freiheits-Partei der Schweiz (Swiss Freedom Party, FPS) in 1994, suffered major defections of its members of parliament to the SVP (Church 2000: 216). It lost all of its national parliamentary seats in the 1999 elections and retained only some mandates in municipal and cantonal parliaments thereafter. The former members of Vigilance, which was dissolved in 1993, switched from the FPS to the SVP. The EDU, LDT, and the Swiss Democrats (the successor to Nationale Aktion, which was founded in 1990) barely survived the 1990s, and none has polled higher than 1.3% in a federal election in the twenty-first century.

In sum, weak party organization and intense factionalism prevented anti-immigrant parties in Switzerland from capitalizing on the significant demand for them. This left space for an established party – the SVP – to fill this void. The history of the SVP begins in 1936 when a group of agrarian parties fused to form the Bauern-, Gewerbe- und Bürgerpartei (Party of Farmers, Traders, and Independents, BGB) to represent the interests of farmers and small traders. Its electoral bastions were German-speaking areas with Protestant majorities, and the BGB became a permanent member of Switzerland's Concordat system under the "Magic Formula" of 1959. Although the party held onto its electoral base, it began to suffer an ideological crisis in the 1960s that was only hastened when it fused with the Democratic parties of the cantons of Graubünden and Glarus and acquired its current name in 1971. During the mid-1970s, the SVP's national leadership tried to appeal to voters beyond the (declining) traditional agrarian base by shifting leftward and adopting social liberal elements. This trend was fiercely resisted, and

ultimately reversed, by the Zürich section of the SVP under the leadership of Christoph Blocher.

Blocher's political views took shape during his years as a student at the
University of Zürich, where he founded the organization Studentenring,
which sought to fight the leftist shift of the generation of 1968 (Hartmann
and Horvath 1995: 43). He joined the Zürich SVP in 1972, and enjoyed
a quick rise both within it and in the chemical firm Ems-Chemie. He
succeeded in transforming both of these struggling organizations into
dynamic players within a matter of years. Ems-Chemie became highly
profitable under Blocher and eventually made him one of Switzerland's
wealthiest people. This wealth would certainly help the SVP later on, but
it was Blocher's organizational skills that revitalized the Zürich SVP, and
later the national party, in the 1970s and 1980s.

One of Blocher's first steps in party building was to found the party's
youth wing, the Jungen SVP (JSVP), in Zürich city in 1977. Members of
the JSVP understood themselves to be at war with left-wing extremists,
but rather than meeting their foes in street skirmishes they took public-
speaking courses to polish their arguments and gestures (Hartmann and
Horvath 1995: 48). The JSVP soon founded sections outside of Zürich
city (although still in Zürich canton). Like other successful youth wings,
the JSVP provided a training ground for future politicians, and many
prominent figures in the SVP cut their teeth in the JSVP (Skenderovic
2007b). The JSVP would also later prove to be Blocher's ally in cantons such as Bern, which disagreed with the direction of the Zürich wing
(Niggli and Frischknecht 1998: 503).

The Zürich SVP made a concerted effort to train its party cadre. The
rhetoric courses that the JSVP pioneered were institutionalized by the
mid-1980s, along with courses by professional journalists designed to
ensure that the SVP would have a strong media presence (Hartmann
and Horvath 1995: 126). Armed with rhetorical skills, SVP members
embarked on a permanent campaign, particularly in the city of Zürich,
where they organized "seniors' afternoons" with free coffee and cake,
"farmers' breakfasts" with free grilled sausage and traditional music,
and regular information sessions (Skenderovic 2007b). Such activities,
while quite common for all parties in Austria, stood out in the Swiss
context, where parties made little effort at mobilization outside of election campaigns. The extensive outreach was most likely responsible
for a rise in party membership: indeed, the Zürich city section of the
SVP increased its ranks by 20% between 1981 and 1982 (Hartmann
and Horvath 1995). The party grew by the same percentage, from ten

thousand members to twelve thousand, in the canton as a whole between 1980 and 1985.

The SVP, under Blocher's direction, thus embarked on a project of extensive professionalization and party building *before* it began to dramatically increase its voteshare and to drift toward right-wing populism. To be sure, the SVP did stress law-and-order themes in Zürich when a left-liberal youth movement began causing public disturbances in the early 1980s, but it would not really enter into debates about immigration until 1985. By forming a joint list with Nationale Aktion, the Zürich SVP signaled its stance on the issue. As the authors of the most extensive study of the party note, "The period from 1985 to 1987 … was the turning point of the neoconservative building project of the Zürich SVP" (Hartmann and Horvath 1995: 99). It was in those years that the party developed its core theme of "internal security," which combined issues related to asylum policy, drug policy, and crime. By the 1990s, the SVP had placed immigration near the top of its political agenda, along with the preservation of Swiss independence from international organizations and support for neoliberal economic policies. In 1992, the party launched the first federal initiative in its history: "Gegen die illegale Einwanderung" (Against Illegal Immigration). The measure would have led to a radical restriction to the right of asylum and was defeated by only a relatively narrow majority (53.7%) in a 1996 referendum.

The SVP also profited by taking an uncompromising position in the intense public debate of the late 1990s over Switzerland's wartime past (Decker 2004: 92). For decades, the official narrative had held that Switzerland had remained neutral, and hence beyond moral reproach, during the Second World War. Any relations between it and Nazi Germany were supposedly designed to preserve Swiss independence in the face of an overwhelming threat. But two allegations against Swiss banks – powerful symbols of Swiss national identity – challenged this interpretation. First, the Swiss were accused of operating an international money-laundering scheme in which the Nazis received convertible currency for gold that they looted from conquered countries and stole from Jews before murdering them. The implicit charge was that the Swiss had helped prolong the war by providing the bankrupt Nazi regime with funds. Second, relatives of those Jews who had opened accounts in Switzerland to protect their assets and had perished in the Holocaust alleged that the Swiss banks would not allow them access to these "dormant accounts." They noted that the banks had demanded the death certificate of the account holder before releasing the money, although they obviously knew that such certificates were not issued at Nazi death camps. A third allegation, which was directed against the country as a whole, was that, although Switzerland accepted 65,000 Jewish refugees, it had closed its borders entirely by 1942 and turned away tens of thousands. It was also at Switzerland's insistence that the Nazis affixed the letter "J" to Jewish passports, so that Jewish refugees could be more easily recognized.

In 1998, the major Swiss banks agreed to pay $1.25 billion to settle all Holocaust era claims against them, Swiss industries, the Swiss central bank, and the Swiss government. The government also established the Independent Commission of Experts in 1996, headed by Swiss historian Jean-Francois Bergier, to investigate Switzerland's wartime behavior. The Bergier commission's report, released in 2002, concluded that Switzerland's refugee policy was "excessively restrictive, and uselessly so," and "contributed to the most atrocious of Nazi objectives – the Holocaust." The report was less critical regarding dormant accounts, arguing that the banks' intransigence stemmed from a desire to preserve bank secrecy rather than from greediness and, on the issue of Nazi gold, concluding that the banks had not prolonged the war.[48]

From the beginning, the Swiss People's Party framed the debate about the past as an attack on Switzerland's sovereignty and national identity by the international community. In March 1997, Blocher delivered a two-hour speech in which he defended Switzerland's behavior during the Second World War and argued that the country "had nothing to apologize for." The SVP distributed several hundred thousand copies of his speech to Swiss households (Niggli and Frischknecht 1998: 439). Later, he suggested that the World Jewish Congress (WJC), which was only one of the groups demanding that the Swiss pay restitution, was leading a blackmail campaign against the country and was interested only in money. This reaction was reminiscent of the Waldheim affair in Austria, in which the Austrian People's Party and the Austrian Freedom Party activated anti-Semitic stereotypes when the WJC charged that presidential candidate Kurt Waldheim had covered up his Nazi past (Art 2006). The debates had similar effects in both countries. On the one hand, they led ultimately to official acknowledgments of complicity in Nazi crimes and a more critical confrontation with history, but on the other, they strengthened forces – particularly the FPÖ and the SVP – that defended the nation's honor against what they viewed as the illegitimate attacks of both international forces out for financial gain and *Nestbeschmutzer* (people who defile their own country).

---

[48] *Financial Times*, March 23, 2002.

The debate about Switzerland's wartime past, like those about asylum and immigration, was part of the SVP's increasing focus on the "politics of identity" and the defense of an idealized Swiss nation against external threats (Decker 2004: 92). Blocher had already staked out a strong position in this arena as early as 1986, when he took a leading role in the mobilization against an initiative for Switzerland to join the United Nations. From 1986 to 2003, he was president of the Aktion für eine Unabhängige und Neutrale Schweiz (Campaign for the Independence and Neutrality of Switzerland, AUNS), an organization that was formed from the efforts to defeat the 1986 referendum. Although it claims to be nonpartisan, AUNS was clearly sympathetic toward the SVP and helped organize party events (Niggli and Frischknecht 1998: 518). In 1992, the SVP and AUNS led the campaign to defeat a referendum on Switzerland joining the European Economic Area, which would have been a first step in accession to the European Union. Membership in AUNS doubled between 1992 and 2002, rising from 16,000 to 32,000 and rendering it an even more powerful satellite organization for the SVP (Mazzoleni 2003: 84).

Blocher's uncompromising defense of Swiss neutrality and campaign against entangling alliances increased his national profile. But the precondition for the party's electoral success of the middle to late 1990s was aggressive party building on the national level. Traditionally, Swiss political parties possessed only a skeletal organization because federalism made national party building difficult. The lack of significant public funding for political parties also reinforces the "militia" nature of the Federal Assembly, which is "composed of amateurs who combine their professional activities with their parliamentary duties" (Kriesi 2001: 60). But as we have seen, Blocher placed great emphasis on improving party organization, and the party extended the Zürich model to Switzerland as a whole. In 1991, the SVP had sections in only fourteen of Switzerland's twenty-six cantons (Skenderovic 2007b). In that year, cantonal SVP sections were founded in Zug, Solothurn, and Basel city; in 1992, in Luzern and St. Gallen; and in 1993, in Appenzell Ausserrhoden. Between 1991 and 1995, the number of SVP seats in cantonal parliaments rose from 22 to 319 (Niggli and Frischknecht 1998: 507). Thus, while the SVP's voteshare in elections for the Federal Assembly rose from 12% to 15% from 1991 to 1995, the party's real achievement was building an organizational presence throughout the country. The party counted 60,000 members by 1997 (Mazzoleni 2003: 29). By 2001, the SVP had sections in every Swiss canton.

The relative consensus within the SVP, and the concomitant lack of infighting and defections, has been another important factor in its success (Mazzoleni 2003: 107). It is true that, beginning in the 1970s, the Zürich section of the party set its own ideological course, which was often criticized by the other powerful and more moderate faction of the party centered in Bern. But the nationalization of the SVP also led to the dominance of the Zürich faction, and therefore to the growing cohesion of the party. Since it was the Zürich faction that played the central role in encouraging party organization in other cantons, its views acquired a dominant position within the party as a whole. This trend was visible within the national delegate's assembly, which elects the party leadership and decides which initiatives to support. Representation in the assembly depends on relative electoral strength in National Council elections, and since the Zürich party began to outpace the Bern faction in this respect, by 1995 it had acquired decision-making power. This shift in the balance of power within the SVP, in which an insurgent nationalist faction from the party's historical bastion prevailed over a more moderate wing in the capital, resembles Haider's putsch from Carinthia against the Austrian Freedom Party liberals in Vienna. However, the conflict between the two factions was never as divisive as in Austria, and the Zürich faction ended up getting its way on most issues without significant opposition. For example, although the Bern faction was uncomfortable with the 1992 referendum against joining the European Economic Area, it eventually conceded. As one leading moderate, Adolf Ogi, conceded in 1998, "The Zürich wing dominates the entire party" (Niggli and Frischknecht 1998: 500).

The SVP possessed three other features that are critical for successful party building. The first two follow logically from my description of the party. First, as a longtime party of government, the SVP benefited from a core of experienced, professional politicians (Mazzoleni 2003: 105). Second, as the party expanded, it attracted experienced politicians from other parties because there was no stigma attached to the SVP and obviously no cordon sanitaire against it. The party was attractive to political entrepreneurs because it wielded meaningful influence in cantonal and national politics and its fortunes were clearly rising. Third, the SVP did not allow itself to be infiltrated by members of Switzerland's right-wing extremist milieu, which scholars, while not downplaying its significance, have characterized as small and weakly organized (Altermatt and Skenderovic 1995: 113).

The rise and radicalization of the SVP have transformed Swiss politics. After becoming the largest party in parliament after the 2003 elections, it changed the "Magic Formula" by gaining a second seat at the expense of the Christian Democrats and "took the country to the verge of systemic change" (Church 2004: 518). Four years later, the SVP ended a half-century of government by consensus by going into opposition. In December 2007, the other major political parties delivered a surprise blow to Blocher by convincing members of parliament not to reelect him as justice minister. Since ministers in Switzerland are appointed in a personal rather than party capacity, the parliament chose to back Eveline Widmer-Schlumpf for the position, a low-profile member of the party's Bern wing. An initially astonished Widmer-Schlumpf accepted the post but was later ejected from the SVP's parliamentary group (although not from the party) along with another moderate, Samuel Schmid, who accepted the SVP's second cabinet position. Since party exclusion is possible only at the cantonal level and since Schlumpf and Schmid have the backing of the Bern section, it is unclear how this situation will be resolved. The future ability of the SVP to mitigate this potentially serious internal conflict is uncertain.

Flash Parties

The leaders of the Danish People's Party, Norwegian Progress Party, and Swiss People's Party needed years to construct professional party organizations, and it was only after they did so that they achieved lasting electoral success. The experiences of New Democracy in Sweden and the List Pim Fortuyn in the Netherlands demonstrate that even spectacular electoral breakthroughs – the LPF became the second-largest party in parliament only three months after its creation – do not necessarily lead to organizational strength and electoral persistence. Although the trajectory of their failure was different from that of the parties discussed in Chapter 3 and although they did not face a repressive environment, the lack of indigenous resources proved as damaging as an abundance of extremists for party development.

New Democracy

The factors that produced anti-tax parties in Denmark and Norway in the 1970s did not exist in Sweden. There was no referendum on EC membership and no resulting surge in nationalist passions. Nor was there a similar tax revolt, even though the overall tax burden in Sweden was as great as it was in the other two states. In 1990, for example, total taxes in Sweden accounted for nearly 57% of GNP. The figures for Norway and Denmark are 46% and 48%, respectively (Svåsund 1998). The fact that Sweden used sales and payroll taxes, in addition to an income tax, to finance the welfare state probably decreased the visibility of taxation levels, and hence the opportunity for mobilization around the issue (Kitschelt 1995: 129).

When a radical right party entered the political arena in 1991, it came in the form of New Democracy. The entertaining history of this party has been told elsewhere (Taggart 1996), but a few of the key details are important for the analysis. The story of ND begins with a meeting between Ian Wachmeister, a count and businessman, and Bert Karlsson, the owner of an amusement park, at the Stockholm Arlanda Airport. The two men discovered that they had similar antiestablishment views: Wachmeister enjoyed writing satirical pieces comparing Swedish politicians to elephants, overweight from too little activity, and to crocodiles, with tiny ears to hear citizen complaints but gigantic jaws to enrich themselves (Rydgren 2006: 57). Karlsson compared parliamentary elections to the Eurovision song contest. The two coauthored an article in *Dagens Nyeter*, Sweden's paper of record, calling for sweeping reforms in Swedish politics. Wachmeister and Karlsson then appeared on the television program *Svar Direkt*. The host of the program announced the results of a specially commissioned poll: nearly one-quarter of the Swedish electorate could potentially vote for "Bert Karlsson's party" (Gardberg 1993: 44).

The duo founded New Democracy seven months before the 1991 national parliamentary elections. They were an odd pair, and the class difference between them gave rise to the nickname "the count and his manservant." Karlsson's notes from one of their first meetings suggest that he enjoyed playing up this dichotomy: "The noble Wachmeister came to the meeting dressed in a smart hat, flowers on his tie and an exclusive document briefcase. The man of the people had sensible shoes, a leather jacket and a plastic sack from the Savings Bank, in which he carried his important papers" (Westlind 1996: 155).

New Democracy promised to inject a bit of whimsy into the staid world of Swedish politics. Its proposal to cut taxes on alcohol was just one part of the 1991 party manifesto that promised "more fun and more money in your pocket." But ND also possessed the core nativist component of radical right parties, even if in a diluted form. Members of the party appeared to be concerned with avoiding charges of racism, but some of their statements on foreign aid and immigration made that difficult. John Bouvin, an ND candidate and later member of parliament, argued during the election campaign that foreign aid was causing overpopulation:

We should help the people in the Baltics, not mess around with misdirected projects in Africa. I have seen the effects. Before they would have ten children, the lions ate up a couple, and then five would die of hunger and then they had three kids that made it. Now, with our money, all of them survive and it's a catastrophe. (Westlind 1996: 148–149)

Rather than distancing himself from Bouvin, Wachmeister defended him and accused African refugees of bringing the AIDS virus to Sweden (Westlind 1996: 149).

Despite these statements, the established political parties simply ignored New Democracy in the run-up to the 1991 parliamentary election. They did not rule out cooperation with it, and in fact the coalition government that came to power in 1991 often found itself reliant on the votes of ND parliamentarians. Since a cordon sanitaire was not in place, Swedish voters did not consider a vote for the party wasted. The media generally treated ND as a "good story," and its reaction was certainly not hostile.[49]

In 1991, the apparently up-and-coming ND captured 6.7% of the vote and twenty-five seats in parliament. Just three years later, however, the party won only 1.2% and no seats. What explains this rapid dissolution?

The answers can be found in the party's internal organization, or more precisely the lack thereof. The party never developed a party bureaucracy, and the two leaders – Wachmeister in particular – opposed efforts to do so (Westlind 1996: 158–159). As one ND politician claimed, "We run the whole party in the whole country with ten people" (Taggart 1996: 122). The party thus had 2.5 members of parliament for each parliamentary staff member, by far the highest ratio of parliamentarians to staff members of parties in the Riksdag (Taggart 1996: 123). Wachmeister controlled the selection of candidates for the 1991 parliamentary election. As Taggart's interviews with ND politicians reveal, the "frequent path for recruitment was that associates, friends, and often friends of friends, of Wachmeister were contacted by Wachmeister and asked if they would like to be on the election list." One New Democrat characterized this

---

[49] Interview with Arne Ruth, former editor in chief of *Dagens Nyheter*, Stockholm, May 2005.

recruitment process as "picking people off the street who were expound-
ing the party programme." Taggart concludes that this style of candidate
selection meant that many of "those who were recruited were those who
had no prior political experience and often no thoughts of even entering
politics" (Taggart 1996: 125).

Yet the popularity of Wachmeister and Karlsson led to the spontaneous
appearance of local parties intending to run under the New Democracy
label. The leadership showed little concern for them until they began to
become a serious problem. Since there was virtually no vetting of candidates at the local level, a number of what one New Democrat described
as "unsavory characters" flocked to the party in 1991. This created much
infighting within local parties, and the national leadership was forced to
intervene and throw many of these personalities out. To ameliorate such
problems, Wachmeister decided to run the party as a business franchise.
He required independent local parties to sign an annual cooperation agreement before they could use the New Democracy label and reserved the
right to annul the agreement if they did not behave as he wished (Taggart
1996: 128; Widfelt 1997: 38). This centralization strategy proved to be
a disaster, creating disenchantment among the party's few local members
and effectively destroying whatever local-level organization the party
ever had. Moreover, given the general lack of personnel and oversight,
local sections still attracted right-wing extremists who had been active in
"Keep Sweden Swedish" and other disreputable organizations and damaged the party's image (Lodenius and Larrson 1994: 73–76; Westlind
1996: 159).

As with the Danish Progress Party, the fact that candidates were
selected with little consideration for their loyalty to the emerging party
led to major defections when the party won parliamentary seats (Rydgren
2006). These defections, coupled with a leadership struggle that soon
erupted between Wachmeister and Karlsson, demonstrated to Swedish
voters, as well as to other political parties, that New Democracy was a
disintegrating party and an unreliable partner. Rydgren's (2006: 85) diag-
nosis is worth quoting at length:

New Democracy's problems within its own parliamentary group can ... be largely
reduced to its peculiar organizational form. The many defections can be put down
to the lack of a coherent ideological glue, the result of the manner in which its
MPs were appointed autocratically by the executive rather than democratically
by the members. Since the party was newly formed at the time of the general
election, the opportunities for internal recruitment were small, and there was
neither the time nor the will to instruct New Democracy's candidates in the field

of politics through internal party work, which usually serves to sift out the less suitable candidates before they reach the nomination stage and which was not the case for New Democracy.

List Pim Fortuyn and the Party for Freedom

Pim Fortuyn was a reasonably well known figure in the Dutch media before his brief political career. A professor of critical sociology at the University of Groningen from 1972 to 1988, Fortuyn was initially a Marxist and member of the Labour Party but migrated toward libertarianism in the late 1980s and 1990s. He left academia when his career as a public speaker at meetings of business organizations blossomed, and he wrote a regular column for the largest weekly in the Netherlands, *Elsevier*, which appeals to a Christian Democratic and Liberal readership. He appeared occasionally on television as well. In August 2001, he announced his intention to run for parliament, although he had not yet decided which party would receive his services (Van Holsteyn and Irwin 2003: 44). On November 25, Fortuyn accepted the position as leader of Leefbaar Nederland (Livable Netherlands, LN), a new political party that grew from various municipal "livable" parties, such as Livable Rotterdam and Livable Amsterdam, that had done relatively well in previous local elections. However, on February 9 an interview was published in the daily *de Volkskrant* in which Fortuyn called Islam a backward culture and recommended that the first article of the Dutch Constitution (which prohibits discrimination on the basis of religion, belief, political opinion, race, or sex) be repealed. The LN subsequently dismissed him as party leader, and Fortuyn immediately founded his own party, the List Pim Fortuyn (LPF).

There is some debate about whether the LPF belongs in the same category as radical right parties such as the French National Front and the Austrian Freedom Party. Fortuyn himself was always clear to distance himself from Le Pen and Haider, arguing that his party was not racist and had no ideological baggage from a fascist past. Scholars have argued that Fortuyn's ideology was a complex mix of libertarianism and right-wing populism (Lucardie and Voerman 2002), and several Dutch experts on the far right have rejected classifying the LPF as radical right (Mudde 2007). Yet whether one places the LPF squarely within the radical right party family or not, it is undeniable that the party was anti-immigrant (Van der Brug 2003; Ivarsflaten 2008). Fortuyn certainly wanted to limit immigration as much as possible and demanded that foreigners living in the Netherlands be assimilated. But this anti-immigrant message was specifically tailored for Dutch political culture. On the campaign trail, Fortuyn repeated the central argument from his 1997 book *Tegen de islamisering van onze cultuur* (Against the Islamization of our culture) that Islam was an intolerant religion and that the increasing number of Muslim immigrants threatened to undermine the Dutch culture of tolerance. To a certain extent, Fortuyn's homosexuality shielded him from charges of xenophobia and certainly made it difficult to place him next to other radical right politicians who had preached traditional family values.

Indeed, the political and media reaction to Fortuyn was dramatically different from their response to the Center parties (see Chapter 3). Fortuyn had generally received positive media coverage before his interview in *de Volkskrant*. His comments about Islam provoked an intense media debate in which the left-wing press accused him of xenophobia, while the right-wing and centrist press largely defended his position. This debate mirrored the political reaction to the LPF. Whereas the Greens and left-libertarian parties attacked him, the center and right were careful not to. Indeed, the Christian Democrats (CDA) never ruled out a coalition with the LPF before the election, and there is some evidence that Fortuyn and the Christian Democratic leader, Balkenende, had agreed not to attack one another (Chorus and De Galan 2002: 102, 250; Van Holsteyn and Irwin 2003: 46). There was thus no cordon sanitaire in effect against the LPF, and the public debate about the nature of the Fortuynist movement meant that the political environment was in fact quite permissive.

The success of the LPF demonstrated that there was significant demand for anti-immigrant parties in the Netherlands. The first signs of this came in local elections in March when the party Leefbaar Rotterdam (Livable Rotterdam) won 35% and seventeen of forty-five seats. This was significant because Fortuyn had been elected leader of this party before his break with Livable Netherlands and because the party emphasized Fortuyn's themes of immigration and native insecurity. In the May parliamentary elections, held only nine days after the assassination of Fortuyn by an animal rights activist, the LPF captured 17% of the vote and twenty-six seats. As Van der Brug (2003: 102) argues, the LPF's support is best explained not by protest voting or sympathy with the murdered leader, but by policy preferences: "Voters voted for the LPF because this was the party they agreed with most on an issue they considered important: immigration."

Shortly after the elections, the LPF entered into a coalition government with the Christian Democrats and the Liberals (VVD). Less than six months later, however, this government would fall and the LPF's electoral base would shrink by two-thirds in the January 2003 elections. Clearly, the sudden loss of Fortuyn was the primary factor in the party's demise. The LPF was, strictly speaking, not a political party but a list of candidates whose only common feature was their support for Fortuyn. Had he lived, it is possible that he could have managed relations between them. Perhaps Fortuyn's own popularity would have shielded his colleagues from charges of incompetence. Of course, we will never know. Yet before we dismiss the collapse of the LPF as the inevitable result of Fortuyn's assassination, three points are worth noting. First, the fact that the LPF received 17% of the vote after Fortuyn's death cannot be explained purely as a result of sympathy for the slain leader: Dutch voters clearly agreed with the party's message. Second, winning 17% of the vote gave the LPF an enormous opportunity to influence policy and to institutionalize itself in the Dutch party system. It is conceivable that a different combination of candidates and activists could have profited from this chance rather than squandered it. Third, and most important, it is plausible that the manner in which the LPF was constructed would have doomed it to failure whether Fortuyn had lived or not.

After announcing his intention to form his own party on February 11 (the day after being dismissed from Livable Netherlands), Fortuyn had to find a slate of candidates by April 1 to qualify for the May 15 elections. In addition to personal connections and recommendations from friends, Fortuyn and his advisers sorted through the thousands of people who had written letters and attached CVs, offering their services in what was hardly an organized application procedure. By all accounts, Fortuyn was not impressed by the overall quality of his recruits: "Oh my God," he once said to an adviser, "how can we do this to our country? These people are incompetent" (Chorus and De Galan 2002). A close ally of Fortuyn recalls him picking through the list, noting which candidates were alcoholics and which were looking to settle political scores, and generally despairing that he did not have a wider range of choices.[50] One former parliamentarian from the LPF paraphrased one of Fortuyn's remarks to his hastily assembled list of candidates as follows: "I'm glad I'm not alone anymore, but I'm really frightened how this is all going to work out."[51]

This amateurish, oftentimes whimsical method of recruiting the LPF's future parliamentary group is widely viewed as "the biggest failure in

---

[50] Interview with Ronald Sørensen (LR), Rotterdam, March 2009.
[51] Interview with Fred Schonewille, former LPF, Utrecht, March 2009.

the history of the party."[52] One of the former leaders of the LPF noted that the weakness of the vetting procedure "killed the party at the end of the day. In a normal party, people get filtered out. You notice [their problems] if you work with them for one or two years."[53] While the perception that many of these candidates were simply "complete weirdos" is shared by both former members and outside observers, the failure to vet candidates properly had some concrete ramifications.[54] For example, the only minister who was chosen from among the LPF's parliamentary fraction, Philomena Bijlhout, was forced to resign just nine hours after the government was sworn in after her participation in the people's militia in Surinam was publicized. Winny De Jong, who claimed that Fortuyn had designated her his heir apparent and formed her own breakaway faction within the parliamentary group before being expelled, suffered from manic depression and was probably not medically able to handle the stress of parliamentary work.[55] But aside from these specific problems, the process of building a new party from self-described "political adventurers" had three predictable consequences.

The first was that the majority of the twenty-six parliamentarians of the LPF had no political experience. Matt Herben, who became the leader of the LPF's parliamentary group after Fortuyn's assassination and was therefore responsible for negotiating the coalition agreement, reluctantly took the post because no one else was capable of doing it or prepared to do it. "Herben was the only one who knew anything,"[56] and one of his first tasks was to provide the twenty-six LPF parliamentarians with basic information about how the second chamber of government worked and what their responsibilities would be.[57] When Herben lost the support of

---

[52] Interview with Schonewille. Fortuyn also apparently chose several candidates largely on the basis of their personal appearance.

[53] Interview with Harry Wijnschenk, former LPF, Almere, March 2009.

[54] Interview with Kraneveldt, former LPF, The Hague, March 2009.

[55] De Jong apparently locked herself in the bathroom for hours after the parliamentary group had expelled her and offered repeatedly to kiss the feet of the LPF's interim leader, Harry Wijnschenk, in order to remain in parliament. Her husband had to be called in to remove her. There were many other LPF parliamentarians who would not have survived more thorough vetting. Lucardie and Voerman (2006: 10) note issues with several: "Martin Kievits, a teacher at a police academy, had been accused of intimidation and physical assault; Fred Dekker, a cardiologist had been under investigation because of his (possibly excessive) bills; Cor Eberhard, a producer of porno-sites and Theo de Graaf, an optometrist, were apparently trying to buy eligible positions on the list."

[56] Interview with Schonewille.

[57] Interview with Matt Herben, former member of LPF, The Hague, March 2009. Herben was a career civil servant who, like many other LPF parliamentarians, wrote Fortuyn a

his parliamentary group less than two months after taking over, he was replaced by Harry Wijnschenk, who had virtually no political experience and had given his business card to Fortuyn only several months earlier, offering merely to help him out with organizational matters.[58] Only in a party like the LPF was such an ascent imaginable from a complete outsider to leader of the second-largest party in parliament within a matter of months. There was an intoxicating element to this; it all occurred "in a blink of an eye, and without having to invest years [in a party] in the classic way, handing out brochures and going to dull meetings."[59] Yet the drawbacks were also obvious: "We were a group of inexperienced people, with no clue what we were talking about, and with our hands full with our own internal troubles."[60]

One implication of this inexperience was that the LPF had no one who was capable of filling the nine ministries and subministries the party had gained during the coalition negotiations. Aside from the aforementioned Bijlhout, *all* of the LPF ministers were selected from outside the group. Exactly how these ministers were recruited is still unclear. The only explanation for the selection of Herman Heinsbroek as minister of economic affairs was that he happened to be a neighbor of one of the members of the LPF. The fact that the LPF ministers came from three different political backgrounds – Labour, Christian Democratic, and Liberal – virtually ensured strife within the LPF's cabinet group. By October 2002, vice-premier Eduard Bomhoff and Heinsbroek were no longer on speaking terms. This crisis convinced the CDA and the VVD beyond a doubt that they could not count upon their coalition partner, and the government fell on October 16, after a mere eighty-six days in power.

There was perpetual infighting within the LPF's parliamentary faction as well as its cabinet group, and this situation resulted from a second predictable consequence of the party's formation: it was riven with opportunists. According to Herben, the inexperience of the parliamentary group might have been overcome were it not for the "job-hoppers," people "who had been denied high places on the list by other parties"

letter in February 2002 expressing his interest in joining the movement. He claims that he never wanted to become the leader and would have preferred to have "remained in the background" had his colleagues not forced him into it.

[58] Wijnschenk claims that he was never interested in entering parliament and agreed to take only a place on the list (number 28) that was not likely to win a seat. Whether this was his choice, or whether he was not offered a higher spot, could not be cross-checked.

[59] Interview with Schonewille.

[60] Interview with Wijnschenk.

and who knew just enough about politics to cause problems and "tear the party apart." Wijnschenk, who ironically helped to topple Herben, before being outmaneuvered by another faction and replaced by Herben again several months later, concurs: "Without a filter system in place, you end up with opportunistic people." The infighting and competition to replace Fortuyn as the true leader of the party created "too much turmoil to get down to business."[61] Although my interviewees were candid about the bitter struggles for power that went on within the short life of the LPF's first parliamentary group, Wijnschenk claimed that "we experienced things you don't want to know."[62]

The third predictable downside of the hastily formed list was that its members had nothing in common besides their brief, initial connection with their slain leader. The entire group of selected candidates met one another less than six weeks before the election, and their training and team-building exercises consisted of only four sessions on Saturday afternoons. When thrust into office, these twenty-six "political adventurers" found it nearly impossible to learn to work with one another in the short order that was required. "Fortuyn was the only thing binding these people together," explains Kraneveldt. "There were no common backgrounds, no common experiences, no common principles." "You need time to build these things," she adds, "but we didn't have it."

The prospects for the LPF were not strong following its disastrous episode in government, a period one described as a "real-life soap opera." The internal bickering helped bring the party down to 2% in a weekly public opinion poll conducted in October.[63] The party had trouble finding a candidate to lead the list in the upcoming elections. Hilbrand Nawijn, the former LPF minister for foreign affairs and integration, was the party's preferred candidate, but Nawijn declined the invitation, claiming that he had received death threats. The job fell again to Matt Herben. All things considered, the LPF did well to receive 5.7% of the vote in January 2003. In March, it received only 2.9% in municipal elections. After several more years of internal chaos, the party revealed its desperation in the 2006 parliamentary elections by airing a commercial in which a new party leader parachuted from heaven as the reincarnation of Pim

---

[61] Interview with Kraneveldt.
[62] At one point, Wijnschenk was threatened at gunpoint by someone within the LPF. Wijnschenk did not mention this event during the interview, but the story was reported by Maxime Verhagen, who was the parliamentary leader of the CDA during the period of the coalition government, in an interview by the magazine *Elsevier* on April 12, 2006.
[63] *De Volkskrant*, October 17, 2002.

Fortuyn. After failing to win a single seat, the LPF finally dissolved itself in January 2008.

Given the assassination of its leader and the nature of its parliamentary list, it is difficult to see how the LPF could have survived its period in government. It was, after all, a party that was still recruiting its parliamentary advisers and staff through newspaper advertisements as late as the summer of 2002.[64] The lack of either a nationalist subculture or a preexisting party network led to the formation of a list of amateurs, opportunists, and "weirdos." Fortuyn's qualms about his personnel were prescient.

Yet even if the LPF was doomed, it was still possible for politicians to learn from the experience. One of those was Ronald Sørensen, the leader of Leefbaar Rotterdam (Livable Rotterdam, LR). In contrast to the other local livable parties that broke with Fortuyn after his statements about Islam, LR not only stayed with Fortuyn but put him first on their electoral list. However, in order to prevent LR from attracting a flood of opportunists hoping to ride Fortuyn's coattails, Sørensen kept Fortuyn's place atop the list secret until the last moment. If the downside of this strategy was that recruiting candidates "was a hell of a job," the upside was that the candidates were arguably more interested in politics, rather than pure power, than many of those on the national list. Furthermore, Sørensen hired a professional mental coach to help manage the interpersonal relations among the seventeen elected representatives of his party. The LR had a problem similar to that of the LPF: people did not know one another. Yet according to Sørensen, the coach helped ameliorate conflicts for about one and half years. His suggestion that the LPF parliamentary faction hire a similar professional fell on deaf ears.[65]

The second politician to learn from the LPF was Geert Wilders. His unabashedly anti-Islamic positions ("I hate Islam," he has repeated numerous times) and bleached-blond hair have kept him perpetually in the spotlight in the past several years. Wilders left the Liberals (VVD) in 2004 after the party came out in support of Turkish accession to the European Union but retained his seat in parliament as Groep Wilders (Group Wilders). He founded the Party for Freedom (Partij voor de

---

[64] This was the recruitment path that Kraneveldt followed. She was first hired to work for two LPF parliamentarians before being asked by Matt Herben to be a part of the LPF's list for the January 2003 elections. She took one of the eight seats that the party won and stayed with it before defecting to the Socialist Party in 2006, according to her as a protest against Nawijn's overtures to the VB.

[65] Interview with Sørensen.

Vrijheid, PVV) in 2006. Like Fortuyn, Wilders contrasts Dutch liberal values with an image of an intolerant, monolithic Islam. Like Fortuyn, he tries to distance himself from anti-immigrant parties by emphasizing that his animosity is directed not toward Muslims, but toward their belief system: "I believe the Islamic ideology is a retarded, dangerous one, but I make a distinction.... I don't hate people. I don't hate Muslims."[66]

The PVV won 5.9% in the 2006 parliamentary elections and nine seats. Like the LPF, however, the PVV's first cohort of elected representatives contains several political novices, such as Hero Brinkman, a policeman nicknamed the Rambo of the Bellamybuurt, a former car salesman, and a real estate developer who grew up with Wilders.[67] Very little is known about the rest of the PVV's parliamentary group, in large part because access to it is so tightly controlled. For example, two former members of LR confessed to their former party chairman that Wilders had prohibited them from speaking with him.[68] The PVV was the only party in this book that refused my request for interviews, and members of the Dutch media have apparently fared little better in their attempts to learn more about the internal workings of the PVV.

One conclusion to draw from this is that Wilders, having seen first-hand how the Dutch media reported daily on the struggles within the LPF, is unwilling to let a similar fate befall his fledgling party. A second conclusion is that Wilders is determined not to let such factionalism erupt in the first place. Technically, he is the only member of the PVV, and there are currently no plans to build a party base. This means he is under no legal obligation to run his party democratically or to report his sources of funding.[69] Wilders personally interviews potential candidates for office and selects only those who will toe his line. A third conclusion is that Wilders is determined that the other members of his parliamentary faction appear competent. Although he often poses as a political outsider, Wilders has worked in parliament for most of his adult life and has an exhaustive knowledge of both parliamentary procedure and tactics. Other parliamentarians noticed early in 2006 that Wilders accompanied other PVV members to debates to help coach them, and the assumption is that he has spent a great deal of time personally training them. The results have been impressive. A parliamentarian from the PVV "is now better than average, to be honest." Aside from a minor scuffle involving

---

[66] *International Herald Tribune*, March 22, 2008.
[67] Bellamybuurt is a district in Amsterdam.
[68] Interview with Sørensen.
[69] Wilders does not apply for state funding and is thus not bound by its constraints.

Brinkman during a tour to the Dutch-administered island of Aruba, the PVV has not suffered from the amateurism and incompetence of the LPF. It is also important to note that the PVV has not been subject to any form of cordon sanitaire in parliament. Even the spokesman from the left-liberal D'66 notes that "we have professional respect for [the PVV]"and that "we sometimes support their motions and form majorities with them."

It is too soon to tell whether Wilders will be able to create an electorally persistent party without members. In his favor is a permissive political environment, one that has shifted fundamentally from the days when members of the Center Democrats were demonized and stigmatized. Wilders has also had time to train his personnel, prepare them for the demands of government, and absorb the lessons of the LPF. The PVV was the biggest winner of the national parliamentary elections of June 2010: it won 15.5% of the vote and twenty-four seats.

On the negative side, the risks of openly working on behalf of the PVV should not be underestimated. Wilders has lived under constant police protection since 2004 (following the murder of Van Gogh) and has had to spend time in army barracks, prisons, and other undisclosed locations. The (credible) death threats from Islamic extremists are likely to be a serious problem for recruitment. The PVV's suite of offices in the Tweede Kamer (the Dutch parliament) are currently sealed off from the rest of the building as a safety precaution and provide a reminder of the costs of working on behalf of the PVV. Finally, the experiences of other radical right parties – and other political parties in general – suggest that a single leader cannot manage all aspects of the party after it reaches a certain size. The leader of the LR predicts that Wilder's management style "will break him in the end. He has to start trusting people, he has to talk with people who are critical of his ideas.... [His system] works with 10 or twelve people, but it won't with more."

Conclusion

Although Wilders may not have any interest in creating a large party, he has certainly worked hard to make sure that the PVV is coherent, competent, and legitimate. In this sense he is similar to Kjaersgaard, Hagen, and Blocher, all of whom had the certain luxury of crafting their respective parties before their electoral success became too large for them to handle. Sequencing thus matters, as does the ability of leaders to learn from prior experience. But the most critical factor was that, while these radical right entrepreneurs skillfully managed party transformation, they were not creating them from scratch.

The List Pim Fortuyn and New Democracy are not the only examples of radical right – or right-wing populist – flash parties: the Schill Party in Germany, the Popular Orthodox Rally (LAOS) in Greece, and the United Kingdom Independence Party (UKIP) would qualify as well. Indeed, the universe of radical right flash parties would include many other cases of local or regional success, followed by rapid disintegration. There is thus no automatic transmission mechanism between voter demand and political supply, and states that lacked a strong far right legacy have thus far witnessed successful radical right parties emerging only from other sources.

6

Reforming the Old Right?

This survey of the postwar radical right ends in the two countries where indigenous fascist movements came to power. Italy was the birthplace of fascism, and Germany was where it found its most murderous expression. Since both regimes spent more than a decade mobilizing their populations, it is not surprising that millions of people remained sympathetic to fascism after its defeat and that some of the old elites would not accept this defeat as permanent. Given these broadly similar starting points, the divergent fortunes of radical right parties in the two former axis powers are particularly striking. In Italy, an unabashedly neofascist party first became a member of the government in 1994, along with a populist regionalist party with an anti-immigrant bent. Although the former has become more moderate while the latter has been radicalized, the radical right remains a powerful force in Italian politics. In Germany, the radical right has amounted to little more than a temporary annoyance in state parliaments, except in the east, where the National Democratic Party has sunk somewhat deeper roots.

As for other radical right parties, these trajectories were shaped by a combination of means and opportunity. Although both states had a large reservoir of fascists, a combination of postwar allied policy and state action divided and repressed the German far right, while the Italian far right not only was permitted to reorganize but was even treated as an ally by the Christian Democrats at certain points. As a result, the German far right became radicalized and was perpetually enervated by conflicts among extremists, who succeeded in controlling the political parties that emerged from this foundation, while the Italian far right coalesced into a tightly organized party underpinned by a subculture where moderates ultimately gained the upper hand. When the Italian party system exploded in the early 1990s and the fascist successor party was granted instant legitimacy by Silvio Berlusconi, it thus had the means to take advantage of this historic opportunity. So too did the Northern League, although the large number of opportunists within it nearly caused it to share the same fate as the List Pim Fortuyn and New Democracy. For the German far right, to which we will turn first, such an opportunity never came.

Germany

To understand the radical right in contemporary Germany, a National Democratic Party rally is a good place to start. This, at least, was my thinking as I set out to observe an NPD march through the Charlottenburg section of Berlin in the spring of 2002. As usual, an antifascist group had discovered the time and place of the march and posted the information on the Internet. I was initially worried that the NPD might have decided to relocate, but the passengers who boarded the S-Bahn toward Charlottenburg convinced me otherwise. Young men dressed in neo-Nazi garb – many of whom appeared drunk at ten in the morning – began to fill up the car. Their language and general demeanor did not make them the best representatives of a party whose members still cling to an ideology of a master race. Police began to appear on the platforms as we got closer to our destination. When we reached Charlottenburg, police lined the station platform and separated the NPD members from the antifascist activists who had begun to gather for their counterdemonstration. I followed the NPD from the station until I reached the police cordon around their meeting point. From the edges I observed a handful of men in their forties in dated suits who tried, without much success, to capture the attention of several hundred young neo-Nazis with speeches about the importance of national identity and the honor of the Waffen-SS. A few minutes before the event was set to begin, several dozen police formed a wall around the front line of marchers to protect them from the antifascists. The march itself was, by design, nearly impossible for an observer to follow: when the head of the procession came to a crossroads, the police guided it in one of three directions. The leaders of the march appeared not to know the route beforehand and simply followed the police escort as it twisted through the streets of West Berlin. After every turn, antifascists raced down different streets and shouted the latest updates into their cell phones. But the police were largely successful in keeping the two sides separated.

Germans, for obvious reasons, take the radical right very seriously. The international community, again for obvious reasons, also reacts to the slightest sign of far right resurgence in the Bundesrepublik. The topic has spawned an enormous academic literature. While I would not want to minimize the threat of parties like the NPD, the attention that the German radical right habitually receives should not blind us to the fact that it has failed to win a single seat in the Bundestag since 1945. Put another way, radical right parties in Germany generate more books, articles, and newspaper stories per vote cast for them than their counterparts anywhere else. Most academic and journalistic studies of German radical right parties seek to uncover the reasons for their success. But given the empirical record, it seems more appropriate to consider why they have repeatedly failed.

Here again, the NPD rally is instructive. Without reading too much into the event, one could observe three dynamics at the microlevel that have, I argue, prevented the radical right from becoming a sustained electoral force.

The first is the tension between the middle-aged leadership of the NPD and its youthful rank and file. This intergenerational coalition within the party dates only from the mid-1990s when NPD chairman Udo Voigt calculated that his moribund party could be saved only if it were opened to neo-Nazis. As I argue later, Voigt's strategy has been successful in many ways. Yet one of the obvious downsides is that the interests of the NPD party elite are often at odds with those of the new recruits. The former want to follow the logic of electoral competition and win seats in parliament, whereas the latter want camaraderie and constituency representation. These objectives are mutually exclusive in the case of the NPD because many party activists seek camaraderie through violence. The contemporary NPD is not committed to parliamentary democracy and embraces biological racism (although the party has become adept at hiding these features to avoid being banned). Yet even within such a party, as within the British National Party, one can speak of "moderates" and "extremists" and highlight the conflicts between them. Such conflicts have been particularly pronounced in Germany, in large part because the reservoir for right-wing extremism is much deeper than in other countries. During the first several postwar decades, unreconstructed Nazis battled with national conservatives who wanted to create a democratic party to the right of the Christian Democrats (CDU) and Christian Socialists (CSU). This fissure ultimately tore apart the NPD in the 1960s and relegated it to electoral oblivion for three decades.

The second dynamic is that of state control. The police, to be sure, were present in large numbers at the rally to protect the NPD from the antifascist activists who outnumbered them. But they were certainly also there to protect the population at large from the NPD. The German state has, writ large, dealt with the postwar far right in the same way. It has banned parties and organizations, monitored their activities, and barred civil servants (a large population in Germany) from joining them. At the same time, the state has actively sought to convert members of far right parties and organizations. Some of the NPD marchers may one day find themselves in a state program designed to help right-wing extremists exit the neo-Nazi milieu and integrate them into society. In the 1950s, Adenauer's government allowed former Nazis back into elite positions in politics and society, on the condition that they swear allegiance to parliamentary democracy and make no attempt to resuscitate their former ideology. The German state has, in short, drawn clear lines between extremist groups and mainstream politics, yet has offered a path of repentance and reentry into mainstream society to those who disavow their extremist pasts.

The third dynamic is the mobilization of antifascist groups against the NPD rally, a scene that has been repeated innumerable times across the country. While their activities have certainly made organization building difficult for a number of far right parties in Germany in the past four decades, it is the broader social reaction of German politics and society that has dramatically restricted these parties' recruitment base. It is with these general dynamics in mind that we analyze the "four waves" of far right political activity in postwar Germany, beginning with the first in the late 1940s and 1950s.

The First Wave

There were good reasons to expect that Germany, in the immediate postwar years, would produce a sizable far right political party. The potential voter base in West Germany included the following: 9 million refugees, expellees, and emigrants from the east; 2 million discharged Nazi officials and professional soldiers; 2 million "late returnees," many of whom spent time in Soviet POW camps; and 4 to 6 million injured civilians. These groups overlapped to some extent, but to the total figure one could add an inestimable number of Germans who had internalized the values of the totalitarian regime they had lived under for twelve years. Public opinion polls by Elisabeth Noelle and Peter Neumann's Allensbach Institute revealed the persistence of National Socialist attitudes. In 1952, for example, 37% of Germans agreed with the statement that "it would be better for Germany not to have any Jews in the country," while only 20% disagreed (Noelle and Neumann 1967: 197). A critical confrontation with the Nazi past was decades away.

Yet no far right party came close to capturing these voters. Although there were some isolated successes, the four major far right parties (the German Party, German Rights Party, Socialist Party of the Reich, and Federation of the Expellees and Disenfranchised) were more or less defunct by the early 1960s, if not earlier. The Niedersächsische Landespartei (Lower Saxon Land Party, NLP) was founded in 1946 and renamed the Deutsche Partei (German Party, DP) in 1947. The DP militated for former Wehrmacht soldiers and German expellees, winning 4.0% of the vote in the national parliamentary elections of 1949, 3.3% in 1953, and 3.4% in 1957. The Deutsche Rechtspartei (German Rights Party, DRP) was also founded in 1946, although it too changed its name, but kept its acronym, in 1950 to the Deutsche Reichspartei (German Reich Party, DRP). The DRP's best result in a national parliamentary election was 1.1% in 1949. It did manage to win 5.1% in a state election in Rheinland-Pfalz in 1959, by far its best electoral performance. The Sozialistische Reichspartei (Socialist Party of the Reich, SRP) was formed by a faction of the DRP in 1949 and captured 11% in state elections in Lower Saxony in 1951. Finally, the Bund der Heimatvertriebenen und Entrechteten (Federation of the Expellees and Disenfranchised, BHE) won 23.4% in the 1950 state elections in Schleswig-Holstein, a state with a particularly high concentration of expellees from the east. The party reached double-digit totals (although often through electoral lists with other parties) in several others states and won 5.9% in the 1953 national elections. However, the BHE's decline in its bastion of Schleswig-Holstein – 14% in 1954 and 6.9% in 1958 – mirrored its deterioration across Germany before its eventual fusion with the DP in 1961.

Three factors were responsible for the failure of the German far right in the first two postwar decades. First, and most obvious, was the fractionalization of the far right landscape. Six far right parties, among the many who stood for office, won seats in state elections between 1949 and 1953. The division of Germany contributed to this outcome: the fact that parties required licensing by one of the occupying powers until 1949 meant that they were geographically contained. None of these parties were ever able to form a truly national organization. Yet long-standing political divisions on the right were even more important. The central ideological divide on the far right was between unreconstructed National Socialists and conservative nationalists (many of whom had joined the

Nazi Party but did not necessarily want to advertise that fact), and this rift was present from the beginning. Within the DRP, for example, these two groups battled with one another before the National Socialists broke off to form the SRP. The BHE contained both a so-called ministerial wing of moderates who did not want to jeopardize their alliance with the CDU, and the extremists who wanted to turn back the clock to before Nazi Germany's defeat. The DP, under the leadership of the monarchist conservative Heinrich Hellwege, expelled many of its members for supporting pro-fascist statements in 1950. In 1953, Hellwege dissolved the entire DP organization in North Rhine-Westphalia because he claimed that it had been sabotaged by Nazi elements (Nagle 1970: 25).

Adenauer's policy of integration was a second major factor that helped eviscerate the far right. As several historians have demonstrated (Friedrich 1984; Frei 1999), one of Adenauer's first priorities was to pass amnesty laws that essentially overturned denazification and allowed former Nazis back into the professions and the government. In a bold statement of this policy, Adenauer appointed Hans Globke, a former Nazi official who had written commentaries on the Nuremberg race laws, to be his chief of staff in 1949. The unwritten, yet widely followed rule in this bargain was that former Nazis would neither defend their pasts nor raise any challenges to the new democratic order. Mainstream political parties, particularly the CDU and the FDP, opened their doors to these people as well. Adenauer was also willing to form coalitions with the DP and the BHE, reasoning that such a policy would exacerbate the conflict between moderates and extremists within each party. For example, although the BHE won only 5.6% of the vote in the 1953 elections, Adenauer offered the party several ministerial posts. The moderates within the BHE leapt at this chance, while the extremists wanted to go into opposition. The result of this feud was that the ministerial wing of the BHE, including the party's chairman and its government minister, left it to join the CDU in 1955. As Nagle (1970: 24) notes, "This process eventually deprived the BHE of its most respected and able leaders and hastened the already apparent decline of the party." A similar dynamic occurred within the DP, as several of its leading figures converted to the CDU in the late 1950s.

The third reason for the far right's failure was the repressive apparatus of the state. The Federal Republic was specifically founded as a "militant democracy" (*streitbare Demokratie*) in which the Federal Constitutional Court (Bundesverfassungsgericht) could ban any political party that was hostile to the Basic Law of 1949. But the fear of banning dates back to the occupation period and contributed to the early fractionalization of the far right. Before the first national election of 1949, for example, leaders of the DP and the DRP (in addition to the smaller NDP) had apparently agreed to fuse their parties. Yet members of the DP were worried that the occupation authorities would willfully interpret the fusion as the founding of a new party and delay licensing it until after the election (Nagle 1970: 18). The agreement broke down, and after the DP won twenty-five seats and two ministerial posts in the elections it was unwilling to discuss a merger.

In 1952, the Federal Constitutional Court declared the SRP illegal and brought the party's meteoric rise to an abrupt end. There is no doubt that the SRP was a party founded by Nazis for Nazis, and there was little attempt to hide this fact. One applicant, for example, wrote the following to SRP headquarters: "I was a member of the NSDAP with the membership number 566,776.... Could you please send me your propaganda material immediately? You can do this without hesitation. I am not a traitor. I am still a convinced national socialist" (Kühnl, Rilling, and Sager 1969: 15). After the ban, many of the SRP's ten thousand members returned to other parties, in particular the DRP. The influx of these extremists led to the banning of the DRP in the state of Rheinland-Pfalz in 1956 and exacerbated internal conflicts within both it and the other far right parties. The threat of banning also led many moderates within far right parties to seek safety and greater stability in the CDU or FDP. The arrest of Werner Naumann, a former Nazi state secretary, who had created a power base within the FDP in North Rhine-Westphalia, also demonstrated that the Allies would not permit unreconstructed Nazis to wield significant political power (Frei 1999).

In sum, the German government adopted a carrot (integration) and stick (repression) approach that succeeded in exacerbating internal conflicts within far right parties and contributed to the balkanization of the far right party landscape. Of course, a fourth factor was undoubtedly important in limiting the electoral appeal of far right parties: the Wirtschaftswunder (Economic Miracle). The extraordinary growth of the German economy in the 1950s led to dramatic increases in the standard of living. This was not a fertile environment for parties that advocated a return to the past. It would take nearly fifteen years before economic growth stalled for the first time and allowed the far right to enter its second wave.

The Second Wave

Desperation ultimately pushed the remnants of the German far right together in the early 1960s. In 1961 the BHE fused with the DP at the national level to become the Gesamtdeutsche Partei (All-German Party, GDP), which won a disappointing 2.8% in the 1961 elections for the Bundestag. The DRP received a mere 0.8% in these elections, and its leader, Adolf von Thadden, feared that the party would not survive the 1965 Bundestag elections without a major change in strategy. After several months of negotiations, the Nationaldemokratische Partei Deutschlands (National Democratic Party, NPD) was founded on November 28, 1964.

Although the NPD consisted of remnants of the BHE and the DP, the new party was essentially a renamed DRP. One of the conclusions Von Thadden drew from the banning of the SRP, and the threatened banning of other far right parties, was that any new party would need a moderate at the helm (Kühnl et al. 1969: 29). He was thus content to let Fritz Thielen (formerly of the CDU and the DP) become the first leader of the new party. Von Thadden also tried to mask the predominance of former DRP members by choosing people from outside the party to become the *Vorsitzende der Landesverbände*, the leaders of the NPD's state-level organizations (Smoydzin 1969: 23). Von Thadden also tried to control the public statements of party members by forbidding them to discuss "the so-called Jewish question" and providing *Musterreden* (model speeches) to which they were expected to adhere (Dittmer 1969: 83). The NPD's propaganda chief, Hess, commanded party members to "take care to avoid the tone that you had once learned," a reference to the fact that many of them had been in the Nazi Party.[1] Party members who ignored this injunction were evicted, and the distribution of model speeches did produce a common discourse. In fact, these were followed so literally that candidates sometimes gave exactly the same response to questions (Kühnl et al. 1969: 41).

None of these cosmetic maneuvers could hide the facts that the NPD was dominated by the DRP and that unreconstructed Nazis were a powerful force within the party. Eight of the initial 17 members of the party's central committee were from the DRP, including Von Thadden, who controlled the party apparatus. Former DRP members accounted for one-half of the NPD's initial party membership and 36 of the 61 (60%) NPD members of state parliaments elected by 1967 (Kühnl et al. 1969: 46). Of the 218 NPD county committee members in the state of North Rhine-Westphalia, 86 (39%) had been members of the NSDAP.

---

[1] *Die Zeit*, no. 17, 1967.

The concentration of former Nazis increased the higher one went within the ranks of the party.

Since the NPD built upon the DRP's membership base, the new party was able to claim 7,500 members and form local and state organizations across Germany by 1965 (Smoydzin 1969: 23). Despite an active election campaign and predictions that they would receive 15% of the vote, the NPD won only 2% in the 1965 elections for the Bundestag and appeared destined to remain yet another fringe party on the far right. Yet two major exogenous developments revived the party's fortunes. The first was an economic downturn in 1966 that led to the largest increase in unemployment yet experienced in the history of the Federal Republic. The number of unemployed rose from 105,743 in August 1966 to 673,572 by February 1967.[2] The second factor was the formation of a grand coalition between the Social Democratic Party of Germany (SPD) and the CDU, which marked the first time the SPD had been part of the federal government. Many conservatives could not countenance the CDU's power-sharing agreement with the left, and their discontent gave the far right access to a potential reservoir of new voters. The NPD enjoyed a strong showing in a series of state elections between March 1966 and April 1968, peaking at 9.8% in Baden-Württemberg in April 1968.

The NPD thus expected to cross the 5% hurdle in the 1969 Bundestag elections. When it received only 4.3% (and no seats), the party entered into a period of internal discord that would confine it to electoral oblivion for more than three decades. Certain factors in its demise were beyond its control. The Grand Coalition ended before the 1969 elections, and an increasing polarization between the CDU and SPD enticed conservative voters to return to the Christian Democratic Union. An economic recovery also led to a decrease in unemployment. The inherent cause of its failure, however, lay more in its long-term internal divisions than in short-term political and economic events.

The NPD had in fact been plagued by internal conflicts between extremists and moderates from the beginning. The first rifts in the NPD actually appeared before it began its meteoric rise. Von Thadden's heavy-handed tactics and fidelity to Nazi ideology had chased off 1,800 members of the moderate wing of the party by the end of 1966 (Kühnl et al. 1969: 47). Among them was Franz Florian Winter, the former

---

[2] *Statistisches Jahrbuch für die Bundesrepublik Deutschland*, 1967.

leader of the NPD's party organization in Bavaria, who denounced von Thadden's wing as "godless fanatics" and published a scathing account of his experience within the party – the first example of what would become a genre in the literature on the far right (Winter 1968).[3] Several months later, the long-awaited conflict between Thielen and von Thadden erupted when the latter tried to squeeze out any NPD functionaries who were not loyal to him. Von Thadden ousted Dr. Lothar Kühne, an ally of Thielen, from the chairmanship of the NPD's organization in Lower Saxony. Thielen's group challenged this move in a Bremen court and succeeded in having von Thadden's election overturned as a violation of the party's bylaws. Thielen proceeded to eject von Thadden and several of his lieutenants from the party, and for a moment it appeared that the moderates had won.

But von Thadden controlled the party apparatus, and Thielen's isolation quickly became clear. Nagle's (1970: 56) description is worth quoting at length:

At this point, the Bundesrepublik was treated to the ludicrous sight of a party chairman in search of a party. Thielen and von Thadden engaged in a series of petty encounters which took on the atmosphere of a low farce. Thielen, as chairman, decided to impound all party records and even the furniture at NPD headquarters. When he arrived there with moving vans and police, however, he found the offices empty. Von Thadden and friends had moved everything out for safekeeping. For the next several weeks, NPD leaders hid keys, envelopes, stamps, and other official party facilities from the party's own chairman.

This inner-party turmoil was probably responsible for the NPD's poorer than expected showing in Schleswig-Holstein. Forecasts suggested that the party would receive at least 10% in this former Nazi bastion (Nagle 1970: 58). When the party received only 5.8%, the consensus among analysts was that the NPD had finally been destroyed by its internal contradictions. Yet after Thielen finally quit in June 1967 after admitting that "at the moment the NPD cannot be cleansed," von Thadden was able to restore order to a party that had shed its moderate wing.[4]

But the radicalization of the NPD would, ironically, fell von Thadden. A generational change was under way in the German far right. Whereas the older cohort – many of whom had been members of the Nazi Party – abided by the democratic rules of the game, the younger generation became increasingly hostile to the system and willing to engage

[3] *Allgemeine Zeitung*, November 2, 1966.
[4] *Der Spiegel*, no. 21, 1967.

in violence (Stöss 1989: 156). At an NPD rally in Kassel, one of von Thadden's bodyguards shot and injured two antifascist demonstrators (Staud 2005: 34). Following the defeat in the 1969 Bundestag elections, the group calling for extraparliamentary action challenged von Thadden's leadership. The NPD tried to control this movement and stem a growing number of defections by creating a group called Aktion Widerstand. This move backfired, however, as Aktion Widerstand turned violent and hastened the balkanization of the party. No longer able to control the new generation of extremists, von Thadden announced that he was "neither ready nor suitable for a dance on a volcano of irrational folly" (Staud 2005: 36) and thus resigned. By 1972, the party had lost all its seats in state parliaments and received 0.6% of the vote in that year's Bundestag elections. For the next three decades, the NPD would be electorally irrelevant. Aktion Widerstand, however, marked the beginning of the growth of a violent neo-Nazi movement in Germany.

The Third Wave

Before the Berlin Wall fell in November 1989, the rise of the radical right Republikaner (REP) party was one of the most important political stories of the year in West Germany. Many analysts predicted that the REP would become Germany's fifth-largest party after it won 7.5% in state elections in West Berlin in January and 7.1% in the European elections in June. Several dissidents from the CSU had founded the party in 1983 after Defense Minister Franz Josef Strauss agreed to a major bank loan for East Germany, which they viewed as a betrayal of the goal of German unification. The REP initially sought to attract German conservatives who were disappointed by Helmut Kohl's failure to engineer his promised "political-moral turnaround" (*politisch-moralische Wende*). After an internal power struggle, Franz Schönhuber, formerly a popular radio talk-show host, emerged as the party's leader. Schönhuber had lost his job after he published an autobiography titled *Ich War Dabei* (I was there) that glorified his wartime service in the Waffen-SS. Resistance to *Aufarbeitung der NS-Vergangenheit* (working through the Nazi past) became one of the REP's central themes. Like radical right parties elsewhere during the 1980s, the REP developed an anti-immigrant and welfare chauvinist discourse.

Although the party still exists, the Republikaner have been irrelevant since the mid-1990s. The most common explanation for their demise is that the world around them changed in two fundamental ways. First, German unification robbed the party of one of its central themes. Before

1990, the REP could plausibly claim that it was the only relevant polit-ical party that had not accepted the division of Germany. Although this issue may have mattered less to voters, it was important to party activists. Second, in 1993 the government modified Article 16 of the Basic Law, which had previously guaranteed asylum to "every politically persecuted individual." This contributed to a dramatic drop in asylum seekers, from 438,200 in 1992 to 127,200 in 1994 (Young 1995), and a decrease in the political saliency of immigration.

The problem with this account, however, is that it overlooks inter-nal factors. There is overwhelming evidence that the REP began to come apart at the seams months, and in some places even days, after its elec-toral breakthroughs. In addition to destabilizing the perpetual balancing act between extremists and moderates, the influx of activists and office holders with no political experience – or with turbulent careers in other parties – kept the party in perpetual chaos. The party membership grew rapidly: from less than 2,000 members in 1984, to 8,000 after its suc-cess in West Berlin, to 25,000 by the end of 1989 (Winkler and Schuman 1998: 99).[5] But even the party leadership realized that such exponential growth was at best a mixed blessing. Schönhuber quipped in 1990 that "he wouldn't even eat together" with many of the party's new recruits and that some – including several of the leaders of the party's state organizations – were "really crazy."[6]

These dynamics were apparent before the West Berlin elections. As early as 1988, after the REP's party organization in Bremen broke off from the national party and founded the Bremische Republikanische Partei, Schönhuber commented on the REP's internal factionalism:

When we suddenly got three percent, a bunch of people piled into our party who assumed that, after having failed in other parties, they would become at least a state secretary, if not a Minister, with us.... Many of the newcomers knew one another, which resulted in fights.... These arguments completely paralyzed our work. I spent weeks doing nothing besides running from one party member to another and asking their lawyers questions rather than spending my time on the legitimate tasks of a party leader; namely, to fight for votes and to prove that this party is necessary.[7]

Breakaway factions of Republikaner emerged at the state and even the local level. By mid-1993, the party had lost at least 25% of its four

[5] Perhaps only half of these members were ever active, however. See *Der Spiegel*, no. 45, 1993, p. 54.
[6] *Der Spiegel*, no. 1, 1990.
[7] Quoted in Jaschke (1993: 88–89).

hundred representatives in local councils.[8] By the same year, eight former national party leaders and eight former state party leaders had either left the REP or been kicked out (Jaschke 1993: 86).

Two examples should suffice to document this turmoil. Less than ten months after his party's electoral breakthrough, the leader of the West Berlin REP formed a new party, Die Deutschen Demokraten (German Democrats). An article in the weekly newsmagazine *Der Spiegel* outlined the factors that had led to this split:

The Berlin REPs produce a wave of party and legal proceedings, brawl during meetings, denounce one another with anonymous dossiers that are sometimes produced by an internal party security service. According to statements from former REP functionaries, the party has not only been infiltrated by right-wing extremists from the Wiking-Jugend, the DVU, and the NPD, but its leading figures possess dubious pasts.[9]

Schönhuber ejected Bernard Andres, leader of the Berlin REP, from the party after informing him that his "executive committee consists of criminals." Schönhuber would later refer to Andres as "a nice guy, but crazy."[10] Franz Degen, who replaced Andres, wrote Schönhuber that he needed "to demand state protection (*Staatsschutzmassnahme*) to protect himself from his own party comrades" (Jaschke 1993: 93). Within months after its victory in West Berlin, the party was in complete disarray and never recovered.

This battle between extremists and moderates was later repeated on the national level. Schönhuber claimed in the spring of 1990 that his party had become overrun by former NPD members, and stepped down as party chairman, to the delight of an extremist faction led by Harald Neubauer. But Schönhuber was reelected as party chairman in July 1990, after which he ejected his rivals from the party and replaced nearly the entire party executive. The extremists then formed the Deutsche Liga für Volk und Heimat, which siphoned off an untold number of members from the REP. Although it appeared that Schönhuber had triumphed over the extremists and was steering the party in a conservative nationalist direction, his meeting with Gerhard Frey of the DVU in August 1994 convinced party moderates that this was a ruse. Fearing that he would lose his reelection bid, Schönhuber stepped down as chairman in 1994.

[8] *Der Spiegel*, no. 25, 1993, p. 59.
[9] *Der Spiegel* no. 38, 1989, p. 112.
[10] *Der Spiegel*, no. 1, 1990, p. 42.

His successor, Rolf Schlierer, has survived to this date but has been unable to reproduce Schönhuber's success.

In sum, the REP was enervated by the same basic conflict between moderates and extremists that split the NPD in the 1960s. It is possible, however, that the REP could have overcome this division if it had been able to attract enough moderates. Yet as I have argued at length elsewhere (Art 2006, 2007), the political, social, and legal reaction to the REP not only made new recruitment exceedingly difficult, but also drained the party of existing members. Every political party represented in parliament enforced an airtight cordon sanitaire against the REP at all political levels. Antifascists routinely vandalized the property of REP politicians and threatened their physical safety. REP party members also stood little chance of holding leadership positions in the voluntary associations and clubs that play an important role in German society. The leader of the REP in one German state claimed that he had lost at least a third of his friends after he joined the party.[11] After its initial success in 1989, the REP lost 40% of its membership within a single year (from 25,000 to 15,000). Most REP politicians attributed this drop in part to the myriad social pressures that members faced.

Although these factors were no doubt important, the reaction of the state played the central role in raising the costs of membership in radical right organizations. In 1972, the West German government of Willy Brandt passed the Decree Against Radicals (*Radikalenerlass*), which forbade people with radical political views to hold positions in the German civil service. The law's primary target was initially the leftist terrorist group Red Army Faction, but it applied to radical rightists as well. Given that the civil service includes groups like teachers and policemen in addition to state bureaucrats, it is not surprising that the law sparked a loyalty check of around 3.5 million people (Braunthal 1990). The Office for the Protection of the Constitution (Verfassungsschutz) also began monitoring the REP in several German states. This gave employers the legal right to ask potential and current employees if they belonged to the party. Since firms appeared to care more about the political views of their white-collar workers than those of their blue-collar workers, this most likely contributed to the predominantly working-class profile of the REP membership that we documented in Chapter 2. The former leader of the REP in Bavaria claimed that he advised white-collar workers to leave the party for the sake of their careers. He also noted that, by end

---

[11] Interview with former REP party leader, Stuttgart, April 16, 2002.

of the 1990s, the party consisted mainly of those who had "nothing else to lose."[12]

Although there has been virtually no research on the social structure of REP party members, the findings from Benno Hafeneger's study of REP representatives in the state of Hessen are consistent with those reported in Chapter 2 (Hafeneger 2000: 33–34). Out of a sample of 165, there were 66 (40%) who identified themselves as workers, 43 (27%) as employees, and 17 (10%) as pensioners. Only 11 (7%) identified themselves as university graduates.

The Fourth Wave

Since the collapse of the radical right REP in the mid-1990s, which marked the end of the "third wave," the German far right has been dominated by two parties: the German People's Union (Deutsche Volksunion, DVU) and a regenerated NPD. The DVU is the personal electoral vehicle of Gerhard Frey, the millionaire publisher of the right-wing extremist weekly *Deutsche National-Zeitung*. Founded in 1987, the DVU has never developed anything remotely approaching a party organization. This has not completely prevented it from making sporadic gains in state elections, however, as Frey has shown himself willing to spend vast amounts of money on mass mailings and door-to-door deliveries of party propaganda to gain parliamentary representation. In 1987, for example, Frey spent DM 2 million, more than all other parties combined, on the Bremen state elections (Winkler and Schumann 1998: 99–100). His efforts netted him a mere 3.4% of the vote and only because of a special provision for the constituency of Bremerhaven, where the DVU won 5.4% – two seats. In the 1989 European elections, Frey spent DM 17 million to circulate 70 million pamphlets, only to receive a mere 1.6%. In the early 1990s, however, the party did manage to surmount the 5% hurdle in both Bremen and Schleswig-Holstein.

The DVU's best result to date came in the 1998 elections in Saxony-Anhalt. The party once again made up for its lack of organization (it had only about thirty members in the entire state) with a mass-mailing campaign and shocked observers by winning 12.9% of the vote (Backes and Mudde 2000: 53). But in Saxony-Anhalt, as in other states in which it has won representation, the party's parliamentary group quickly collapsed amid bickering and incompetence. One-quarter of the group defected to other parties within the first year, and the DVU won less than 2% of

---

[12] Interview with Johann Gärtner, Kissing, April 22, 2002.

the vote in the 2002 state elections (Rensmann 2006: 73). In 2004, the DVU won 6.1% and six seats in the Brandenburg state parliament. Five years later, however, the parliamentary group had collapsed and the party won only 1.2% of the vote in state elections. The DVU has thus been a phantom party throughout its history, with small electoral breakthroughs leading quickly to internal breakdown and defeat. The new NPD, however, represents a very different type of party.

There are two central differences between the NPD of the 1960s and that of this decade. First, the old NPD was a party of old Nazis; the new NPD is primarily a party of the young. Second, the old NPD obviously operated in West Germany; today, despite a strong showing in state elections in the Saarland in 2004 (4%), the NPD is concentrated in the east. Immediately following unification, extremists from the west rushed to the east and founded local organizations. The neo-Nazi leader Michael Kühnen described the situation immediately after the *Wende*: "There are tens of thousands of youths there [in the east] that are sympathetic to us. This is of course a situation that awakens close to erotic feelings in every politician. It is fabulous" (Staud 2005: 46).

The collapse of East German social institutions provided neo-Nazi organizations with a fertile environment for recruitment. In the DDR, a plethora of youth organizations had provided adolescents and young (overwhelmingly male) adults with activities and structure after school. These possibilities disappeared virtually overnight, and the NPD, following on the heels of the extraparliamentary neo-Nazi movements, stepped in to fill this vacuum. The party venerated many of the same values as the Communists, such as order and discipline, and in this sense the ideological legacies of the DDR also contributed to the party's success. Since then, a high level of unemployment and pessimism about their life chances has brought a large number of young males into the party, or into the party's broader milieu.

Yet these chances might have been squandered had Günther Deckert, the NPD's chairman from 1991 to 1996, remained at the helm. Deckert's obsession with Holocaust revisionism and his inability to tap into disillusionment with unification nearly marginalized the party in the east. Udo Voigt, elected party leader in 1996, changed all this. The party slowly began to adopt anticapitalist rhetoric and highlight socioeconomic problems. This was part of a general strategy of moderating the NPD's extremist ideology (at least on paper) and of cutting a more respectable image among the electorate.

This strategy finally bore fruit in the 2004 state elections in Saxony. In slogans that could have been written by the extreme left, the NPD stressed "social security and justice" and railed against the "unwinding of the German welfare state."[13] The explosion of protest against Chancellor Gerhard Schröder's liberal labor market reforms provided the NPD with an ideal political opportunity. Members of the NPD led demonstrations against the Hartz IV reforms and sometimes hijacked protests organized by other political parties. Although the party certainly did not shy away from its xenophobic rhetoric, there was a concerted effort to make the party seem as respectable as possible to disenchanted voters. After nearly thirty-six years in the political wilderness, the NPD won 9.2% of the vote in Saxony (the SPD managed only 9.4%), thereby capturing twelve seats in the Dresden state parliament. In 2006, it won 7.3% of the vote and six seats in state elections in Mecklenburg-West Pomerania.

Although ideological repositioning mattered in this case (see Rensmann 2006), the NPD could not have succeeded without mobilizing a constituency to work on its behalf. Whereas Deckert had tried to hold the neo-Nazi youth subculture at arm's length, Voigt saw the possibilities in it. To acquire the necessary signatures for the party to appear on the ballot in the 1998 parliamentary elections, for example, Voigt stated that he "simply drove through the villages and stopped when he saw three or four skinheads standing at the marketplace" (Staud 2005: 23). Voigt opened the NPD to neo-Nazis because it was impossible to find the manpower for grassroots mobilization from any other source. This tactic, however, fit uneasily with the overall strategy of moderating the party ideology to attract voters and to avoid banning by state authorities.

The party tried to square this circle by urging its members to modify their public image. Although the NPD did little to control the violent activities of its members, it did try to steer them into local community work. Many NPD politicians cast off their jackboots and donned suits while organizing programs to benefit the youth and the elderly. They founded bars, discos, and clubs for adolescents and young adults. For many eastern Germans, the NPD's emphasis on discipline and national pride do not place it outside the spectrum of legitimate political movements. The social sanctions that have had such a powerful negative effect on other radical right parties elsewhere in Germany are therefore not as strong in the east.

[13] http://www.sachsen.npd.de/npd_sa_info/wahlen/2004/unser-wahlprogramm.html.

The combination of social legitimacy and violence has worked. In marked contrast to the DVU, the NPD has dense networks in many eastern German towns, particularly in Saxony and Brandenburg. Observers have been warning of this for some time. The *Zeit* journalist Toralf Staud, among others, has long been reporting that the NPD has become acceptable (even hegemonic) in many eastern German towns. In 2001, he wrote that "right-wing extremism in the east is not a phenomenon of marginal groups. It is not a sub-culture, but rather dominates the youth scene in many small cities and towns. Racism and anti-Semitism are in fashion." In short, "Nazis are chic."[14] In 2002, the neo-Nazi scene even received its own designer brand apparel: Thor Steinar. Far from jackboots and bomber jackets, the fashion line contains items that might appear in an Eddie Bauer or J. Crew catalog. Thor Steinar's logo, however, was constructed from obscure images from the Third Reich, meaning that insiders can demonstrate their affiliation without drawing the attention of the police or antifascist groups.[15]

The control of the NPD over some eastern German towns is remarkable. Some mayors in eastern towns lament that the only youths who are active in the community are those from the extreme right milieu. Neo-Nazis have declared some areas to be *national befreite Zonen* (nationally liberated zones). Although neo-Nazis are not literally in control of these regions, the German government's Office on Foreigners' 1997 yearly report maintained that there were at least twenty-five "no-go zones" for foreigners.[16] In the same year, the state of Brandenburg reported that at least nine towns within its borders had become centers of neo-Nazi activity and warned foreign construction workers that they could be the targets of attacks.[17] If the international reaction to neo-Nazi violence in the 1990s and predictions of the return of fascism was alarmist, reports of the current dominance of some eastern German environs by right-wing extremists are accurate and unembellished.

Yet it is precisely fear of this development that has motivated many elites in small towns to downplay the extent of right-wing extremism. Concerned about their cities' reputations, mayors have treated neo-Nazism as a passing phenomenon and routinely deny that "their" youths are ideologically committed to radical right politics. The local media in

[14] Toraulf Staud, "Nazis sind chic," *Die Zeit*, no. 8, 2001.
[15] Toraulf Staud, "Der braune Pop," *Die Zeit*, no. 40, 2004.
[16] Toraulf Staud, "Der braune Pop," *Die Zeit*, no. 40, 2004.
[17] *Frankfurter Rundschau*, January 23, 1998.

eastern German locales have also made right-wing violence much less an issue than have their counterparts in the west, for fear of damaging the town's reputation or appearing traitorous.[18] Moreover, police in the east have generally not combated neo-Nazi groups as aggressively as the law allows. Although there are undoubtedly exceptions, even a brief visit to NPD strongholds in Saxony leads one to Staud's (2001) conclusion about the differing perceptions of right-wing extremism in east and west: "In the west a clear climate against right-wing extremism dominates, in the east fear and indifference dominate."

The NPD, not surprisingly, immediately became a breeding ground for neo-Nazi violence. During the early 1990s, neo-Nazi gangs burned asylum homes and attacked foreigners. In the summer of 2000, another wave of attacks prompted German elites to call for the banning of the NPD. This set off an intense public debate about the legitimacy and utility of banning a right-wing extremist group. Critics argued that a democratic society needed to leave room for all political views, no matter how distasteful. Besides, with the NPD polling less than 1% in national parliamentary elections, some observers argued that it was helpful to allow the party to contest elections and demonstrate just how marginal it was. Others argued that Germany had become a "vigilant democracy" (*eine wehrhafte Demokratie*) given its history of political extremism and that banning a party that rejected the Basic Law was necessary. Allowing an antidemocratic party to receive state funds was also, from this perspective, ethically wrong. From a utilitarian perspective, many argued that banning the NPD would make it more difficult for the state to keep track of right-wing extremists. The NPD had been deeply penetrated by agents working for the Office for the Protection of the Constitution (Verfassungsschutz), and many were unwilling to sacrifice this achievement. In the end, the case for banning won but was derailed by the success of the state's covert penetration. It turned out that NPD members called upon to give testimony against the party, and specifically to provide evidence that the NPD was seeking to overturn German democracy, were paid informants. Germany's Constitutional Court was forced to throw out the government's case against the NPD.

The state may yet again try to ban the NPD, although the public pressure to do so has receded in the past several years as the party has stumbled. Despite signing a "pact for Germany" in 2004 with the DVU in which the two parties agreed not to compete against one another, the NPD

---

[18] This point emerged in dozens of interviews with members of the German Bundestag.

won only 1.6% of the vote in the 2005 Bundestag elections. Although this total was four times larger than the party's 2002 performance, it was clearly a disappointment. The newly formed Left Party (Die Linke), a conglomeration of the former Communist Party (the PDS) and Oskar Lafontaine's left-wing breakaway faction of the SPD, appealed to many of the same voters as the NPD. Although on the other end of the political spectrum, the Left Party mobilized discontented voters who blamed both globalization and the political elite for their problems, were nostalgic for the DDR, and held ethnocentric attitudes (Rensmann 2006: 84).

Once again, then, the future of the NPD is unclear. On the one hand, the party draws strength from a right-wing extremist subculture that is unlikely to dissipate anytime soon. Yet the party's reliance on this group for mobilization means that any moderates within the party (of which there are very few) will be unable to move it farther away from an extremist program that still limits its appeal among voters. It also faces competition from the Left Party for the so-called losers of modernization, globalization, and German unification. Moreover, criminal behavior may destroy the party from within. The arrest of the party's treasurer, Erwin Kemma, in February 2008 on the charge of embezzling nearly $1 million precipitated the NPD's largest crisis in a decade.[19] The affair not only left the party nearly bankrupt, but also touched off a leadership struggle that continued throughout 2009 and early 2010. The party struggled mightily during the elections of 2009, winning only 1.5% of the vote nationally and failing to surmount the 5% threshold in any state aside from its stronghold in Saxony. Even there, however, it won only 5.6% of the vote, down from 9.2% in 2004. Thus, while the NPD will probably continue to serve as a focal point for Germany's extreme right subculture, the most successful radical right party in Germany's history is still nothing more than a political irritant. The situation is very different in contemporary Italy.

Italy

The Italian Social Movement

Although the Second Italian Republic was founded on an antifascist consensus, the personal and ideological remnants of the old regime survived the immediate postwar period and, only several years after their defeat, were contesting elections and entering into limited alliances with the

[19] *Der Spiegel*, no. 25, 2008.

Christian Democrats. Former fascists emerged from a period of internment, hiding, and clandestine activity after the granting of a general amnesty on June 2, 1946. The amnesty marked the end of the postwar purge (*epurazione*), which, as in other European states, proved to be a failure. Given the massive number of fascists – membership was obligatory for civil servants – a thorough housecleaning was bound to be difficult; a judiciary composed of former fascists made it impossible. For example, a leading fascist such as Paolo Orano, Mussolini's chief of staff during the March on Rome and later a member of the Fascist Grand Council, was acquitted because the court could not find a "causal link" between his actions and the destruction of democracy (Ginsborg 1990: 92). At the same time that fascist leaders were escaping punishment, the purges concentrated on the fascist rank and file. The first movement to capitalize on this discontent was the Front dell'Uomo Qualunque (the Common Man's Front), led by Guglielmo Giannini and funded in part by former fascists (Ginsborg 1990: 92). First a newspaper and later a political party, the Uomo Qualunque (UQ) attacked antifascism and the legitimacy of the power holders in general. Giannini's UQ won 5.3% of the vote in the 1946 elections for the Constituent Assembly. It did even better in local elections four months later, winning 20.7% in Rome, 19.7% in Naples, 24.5% in Palermo, and 46% in Bari (Chiarini 1995: 24).

The end of the purges, the success of the UQ, and the onset of the Cold War (which meant that communists were suddenly viewed as more dangerous than former fascists) convinced a group of fascist veterans to create their own political party and thereby avoid having to rely on the mercurial Giannini. The Italian Social Movement was thus founded on December 26, 1946, and contested its first election, for Rome's city council, in October 1947. In 1948, the MSI won 2.2% of the vote in the parliamentary elections. The fact that nearly 70% of the party's vote and all of its six parliamentarians came from the south led to a shift in the balance of power between the two principal factions of the party. The first faction, led by Giorgio Almirante, was concentrated in the north and identified with the radical, utopian, and socialistic strand of fascism that predominated before the consolidation of Mussolinis rule and again during Salò.[20] The second faction was more moderate and represented the authoritarian, clerical, and traditionalist tendencies of the fascist regime and the preferences of the southern notables (De Felice 1969; Ignazi

---

[20] Salò is the common term for the Italian Socialist Republic, the Nazi puppet state that existed in northern Italy from 1943 to 1945.

2003: 36–37). The 1948 elections demonstrated the electoral hegemony of the second faction, and Almirante lost a power struggle with Alfredo De Marsanich.

Although the extremist faction would persist and Almirante himself would return to head the party in 1969, the MSI's electoral bastion would remain Rome and the south (Ignazi 1998: 366). There are several compelling reasons for this. As Ginsborg (1990: 144) notes, many MSI voters lived in places like Flaminio, a quarter of Rome that had benefited from large construction projects under fascism and had been employed by the old regime. Those who equated fascism with modernization were not ill-disposed toward a party of fascist nostalgists. Neither of the two major subcultures that dominated postwar Italian politics, the Catholic and the Communist, had penetrated southern society, leaving the MSI with political space (Chiarini 1995: 24). Furthermore, antifascism and the partisan struggle had been concentrated in the north. In the south, antifascist prejudice was muted and "in vast sectors of the electorate it was practically nonexistent" (Carioti 1996: 60). Finally, the MSI's initial strength in the south allowed it to develop clientelistic networks there that would enable it to consolidate itself in politics and society to an extent that was impossible in the north.

The extremist (Almirante) faction of the MSI was initially opposed to seeking alliances with other political parties, fearing that doing so would dilute the party's ideology and identity (Chiarini 1995: 27). This changed when De Marsanich took over and embarked on a strategy of democratic legitimation through cooperation with the Christian Democrats (DC) in particular, as well as with smaller conservative parties like that of the Monarchists that were not insignificant in the south. The MSI did form coalitions with the latter, allowing it to govern in such southern cities as Naples, Bari, and Catania in the early 1950s. Yet for this policy of cooperation to succeed, the MSI needed the DC to deviate from its official position of unqualified antifascism. It proved willing to do this at the local level, and in 1952 the MSI and DC were part of a joint anticommunist list for municipal elections in Rome. At several points in the 1950s, the DC government relied on the votes of the MSI. In 1960, the DC government *required* the support of the MSI to take office, marking the first time in postwar Europe that a government had come to power thanks to the far right (Ignazi 2003). But the very success of the MSI's strategy produced a more repressive political environment for it. To thank the MSI for its votes, the DC government under Fernando Tambroni allowed the MSI to hold its national congress of 1960 in Genoa. The city had been a center of antifascist resistance, and the MSI's planned congress provoked leftist parties and activists to take to the streets. Rioting soon spread from Genoa to other cities, leading to several deaths, the banning of the party congress, and the fall of Tambroni's government. The DC's maneuvers had violated Italy's antifascist consensus, and the party adopted a strategy of marginalization toward the far right for the next several decades.

The failure of the MSI's integration strategy sparked a decade of inner-party turmoil and a decline in its share of the vote. Extremists abandoned the electoral road to power and embarked on a "strategy of tension" (*strategia della tensione*) that would result in a decade of political violence known as the "years of lead" (*anni di piombo*). The extraparliamentary right sought to convince the public that a left-wing takeover was imminent and thereby provoke right-wing elements into suspending democracy and installing authoritarian rule. Following the massive student protests and labor strikes that crippled northern Italy during the "hot autumn" of 1969, this scenario was not as fanciful as it appears to be in hindsight.

The spike in political violence created both a challenge and an opportunity for the MSI. The challenge was to maintain its hegemony over the far right spectrum and prevent its supporters from defecting to the extraparliamentary right, while the opportunity came in the form of an Italian public that was suddenly sympathetic with the MSI's traditional emphasis on law and order. When Almirante returned to lead the MSI in 1969, he developed a "two-pronged strategy" (*strategia del doppio binario*) to address this situation. On the one hand, Almirante reached out to other rightist forces and tried to make the party attractive to conservatives who had lost confidence in the ability of the DC to combat the leftist threat. To this end, the MSI merged with the Monarchist Party under the new name Destra Nazionale (National Right) and attracted a number of respectable notables to stand for office (Chiarini 1995: 33). On the other hand, Almirante tried to reclaim defectors to the extraparliamentary right by supporting violent actions against left-wing opponents. The strategy appeared to work in 1972, when the Destra Nazionale captured 8.7% of the vote and inspired imitators across Europe, most notably, as we have seen, in France. But as Ignazi (2003: 39) points out, Almirante's "two-track strategy" was based on a contradiction: the party tried to present a respectable face to its potential voters while encouraging radicalism.

Put another way, Almirante tried to attract both moderates and extremists to the party. As we have seen in other cases, this proved to be a volatile mixture. As the death toll from the "lead years" mounted, conservatives who may have voted for the Destra Nazionale rejected terrorism and withdrew their support. The DC also stepped up its attacks on the MSI and blamed it for the rising tide of violence. In the 1976 parliamentary elections, the Destra Nazionale won only 6.1%, which led to a split from the moderate faction that sought respectability above all else. This group formed the short-lived National Democracy Party, which collapsed after winning only 0.6% in the 1979 national elections.

By the early 1980s, the MSI had distanced itself from extraparliamentary right-wing extremism and tried to position itself as a party of protest against the "partocracy" that it claimed was strangling Italy (Ignazi 2003: 41). It underwent a number of strategic shifts over the next decade, including an attempt by Pino Rauti in the early 1990s to turn the MSI into an antiracist party. Rauti had ousted the young Gianfranco Fini, who an ailing Almirante had chosen to succeed him in 1987, from the position of party secretary in 1990 after Fini appeared unable to reverse the MSI's electoral decline. Yet Rauti's attempts at ideological renewal proved wildly unpopular, and Fini was able to reclaim the party leadership in 1991.

The 1980s also witnessed the first overt flirtations with the MSI by mainstream political parties since the fall of the Tambroni government. Socialist Prime Minister Bettino Craxi, following the lead of Bruno Kreisky and François Mitterrand, calculated that an invigorated extreme right would steal votes from his primary competitor (the DC) and therefore tried to improve the MSI's image. Craxi declared during a parliamentary debate that he would treat every parliamentary group equally, and shortly thereafter MSI leaders were invited to appear in public with antifascists (Ignazi 2003: 41). The MSI also began to be treated like any other political party in parliamentary committees (Chiarini 1995: 35). While this did not mean that the MSI was suddenly seen as a potential coalition partner, the diminution of hostility toward the far right in the 1980s paved the way for Berlusconi's alliance with it a decade later.

What was the state of the MSI's party organization on the eve of the *mani pulite* investigations?[21] The answer, with minor exceptions, is very much the same as it had been since the early 1950s when the leadership adopted a mass-party model. Although reliable figures are lacking, the MSI clearly had the largest membership of any far right party in

---

[21] The *mani pulite* (clean hands) investigations of the early 1990s were judicial investigations into political corruption that led to the collapse of the Italian party system.

Western Europe. It had local sections (*sezioni*) across the country and a range of auxiliary organizations that helped maintain a political subculture that proved as tenacious as the larger Communist and Catholic ones (Tarchi 1997: 402). The party elite reached their positions after years of activity within the party and, in most cases after the 1960s, in far right youth organizations. They were thus highly experienced, in addition to being well-educated. Although factional divisions existed, the MSI possessed a high degree of internal coherence. This was not surprising for a party whose defining features were faith in fascism and defense of the old regime. Drawing from the seminal works of Ignazi (1989; 1998) and Tarchi (1997), I shall expand on some of these points here.

The only membership figures that exist for the MSI are those provided by the party, beginning in 1960. This "official figure" ranged between about 160,000 and 240,000 from 1960 to 1993. These numbers are probably twice as high as the actual figure (Bardi and Morlino 1992), but there is no way of knowing for sure. Like parties elsewhere, the MSI has an interest in inflating its membership figures to demonstrate its strength. Some of its claims bordered on the ridiculous. For example, De Marsanich's contention that the party had 500,000 members in 1950 seems fanciful considering that 30,000 was a reasonable estimate of party membership in 1947 (Ignazi 1989: 291). The MSI's "official data" on the number of local sections – it claimed between 3,000 and 4,000 for every year since 1950 – are unfortunately no more reliable than those for party membership. Yet even if the MSI's own figures on membership and local sections are reduced by half, they would still dwarf those of any other extreme right party during the postwar period, with the exception of the Austrian Freedom Party. As previously noted, the MSI had a natural constituency of fascist sympathizers who numbered in the tens of thousands. During the first half of the 1950s, the MSI certainly succeeded in increasing its membership and founding local sections across the country (Ignazi 1989: 292), particularly in the Mezzogiorno (the south). Since the children of MSI members tended to share the views of their parents, the MSI's reservoir of recruitment did not dry up after it had tapped all those with personal memories of the fascist regime.

While the MSI sought to create a mass membership, it balanced this goal with the maintenance of internal cohesion. A potential member required the signatures of two current members to fill out the application form, which was then screened first by the secretary of the local section and then by the federation (Ignazi 1998: 161). Even if, as Tarchi argues

(1997: 165–166), recruitment was more open than the formal rules suggest, it was still a controlled process. The party used two primary criteria contained in the party statutes – "indignity" and "incompatibility" – to disqualify potential recruits and to expel or control dissident members (Ignazi 1998: 161).

Although the data are thin, we know more about the MSI's party elite than we do about the rank and file. The first, unsurprising, characteristic is the elite's continuity with the old regime. Five of the seven members of parliament (MPs) elected in 1948 had a clear fascist past (Ignazi 1998: 158). One-third of the twenty-seven MPs elected in 1953 had been members of the fascist government, and practically every one had a fascist past of some sort (Ignazi 1989: 315). As the party built its organization, it began to recruit its leaders and candidates for office internally. Except for the early 1950s, when the party recruited fascist notables who were not party members to stand for office, and the 1970s, when the Destra Nazionale included conservative notables on its electoral lists to appeal beyond the MSI's traditional electorate, long-standing service within the party was a requirement to run for elected office or reach the upper echelons of the party hierarchy. Ignazi (1989: 344) found that one-third of MSI politicians waited at least twenty years before gaining a seat on an elected assembly.

The MSI cadre also appears to be relatively well educated. A survey conducted at the MSI's 1979 party congress ($n = 214$) revealed that 62.6% had graduated from university (Ignazi 1989: 336). A similar survey of educational background and professions was conducted at the MSI party congress in 1989, and the results, reported in Table 6.1, were broadly consistent with those from 1979 (Ignazi 1989: 336–337).

The only other analysis of the professional background of the MSI cadre, reported in Tarchi (1997: 264), was conducted by the party itself and published in the party newspaper, *Secolo d'Italia*, on January 22, 1977. There are data for 280 of the 334 members of the Comitato Centrale. Of these, 76 (27%) were lawyers, 29 (10%) were directors or functionaries at state or parastatal institutions, 28 (10%) were teachers, and 29 (10%) were medical or university students. Verzichelli's (1996) analysis of the professional background of the 105 Alleanza Nazionale (the successor to the MSI) deputies elected to parliament in 1994 (see Table 6.2) is consistent with previous findings. Nearly one-quarter of the AN deputies were lawyers, more than one-fifth were professional politicians, and nearly one-tenth were teachers.

TABLE 6.1. *Occupations of Delegates to the 1989 Italian Social Movement Party Congress*

Occupation	Percentage of MSI Delegates ($n = 210$)
White-collar workers/teachers	29.9
Liberal professionals	28.5
Other workers	12.8
Retired	9.5
Students	7.6
Managers/executives	7.6
Unemployed	5.2
Other	0.6

TABLE 6.2. *Occupations of Alleanza Nazionale Deputies*

Occupation	AN Deputies, %	Total Deputies, %
Lawyers	22.9	10.3
Professional politicians	21.0	16.8
Other professionals	19.0	16.8
Teachers	9.5	10.5
Civil servants	7.6	5.1
Other	4.8	7.2
Craft merchants	3.8	6.4
Professional union leaders	3.8	3.0
Entrepreneurs	2.9	4.3
Public administrators	2.9	5.4
Business managers	1.0	3.5
Laborers	1.0	1.6
University professors	0.0	10.1

A final important characteristic of the AN and the MSI are their high levels of professionalism. Verzichelli (1996) found that the AN's parliamentary group contained the lowest percentage of amateurs (11.4%) of any party, with the exception of the heirs to the Italian Communist Party (PCI).[22] The 1994 parliament contained a higher percentage of freshmen deputies than any other in the postwar period, with the exception of the one immediately following the war in 1946 (Verzichelli 1996: 116). In a parliament in which 35% of the representatives were amateurs, the professionalism of the AN would prove to be a distinct advantage.

[22] Verzichelli (1996) defines "amateurs" as "those who have never held, before their election to Parliament, local elective office or party duties at least at the regional level."

The Lega Nord

As of 1994, the Lega Nord was Italy's best-organized political party (Bull and Gilbert 2001: 32). To be sure, the collapse of the Italian party system had eliminated the usual contenders for this title, and most of the new parties – including Forza Italia – had been thrown together to contest the 1994 parliamentary elections. Yet the disarray of its competitors should not detract from the LN's achievement in building a party machine that, as several scholars have argued, depended on a large, highly motivated base (Ruzza and Schmidtke 1993; Bull and Gilbert 2001). As Cachafeiro (2002: 141) correctly notes, most analyses of the LN either do not consider its organizational features or simply treat them as reflecting the will of Umberto Bossi. There is no doubt that Bossi was keenly attuned to organizational issues and created a degree of party centralization that has often been likened to the "democratic centralism" of Stalinist parties. If his autobiography (Bossi 1992) is to be believed, Bossi was obsessed with party organization "even at a time when the entire active membership of the movement could have met in his new partner's one bedroom flat" (Bull and Gilbert 2001: 12). The following paragraphs will demonstrate how Bossi's attention to organization helped prevent the LN from becoming a flash party. Although the preexisting networks of linguistic enthusiasts, amateur historians, and regional leagues provided some resources for radical right party building, the LN started out building from close to scratch. Bossi's rigid control of recruitment and mobility within the organization dampened tendencies toward factionalism and defection. Yet given the overwhelming lack of political experience of LN politicians and activists, the newness of the party, and the weak ties of many LN representatives to it, Bossi proved incapable of avoiding such problems entirely.

What accounts for the appearance of this novel political force? A full answer to this question would require attention to the following four factors: Italy's incomplete nation building, which left regional identities strong and intact (Gold 2003); the deepening of the historical cleavage between north and south (Tambini 2001); growing disenchantment with the Italian partocracy, particularly once the Christian Democrats and Communists were unable to deliver the patronage they had in the past (Kitschelt 1995); and the impact of economic globalization on the "third Italy" (Bull 1993; Bull and Gilbert 2001). Significant as these forces were, it is nevertheless possible to offer a more prosaic story of the LN's origins, which Bossi once referred to as the "primordial chaos" from which his movement developed (Biorcio 1997: 36).

The LN was an amalgamation of regional leagues, also referred to as autonomous leagues, which emerged in the 1970s. The first leagues appeared much earlier in the so-called special regions that, by virtue of the presence of linguistic minorities, enjoyed more autonomy than the "ordinary" regions (Cachafeiro 2002: 45–63). The most significant of these was the Union Valdotaîne, led by Bruno Salvadori, which claimed to represent the interests of French speakers in the small region of the Aosta valley. In 1979, several members of the Società Filologica Veneta, a group that valorized the culture, history, and dialect of Venice, founded the Liga Veneta (Biorcio 1997: 43). This marked the first time an "ordinary" region produced its own league; over the course of the 1980s, similar leagues would emerge in Piedmont, Liguria, Emilia-Romagna, Tuscany, and Lombardy. Like the Liga Veneta, they drew their initial members from regional linguistic and historical societies, as well as from friendship and family networks (Tambini 2001: 120). Their political program amounted to "local chauvinism," as they demanded preferential treatment for the regional group in public housing, health care, education, and jobs (Bull and Gilbert 2001: 10). They also engaged in polemics against southern Italians, foreshadowing the discourse of the LN (Biorcio 1997: 45). The Liga Veneta, led by Franco Rochetta, appeared to be the strongest of the leagues in the early 1980s, winning 4.3% of the vote in the Veneto in the 1983 elections and sending one deputy, Achille Tramarin, and one senator, Graziano Girardi, to parliament.

But it was the Lombard League, rather than the Liga Veneta, that would enjoy a far larger electoral breakthrough in the late 1980s and, by virtue of its strength, amalgamate the other regional leagues into an expanded version of itself. The founder of the Lombard League was Umberto Bossi, whose career in politics began with, according to LN party lore, a chance meeting with Salvadori in 1979. Born into a working-class family in Varese, Bossi had worked alternatively as a laborer, math tutor, and guitarist before beginning his medical studies in his late twenties. Salvadori apparently convinced Bossi to devote himself to the cause of Lombard autonomy, which he did by founding a small newspaper (*Nord Ovest*) and a political movement, the North-West Lombardy Union for Autonomy (UNOLPA). He also agreed to build up the Union Valdotaîne's support in Varese and incurred a debt of 20 million lira in the process. Following Salvadori's death in a car crash in 1980, Bossi became liable for the entire sum. He was unable to finish his medical studies and his marriage collapsed (Bull and Gilbert 2001: 12).

Perhaps precisely because the costs of entering politics were already so high, Bossi threw himself into the autonomist cause. The UNOLPA was replaced by the Lega Lombarda (LL) in 1982. Thanks to tireless mobilization efforts described later, the LL succeeded in winning 3% of the vote in Lombardy in the 1987 elections, which translated into one seat each in the Chamber and the Senate. Bossi took the latter seat, and with it the media's ironic designation Il Senatúr (the Senator). The elections for the European Parliament in 1989 marked the LL's true electoral breakthrough, however, as the LL gained 8.1% in Lombardy and became the fourth-largest party in the region (Betz 1998a: 46). It followed up on this score with 19% in the 1990 regional elections. The electoral superiority of the LL relative to the other regional leagues allowed Bossi to unite them into a single league. The Lega Nord (Northern League) was ratified at its first party congress in 1991. Although the LN preserved its federalist origins by dividing the movement into twelve regions (or "nations"), the LL extended its own organizational structure to the new party, and power remained concentrated in the hands of Bossi and his small band of *fedelissimi* (loyalists).

Why was it the LL, rather than the initially more successful Liga Veneta or Piedmont Leagues, that became an electoral force and united the other leagues around itself? The simple answer is that both of the LL's possible challengers were torn apart by internal squabbles. Dissidents from the Union Piemonteisa formed their own party, the Piedmont Autonomista, to contest the 1987 elections. A similar leadership struggle erupted in the LV when Tramarin refused to resign as the party's general secretary after winning elective office in 1983, as the party statutes demanded. The dispute between the Tramarin and Rochetta factions ended in a court decision that granted the latter use of the party name and symbols. Tramarin responded by founding the Serenissima Liga Veneta in 1985, while Ettore Beggiato founded the Union del Popolo Veneto in 1987. These fissures were widely reported in the local media and damaged the reputation of the belligerents and litigants (Cachafeiro 2002: 72). Moreover, the doubling of the challengers for the already small constituency of the leagues in Piedmont and the Veneto prevented any of them from winning parliamentary representation.

Bossi undoubtedly absorbed these lessons. As noted earlier, he was obsessed with organization even when his party, like the other leagues, consisted of little more than a group of friends. He conducted a "purge" of the LL's founding members in 1986 to prevent challenges to his authority (Vimercati 1990: 32–33). In the same year, Bossi instituted perhaps his most important organizational innovation by introducing a distinction between *soci ordinari* (ordinary members) and *soci militanti* (supporters). The nomenclature is confusing, for it is the ordinary members who possess the right to vote in internal party matters, to stand for elective office, and to become leaders of local sections. There were various modifications to the process of becoming an ordinary member over the course of the LL's, and later the LN's, history, but the following describes the situation as of 2001:

All would-be members have to begin as 'Supporters' and have to prove their worth to the movement during a six-month trial period. At the end of the period, the 'Supporter' may present his or her request for promotion to the municipal section of the party. Rather like the bans before a marriage, this application is openly exhibited for 20 days in order to give objectors time to formulate their doubts. The leaders of the municipal section then forward a report on the individual to the provincial party leadership, which makes a final decision. No 'Supporter' can be made an 'ordinary militant' in the month preceding a provincial, national, or federal Congress.... 'Ordinary Militants' may also be degraded to the status of 'Supporter' for a full year if, in the view of the local section management committee, their political activity has been insufficiently zealous. (Bull and Gilbert 2001: 234)

The goals of such rules are clear: to prevent infiltration of the movement and create an inner-party elite loyal to Bossi, who, in practice, controlled the selection of the *soci ordinari*. A secondary, but important objective was to create a common party culture by introducing a strong element of socialization into the recruitment process. It is important to stress that Bossi devised these mechanisms before the LL achieved even its modest electoral breakthrough in 1987. The party was therefore somewhat prepared for the flood of new members that followed its electoral victories in the late 1980s and early 1990s. According to the party's own statistics, the LL counted 16,912 members in 1991 and 19,951 in 1992. This was massive growth for a party that probably counted only a few hundred members in 1987. By 1993, the LN had grown to 43,308 members, 26,334 of whom were from Lombardy. The party also first reported the breakdown of party members by type in 1993: 6,093 ordinary members and 37,215 supporters. In 1994, total membership numbered 44,186, with 9,090 ordinary members and 35,096 supporters. These figures, reported by Cachafeiro (2002: 147), indicate two important trends: (1) that there were between five and six times as many supporters as ordinary members during the party's period of growth and (2) that, judging from the promotion to ordinary member of only about 3,000 of the possible 37,215 supporters, the party apparatus actively controlled inner-party mobility.

There can be little doubt that the LL's and LN's electoral success led to a surge in members. But it is also important to note that Bossi devoted enormous energy to recruitment. During the early days of the party, Bossi and his inner core spoke at every opportunity to "semi-deserted school halls and social clubs" (Gilbert 1995: 51). These efforts were probably not nearly as effective as the LL's graffiti actions, which Bossi participated in and which many members of the Lega remember as their introduction to the movement's politics (Biorcio 1997: 212). As the movement gained momentum in the late 1980s, the Lega began to recruit in nonpolitical venues such as bowling halls, soccer games, and bars (Diamanti 1993: 83; Ruzza and Schmidtke 1993: 11; Tambini 2001: 40).

Who were these new recruits? Gilbert (1995: 54) provides the following description of the median Lega politician: "Local league candidates tended to be people of no particular academic or social distinction – bar room philosophers – who were nevertheless well-known in their communities and who could count on a considerable personal vote." They were, in short, unlikely to be the types of marginal figures who populated parties like the Front National in Belgium, Center Democrats in the Netherlands, or the Sweden Democrats. According to an internal study, league activists were also predominantly drawn from the independent middle class (Lucchini 1992: 5). An analysis of LN members in the province of Como revealed that 38% were artisans, entrepreneurs, or liberal professionals, 15% worked in commerce, 15% were white-collar workers, 7% were students, 5% were pensioners, and 4% worked in the public sector. The only category that was clearly blue collar was that of wage earners, which was 15% of the total (Bull and Gilbert 2001: 70).

The data from Como are consistent with those from Roberto Biorcio's independent study of party members at the LN's third annual congress in February 1997 (1997: 224). The respondents filled out a questionnaire in which they were asked about their most important political concerns, their trust in different political institutions, and their political and religious orientations. More important for our purposes are Biorcio's division of the members between simple militants and party cadre (presumably equivalent to the distinction between militants and ordinary members) and the socioeconomic profiles of each category. The data presented in Table 6.3 confirm that the socioeconomic composition of the LN party cadre (but, significantly, not of LN voters) is thus very different from that of parties like the Sweden Democrats and the Belgian Front National, which, as we saw in Chapter 2, contain a high percentage of manual workers, retirees, and unemployed.

TABLE 6.3. *Occupations of Lega Nord Militants, Cadre, and Voters*

Profession	Militants, % (n = 187)	Cadre, % (n = 107)	Voters, % (n = 552)
Entrepreneurs, executives, managers, or liberal professionals	35.1	52.4	2.5
Office workers	21.6	13.1	14.4
Merchants or artisans	18.9	16.9	7.4
Retired	7.6	2.8	16.1
Blue-collar workers	7.0	3.7	28.2
Other	3.2	4.7	1.1
Students	3.2	5.6	9.1
Farmers	1.6	0.0	0.2
Housewives	1.1	0.0	18.5
Unemployed	0.5	0.9	2.5

The six-month training period required to become an ordinary party member, coupled with the threat of demotion from ordinary party member to supporter for lack of commitment, was designed to create loyalty to a new political organization that lacked deep roots in Italian society. Party rituals and iconography, in addition to raising money and attracting media attention, served a similar goal. The LN produced its own watches, ties, pins, flags, coins, and paper currency. The party wrote its own anthem and created ceremonies in which new members swore their allegiance to the movement (Ruzza and Schmidtke 1993: 11). Among the LN's many party events, the most significant are certainly the rallies at the tiny northern town of Pontida. This was the site where the members of the Lombard League had sworn to fight the Holy Roman Empire in the twelfth century, and LN politicians reaffirm their loyalty to the movement by taking a similar oath. The first rally at Pontida, in 1990, was attended by only about five hundred members, according to the League. But by the early 1990s, the daily *Corriere della Sera* was reporting attendance of about ten thousand. As the following participant observation suggests, Pontida is very similar to the Front National's Fête des Bleu–Blanc–Rouge:

Pontida is a feast of flags, symbols, customs, food, and singing. One has the opportunity to listen to autonomist hip-hop and rap in the local dialects, participate in raffles and eat *panini*. Posters covered with the phrase 'Bossi, you are the Mike Tyson of the North' and the flags of Lega Nord surrounded the stage. It is a public rally and a public feast in the traditional sense and it recalls the traditional feasts organised by the Communist party. (Cachafeiro 2002: 157)

In sum, both the LN and the MSI possessed large organizations before the collapse of the Italian party system in the early 1990s. Yet both were still viewed as perpetual outsiders: Bossi, as his nickname, Il Senatúr, implied, was viewed with derision, while the MSI was still considered beyond the political pale. That all changed in 1993.

Creating Legitimacy

Silvio Berlusconi, the media tycoon who formed his own party, Forza Italia (Go Italy), overturned the MSI's status as a pariah party within a matter of months. His first important action was to express support for Gianfranco Fini, the ambitious young leader of the MSI, who was a candidate for the mayor of Rome in November 1993. Berlusconi's endorsement, "If I were in Rome I would certainly vote for Fini," made headlines across Italy.[23] Although Fini did not win the elections, he placed a strong second, winning 47% of the vote. Alessandra Mussolini, the granddaughter of the Duce, also posted a remarkable showing, winning 43% in the second round of the municipal elections in Naples. Although she too failed to win the mayor's office, she described the results as "a victory for my family, for my grandfather."[24]

The next step in the so-called customs clearance (*Sdoganamento*) of the MSI occurred when Berlusconi entered into an electoral coalition with Fini's newly founded Alleanza Nazionale. After his success in Rome, Fini sought to revamp the public's perception of the extreme right and succeeded in convincing party delegates to dissolve the MSI in favor of the AN, which Fini described as "a common home of all the right." The merger eventually occurred at the party congress in Fiuggi in 1995 (Bull and Newell 1995). Although interviews with the party rank and file suggest that the neofascists had changed in name only, Berlusconi announced that he was forming an electoral alliance (the Freedom Alliance) with both the AN and Umberto Bossi's Northern League to contest the 1994 parliamentary elections.

Berlusconi's near monopoly of Italian private television, which allowed him to "swamp the television screens with endless political commercials," was another critical factor in legitimating the AN (Statham 1996: 96). Fini and Bossi were presented as legitimate politicians like any other, and their electoral alliances with Berlusconi brought them favorable news coverage at virtually no cost. In the event, the AN received 13.5% of the

[23] *La Republica*, November 24, 1993.
[24] *Economist*, November 27, 1993.

vote in the 1994 elections, nearly tripling its total from two years earlier and earning five places in Berlusconi's cabinet.

The AN's achievement of political respectability within only a few years occurred without the party truly changing its attitudes toward the past. Fini's 1994 description of Mussolini as the "greatest statesman of the 20th century" sparked a minor uproar from the left, but it did not come close to disqualifying him from public office. Nor did an interview with the newspaper *La Stampa*, in which Fini said that "there are periods in which liberty is not the most important value. Fascism suppressed liberty of association for the benefit of social progress."[25] Outright praise for fascism was also common among other AN politicians. One of Fini's allies in Milan, Ignazio La Russa, described Mussolini as the historical figure he most admired. Roberto Predolin, La Russa's running mate, reserved that distinction for the Romanian fascist Corneliu Codreanu.[26] Interviews with AN rank and file demonstrate that historical apologia and revisionism are widespread.[27]

In marked contrast to the situation in Germany, historical memory in Italy did not preclude a far right party, and indeed a party that traced its roots directly to fascism, from forming coalitions and coming to power in Italy. This newfound permissiveness must be understood in the context of a general reevaluation of, and even a certain nostalgia for, the fascist era in Italian politics and society since the late 1980s. As Paul Ginsborg notes, the Italian left also played a role in allowing this historical revisionism by speaking the language of "national reconciliation" and letting "bygones be bygones." Francisco Rutelli, the left-of-center mayor of Rome, even proposed naming a square after Giuseppe Bottai, a supposedly liberal fascist leader (Ginsborg 2004: 155). In 1996, Luciano Violante, a former Communist and president of the Chamber of Deputies, used his inaugural address to commend the "men and women of Salò" and urged Italians to put the past behind them (Gallagher 2000: 81). Against this backdrop of revisionism, Berlusconi's claims in 2003 that Mussolini had "never killed anyone" and "used to send people on vacation in internal exile" becomes more understandable.[28] And with Alessandra Mussolini regularly praising her grandfather on the Italian talk-show circuit, it is little wonder that Berlusconi's remark did not provoke the political fallout that a similar one in France or Germany would have engendered.

[25] Quoted in Gallagher (2000: 76).
[26] Gallagher (2000: 73).
[27] Ignazi (2003).
[28] *International Herald Tribune*, October 29, 2003.

The Italian left, particularly in the early 1990s, also did not take as strident a position toward the MSI as one might have expected from the most vociferous defenders of the postwar antifascist consensus. Compared with that of their counterparts in Germany or even Austria, the Italian left's protest against the regeneration of the far right was muted. This behavior can be explained by the left's and the MSI's common position and interests in the fluid Italian party system. Both forces had a common interest in preventing the coalescence of a center party – such as the Christian Democratic Party – that would effectively marginalize both. "This explains why," James Newell (2000: 481) suggests, "the leadership of the two parties have gone out of their way, in political contests, to avoid the old battle cries of 'anticommunism' and 'antifascism.'" In the 1990s, both had an interest in seeing the other succeed.

The first attempt at governing with Berlusconi, short as it was, affected his two coalition partners very differently. The MSI/AN undoubtedly profited from the experience. Fini's national popularity allowed him to sanitize his party without losing control of it. The MSI/AN acted like a reliable party and appeared moderate compared with its coalition partners. For the LN, on the other hand, the alliance with Berlusconi would nearly destroy the party. In the end, Bossi was forced to bring down the government to save his movement. To resuscitate it, Il Senatúr embarked on a wild theatrical scheme that involved founding the virtual state of "Padania." This move, part of a general radicalization, ultimately saved the Lega from extinction but at the same time dramatically limited its electoral appeal. To a large extent, these divergent trajectories following Berlusconi's first electoral alliance were attributable to the internal state of the coalition partners. The MSI's half-century in opposition had produced a cohesive, professional, tightly organized party that was able to govern, if given the opportunity. Despite his attempts to limit infiltration by opportunists, limit dissent and factionalism, and foster loyalty to the movement through symbolism, Bossi could not reproduce within a couple of years the internal discipline that the MSI had created over several decades.

Let us begin with the Lega. Bossi's decision to enter into an electoral alliance with Berlusconi was unpopular with the rank and file from the start. This opposition stemmed not only from Berlusconi's alliance with the MSI, a party whose core values could hardly have been farther from the LN's, but also from his association with the disgraced Bettino Craxi (Bull and Gilbert 2001: 32). Furthermore, many LN activists could not understand why a party advocating regional independence that had railed against Roma Ladrona (Thieving Rome) was now becoming a part of the hated national government. Bossi, it appears, was worried that Forza Italia would wipe out the LN under the new electoral system, in which 75% of the seats were contested using first-past-the-post and 25% under proportional representation (Bossi 1996: 6). In retrospect, Bossi should have been more concerned about Forza Italia wiping out the LN's 117-member group in parliament. The problem, as Bull and Gilbert (2001: 34–35) note, was that many of the LN parliamentarians had been elected on Berlusconi's coattails:

> Long used to running the Lega as a personal fief, [Bossi] now had to face the task of holding together a movement whose leadership élite no longer needed to look to him alone for advancement. He could no longer lay down the law within the movement without risking the defection of large numbers of senior figures to Forza Italia. A 'ministerialist' party swiftly formed within the Lega, contrasting the 'independentists', and Bossi was forced to balance on both of these horses together.

This balancing act lasted less than nine months. When Bossi engineered a no-confidence vote against the government, nearly one-quarter of LN members of parliament refused to follow the party line. Although Berlusconi ended up resigning (there were enough votes from the LN and the opposition to topple the government), Bossi's party was devastated. Fifty-nine of the LN's 117 parliamentarians defected over the course of 1994, and many of them joined Forza Italia (Cachafeiro 2002: 152). Party membership plunged from a total of 44,186 in 1994 to 19,501 in 1995. The decrease was due entirely to a hemorrhaging of "supporters" (the number of ordinary members actually increased from 9,090 to 9,986) from 35,096 to 9,515 (Cachafeiro 2002: 147). The LN seemed destined to suffer the fate of flash parties like New Democracy and the List Pim Fortuyn.

Bossi calculated that the LN needed to differentiate itself even more strongly from Forza Italia to survive. Furthermore, his earlier unpopular decision to enter into a national coalition government made it necessary for him to reestablish his secessionist credentials. The absurdity of Padania must be understood in this context. In 1995, he created the "Parliament of the North," which was composed of LN elected officials and charged with writing a constitution for the new independent state in the north. The fact that a Padanian identity was Bossi's invention did not stop the league from creating Padanian traditions and claiming a collective historical memory on behalf of Padanians (Tambini 2001). Although he was ridiculed for this attempt at instant nation building, Bossi's radicalization of the LN's long-standing secessionist demands helped the LN to win 10.1% in the 1996 parliamentary elections, a 25% increase over its 1994 performance. Bossi then pressed further: in September 1996 he announced the independence of Padania in an elaborate ceremony that drew several hundred thousand participants and journalists from around the world. Over the next several years, however, the Padanian project would lose steam and contribute to a number of high-profile defections and ejections of LN activists who considered the venture misguided. Yet such a result might have been one of Bossi's goals: according to Ilvo Diamanti (Bull 1993: 111), Bossi viewed Padania as a means to "close ranks and to re-take control of an organization and a mass membership that had become too diverse in character and contradictory in their views." This he accomplished, although the push toward secession alienated the LN from its traditional voting base of small business owners who saw little economic interest in Bossi's dreams, particularly after Italy had met the requirements for the European Monetary Union (Albertazzi and McDonnell 2005: 955). The European elections of 1999, in which the LN mustered only 4.5%, marked the end of the Padanian gambit.

As Bossi gradually dropped secessionism in favor of the more modest goal of devolution, he looked for additional ways of distinguishing his party from Berlusconi's. The transformation of the LN from a regional populist party that flirted with xenophobia to a radical right one dates from this period. Especially after 1998, the Lega built connections with other radical right parties abroad, including the Vlaams Blok, Front National, and Austrian Freedom Party, and took up the typical radical right themes of anti-immigration, islamophobia, homophobia, and opposition to the European Union (Scaliati 2006). The LN has since built up a record of public xenophobic statements whose virulence surpasses that of most of its counterparts. Bossi infamously suggested "blowing out of the water" boats carrying immigrants to Italy and referred to African immigrants pejoratively as "bingo-bongos."[29] The mayor of Treviso (LN) once said that "we ought to dress up immigrants like hares and go 'bang, bang, bang' with a rifle." And an LN councilman in Treviso said in a council session, "With immigrants, we should use the same system the SS used, punishing 10 of them for every slight against one of our citizens."[30]

The LN's participation in Berlusconi's second government (2001–2005) resuscitated a party in decline. As Albertazzi and McDonnell (2005)

[29] *Times*, April 16, 2008.
[30] *Guardian*, April 9, 2008.

convincingly argue, the LN's second spell in the House of Liberties coalition (CDL) was far more successful than its first. The same Bossi who had brought down Berlusconi in 1994 and repeatedly insulted him in public thereafter became the prime minister's loyal ally. At the same time, the LN's attacks on the other member of the CDL, the AN, allowed it to present itself as a party of opposition as well as of government and maintain its populist essence. Indeed, it appears that this strategy has resolved a long-standing tension within the LN between an anti-establishment rank and file and a party elite that seeks power and privilege, as it satisfies both. Not surprisingly, the LN has not experienced the same magnitude of splits and defections since joining the coalition in 2001. The party also weathered a period of almost two years during which Bossi recovered from a nearly fatal stroke, an achievement that probably would not have been possible a decade earlier. To quote Albertazzi and McDonnell (2005: 960), "Bossi has had 20 years to build up an inner circle of ... devotees and the likes of [Roberto] Maroni, [Roberto] Castelli, Giancarlo Giorgetti and Roberto Calderoli not only subscribe (at least publicly) to the maxim of 'the Lega is Bossi and Bossi is the Lega', but have also proved capable both of serving at the highest levels of government and guiding the party during Bossi's absence over the last year."

While the LN became radicalized, the AN moved in the opposite direction. The AN itself was formed to create distance between the party's fascist nostalgia and to rebrand the old MSI as "a common home of the right." But the change in the party's name did not produce a simultaneous change in the political culture of its members. Fini's positive evaluations of Mussolini and his unwillingness to condemn fascism in the mid-1990s were most likely designed to retain the support of the old guard as he moved the party toward the center. It was no accident that the five key speeches at the launch of the AN were delivered by moderates (Bull and Newell 1995: 78). When the faction around Paulo Rauti was unable to repudiate the fascist label and defected from the AN and formed the Fiamma Tricolore, it marked another important step in the party's search for respectability (Gallagher 2000: 78). Yet most of the old guard chose not to defect and to instead support Fini's course. Some found an admirable parallel between Fini's shift and the notorious opportunism of the Duce. Indeed, Alessandra Mussolini initially blessed Fini's strategy by noting that "if he had lived today ... my grandfather would have done what Fini is doing."[31]

---

[31] *Economist*, October 8, 1994.

Although the AN's first foray into government was to be short lived (Berlusconi's Freedom Alliance lasted only nine months), the party, and Fini in particular, profited enormously from the experience. By early 1995, public opinion polls showed that Fini had become the most popular politician in Italy, with the media regularly speculating whether he would soon replace Berlusconi as prime minister.[32] Compared with Bossi and Berlusconi, Fini appeared to be calm and competent. In contrast to the LN, the AN proved to be a reliable coalition partner and suffered from virtually no defections. In the 1996 elections, it improved upon its 1994 score with 15.7%. As the party went into opposition in 1996, many observers predicted that it would overtake Forza Italia as the largest formation on the right.

While this did not occur, the recovery of Forza Italia and the formation of the CDL in 2001 pushed the AN farther toward the center. Fini became foreign minister, a position that both signaled the respect the AN had won from the international community and required him to break even more with the party's fascist past. In November 2003, he visited Israel and denounced fascism as an era of "absolute evil" in Italian history.[33] On the sixtieth anniversary of the liberation of Auschwitz (January 27, 2005), Fini spoke of a "moral duty to transmit to future generations the memory of this atrocity which must never be repeated, in any form." He even noted that "there are some people in Italy who, either through ignorance or bad faith, tend to minimize saying that the 1938 [anti-Semitic] laws did not have an important and tragic role in the persecution and extermination of the Jews."[34] It was statements like these that led Alessandra Mussolini and other hard liners to bolt from the AN. Yet Fini silently welcomed the exit of these extremists, just as he had the defection of the faction surrounding Rauti following the dissolution of the MSI and founding of the AN at the Fiuggi congress in 1995. For a party seeking to position itself as center-right, the loss of the Duce's granddaughter was hardly a negative development. Although many of the rank and file, and certainly some elected officials, still view the fascist era positively, the leadership has effectively intervened to prevent them from airing these ideas publicly (Ignazi 2005: 347).

The AN has also sought to project a moderate image on immigration. Here it is important to note that anti-immigration was never part of the

---

[32] *Corriere della Sera*, February 27, 1995.
[33] Agenzia Nazionale Stampa Associata, November 24, 2003.
[34] Agenzia Nazionale Stampa Associata, January 27, 2005.

MSI's program (Veugelers and Chiarini 2002), meaning that Fini did not risk as big an internal row within the party as he did with his break from the fascist legacy; he has thus been free to adopt a variety of positions on the issue. For example, the Fini–Bossi immigration law of 2003 imposed tighter restrictions on new immigrants while simultaneously offering an amnesty to, and legalization for, 700,000 illegal immigrants, making it one of the largest amnesties of its kind (Pastore 2004; Albertazzi and McDonnell 2005: 962). In 2001, the AN recognized that, given the country's low birthrate and enormous pension obligations, immigration was "necessary for Italy's very survival" (Albertazzi and McDonnell 2005: 963). In 2003, Fini staked his most liberal position yet on immigration by proposing that legal immigrants (non-Italian citizens) be allowed to vote in local elections. Fini had thus steered the AN away from radical right positions before he stepped down as its leader to become president of the Italian Chamber of Deputies in 2008. In March 2009, the party officially dissolved itself and merged with Forza Italia to form the People of Freedom (PdL).

Conclusion

Although the AN no longer exists, it is nonetheless true that the ideological descendants of fascism, in addition to a virulently anti-immigrant regionalist party, have attained a degree of power and legitimacy in Italian politics that is unimaginable in contemporary Germany. This chapter has argued that this divergence is both the product of immediate postwar confrontations with fascism and ongoing debates about the fascist past. The German state succeeded in dividing and conquering the far right in the early postwar period, and the institutionalization of norms against radical right movements raised the costs of activism to unacceptable levels for most potential activists. We have seen how the predominance of extremists led to the collapse of each of the first three waves of the German far right. In eastern Germany, where these norms were not as well institutionalized, the National Democratic Party has found a more hospitable environment to build an organization. Yet even here, the behavior of extremists has threatened the tear the NPD apart once again. In Italy, despite the official antifascist consensus, the Italian Socialist Movement was allowed to persist and found a particularly permissive environment in the south. When Berlusconi announced that he would cooperate with a party that had yet to distance itself from fascism, the MSI was prepared to take advantage of this historic opportunity, as was the Lega Nord. In sum, the radical right in Germany had neither means nor opportunity, with the exception of the NPD in eastern Germany. The Italian case demonstrates that means alone are not enough: without the collapse of the Italian party system and Berlusconi's stamp of approval, the resurgence of the Italian far right would not have been possible.

7

Conclusion

One of the central messages of this book is that there has been no common political response to the structural transformations – immigration, globalization, post-Fordism – that have characterized all Western European countries over the past several decades. These transformations created opportunities for radical right parties to succeed in the long term, but our cross-national historical analysis has demonstrated that they were able to do so only under certain circumstances. The political effects of sociostructural change and exogenous pressures were refracted through national-level variables. In the case of radical right parties, these were not the variables one might immediately suspect, such as the electoral system or other formal political institutions, and this book has focused on two in particular. First, while radical right parties, like fascist movements, are the product of a distinct historical epoch, their success and failure cannot be understood in isolation from the movements that preceded them. Second, the degree of legitimacy accorded to radical right parties – in part because of historical factors, in part because of tactical calculations by other political actors – created opportunities in some cases and major hurdles in other. Thus both historical legacies and political culture were the critical intervening variables between sociostructural transformation and political outcomes.

To support this broad point, this book focused on the microlevel processes of party building. It demonstrated how history and political culture affected both the number and type of activists that were willing to work on behalf of radical right parties. It then showed how these activists either succeeded or failed to craft a message that resonated with a relatively broad sector of the electorate and build a strong party organization. The conclusion that organization matters in particular will come as no surprise to radical right activists themselves. Indeed, no other variable was as consistently cited by my interviewees as the ultimate source of their parties' successes and failures. As we have seen, many of the members of unsuccessful radical right parties were brutally honest about the limitations of both their rank and file and their leaders. While they blamed stigmatization for their inability to find capable people, it was striking how often they attributed their weaknesses to organizational pathologies and self-inflicted wounds. In addition to pointing a finger at the violent extremists, criminals, and mentally unstable people who sometimes populated the ranks of their parties, some radical right activists blamed themselves. They spoke of being overwhelmed in municipal councils, intimidated by the more experienced and better-educated politicians from other parties. While successful radical right parties contained these individuals as well, the presence of a core of experienced politicians and internal training mechanisms helped them to upgrade their human capital. When unprompted, members of these parties spoke somewhat less about the importance of organization and instead attributed their success to meeting the legitimate demands of voters. This, however, was largely because they had come to take for granted a high degree of organizational capacity and professionalism.

This book differs from most studies of the radical right in placing history at the center of the analysis. But it also focuses on another factor that has been strangely and conspicuously absent from this literature: politics. Clearly, the internal political dynamics of radical right parties are important for understanding their success and failure. The struggles for power within these parties, the battles between various factions, and the strategies of leaders and activists assume a central role in this book's narrative. So too do the strategies that mainstream political parties and groups in civil society adopted toward the radical right. These forms of intentional action have been ignored or obscured in most analyses of the radical right, particularly those that view it as the inevitable outgrowth of broad socioeconomic forces.

In this sense, the argument here ties into a long-standing debate concerning the role of socioeconomic structures versus agency in the study of the far right, and of fascism in particular. The "losers of modernization" thesis (Betz 1994) is reminiscent of Lipset's contention that modern capitalism created status anxiety among the petty bourgeoisie and turned them toward fascism (Lipset 1960). The idea that economic realignment has produced a cross-class coalition for the radical right finds parallels in both Barrington Moore's (1966) and Gregory Luebbert's (1991) claim that fascism was the inevitable product of specific patterns of class alliances. For all of these theorists, political agency, on the part of either fascist parties or their erstwhile competitors, had little bearing on political outcomes. Reacting to these sociological and Marxist analyses, Linz and Stepan (1978) asserted the centrality of political reactions to fascist challengers, noting that a key variable in fascist success or failure was whether mainstream conservative forces remained loyal, semiloyal, or disloyal to the democratic regime. More recently, Capoccia (2005) has developed and extended this analysis by demonstrating that the defense of democracy in interwar Europe depended on the repression of fascist parties by political elites. Richard Hamilton's (1982) study of Nazi Germany argued that the reactions of political parties created opportunities for the Nazis, and that the Nazis' organizational capacities enabled them to take advantage of those opportunities.

While my perspective on the radical right is clearly more in line with the latter group of theorists, I am not claiming that radical right parties had unlimited room for maneuver. The protagonists in this book – radical right activists and their opponents and partners from other camps – did make political choices that mattered and were in this sense not "hapless victims" of external circumstances (Berman 1997: 102). They were constrained, however, by historical legacies and norms concerning the acceptability of radical right politics. Activists in these parties could see the strategies that led to success in other countries, but were often unable to imitate them because their state's history and political culture had ruled them out. In the end, then, past choices and intentional action by other political and social actors determined both the number and the nature of radical right agents.

The radical right is connected with a nexus of issues that are of fundamental concern to both students of European politics and Europeans themselves. So long as scholars are concerned with the crisis of representative democracy, the challenge of integrating immigrants with radically different cultural values, and the reaction to globalization and European integration, scholarly interest in radical right parties will remain high. As these parties persist and take on new political roles, for instance as governing parties (Heinisch 2003; De Lange 2007b), they will no doubt continue to inspire more research. This research should not simply cast the radical right as a political enemy, as many studies in the 1980s and 1990s did, or shy away from fieldwork. Moreover, to remain relevant to the rest of the field, this research must connect to broader methodological and substantive issues in party politics and comparative politics in general, a point that Erik Bleich (2008) has made regarding the literature on immigration and integration. In this spirit, I would like to emphasize two other substantive themes that have guided the analysis, before concluding with some general remarks on the politics of ethnicity in Europe, past and future.

The first is the utility of looking inside political parties, social movements, or other types of organizations that are considered to be radical in some respect. Our knee-jerk response is to view the activists of these groups as ideologically homogeneous. Yet even among those organizations in which members risk their lives for a cause, such as terrorist groups, one can draw distinctions between moderate and extremist elements (Crenshaw 1981). Using this simple dichotomy, analysts have linked the internal properties of terrorist organizations to the outcome of negotiations with governments (Kydd and Walter 2002) in order to explain why governments would negotiate with terrorists in the first place and to demonstrate why terrorist organizations often become more militant following concessions by governments (Bueno de Mesquita 2005). An important strand in the literature on ethnic conflict has also used the moderate–extremist distinction to explain outcomes of interest (Fearon and Laitin 2003). In the realm of democratic politics, we have already noted how Kitschelt (1989) used a tripartite typology of Green activists to understand these parties' electoral and organizational strategies.

This sort of work carries with it certain risks; indeed, of the aforementioned analysts only Kitschelt actually measured, as opposed to assuming from observed behavior, the relative distribution of different types of activists within an organization. The moderate–extremist dichotomy may also be too crude and mask other forms of internal differentiation that may affect political outcomes. Conducting the type of fieldwork that would enable one to identify and measure the relevant factions within an extremist organization is likely to be some combination of costly, difficult, and dangerous. But the broad point is that, even by breaking down radical groups into two constituent parts, one can often gain more analytical leverage than by maintaining the unitary actor assumption that still guides much theorizing about political extremism. Moreover, by making this analytical move, one can demonstrate how exogenous forces influence the distribution of activists within an organization, and thereby link structure, agency, and outcomes.

The second substantive theme is the relationship between mainstream political or societal actors and more radical ones in democratic states. At some points in history, such as in interwar Europe, the stakes of this interaction have been extremely high. Bourgeois parties first deemed Hitler and Mussolini acceptable coalition partners before being destroyed by them. This lesson was not lost on political leaders in some other democratic states, who successfully repulsed the domestic fascist challenge before falling to the Nazi (Belgium, Czechoslovakia, France) or Stalinist (Finland) war machine. Although mainstream party behavior was not the only factor that led to democratic breakdown or persistence, it was certainly an important one. The stakes have not been nearly so high for center-right parties confronting radical right parties in contemporary Europe, or for a mainstream leftist party like the Social Democratic Party of Germany, which has long appeared tormented about how to deal with the heir of the East German Communist Party. Yet in one important sense the outcomes were similar: by cooperating with radical challengers, or at least failing to erect a cordon sanitaire against them, mainstream parties gave them much needed legitimacy and rendered them stronger. Like Pierre Poujade, whom we first encountered at the beginning of this book, French conservatives may have believed in the 1980s that the French National Front would soon disappear. Like Austrian Chancellor Wolfgang Schüssel in 1999, they wagered that they would be the only ones to profit in the long term from a temporary marriage of convenience with the radical right. Although there is no postwar equivalent of Von Papen's famous quip about Hitler ("We have hired him"), many a mainstream politician certainly saw radical right challengers as either unthreatening amateurs or forces that they themselves could tame. Unlike German and Italian politicians in the interwar period, however, this calculation – even if ultimately wrong – may still have ultimately been worth it to them. We have seen how the rise of the radical right has created bipolar party systems in states where they did not exist previously, such as Austria, Denmark, and Italy, thereby giving the mainstream right a coalition partner whose policy positions may be closer to their own than the alternatives.

Cooperation and noncooperation (the strategy of the cordon sanitaire) obviously do not exhaust the range of options open to mainstream forces facing challengers on their left or right flanks (Eatwell and Mudde 2004). Another possible, and indeed ubiquitous, response is for parties to try to co-opt the message themselves and thereby weaken challengers by, to quote Anthony Downs (1957), "taking the wind from their sails." Throughout this book, we have witnessed numerous examples of this practice, although we have not analyzed it in detail. Whether it has worked at all is difficult to tell (Schain 2006). My own view, although one that would obviously require further testing, is that a phenomenon equivalent to "ethnic outbidding" occurs when mainstream parties attempt to co-opt the radical right. The former is never able to match the latter's ferocity of discourse or extremity of policy positions without leading to damaging internal splits. As a result, radical right parties are able to "up the ante" whenever the mainstream right approaches its own policy position (Bale 2003).

Co-optation has nevertheless led many conservative parties to take more strident positions on questions of immigration, law and order, and national identity. The European Commission against Racism and Intolerance declared in March 2005 that "the use of racist, anti-Semitic and xenophobic political discourse is no longer confined to extremist political parties, but is increasingly infecting mainstream political parties, at the risk of legitimising and trivialising this type of discourse." The magnitude of this shift is debatable, and mainstream parties have thus far had difficulty in calibrating their message on immigration to attract potential radical right voters without alienating their traditional core (Bale 2008). Playing the immigrant card is not always a winning strategy: the Christian Democrats' election campaign slogan in state elections in North-Rhine Westphalia in 2000 of "Kinder Statt Inder" (Children Instead of Indians) backfired.[1] Yet other parties and politicians, like Nicolas Sarkozy of the Union for a Popular Movement (UMP), have been much more successful, and there is no reason to believe that others will not be so in the future. Immigration and integration do raise a host of legitimate questions for European societies, ones that mainstream parties must address. Yet conservative parties in particular need to debate the extent to which they are willing to subsume what have hitherto been radical right positions on these issues. It is not out of the realm of possibility that certain conservative parties adopt something akin to the U.S. Republican Party's so-called southern strategy and seek electoral gain in the politics of ethnic backlash. One would be naive to deny that such a backlash exists or that it represents a viable route to electoral power.

As the party system in Western Europe becomes increasingly fractured, the dynamic interaction between mainstream parties and challengers on their left and right flanks will become increasingly important. If the argument here is correct, mainstream parties have an important tool at their disposal in the opening and closing of coalition markets. When coalitions

[1] The slogan was a reaction to the Schröder government's announcement that it would grant green cards to qualified foreign workers, such as Indian computer specialists.

are credibly ruled out from the beginning, challengers will have great difficulty recruiting the type of people necessary to build a viable party. The opposite pertains when coalition markets are open or when they have been open at some point in the past.

Yet the reaction of civil society matters as well. Indeed, we have seen how radical right parties have been able to flourish when the social climate was permissive, even when the political one was not. Examples of this include the Vlaams Belang in Flanders – particularly in Antwerp – and the National Democratic Party in eastern Germany. We have also seen how potential radical right activists have been deterred by the perceived social and economic costs of activism in other cases. Indeed, the fear of losing one's job and standing in the community is likely to be a much more powerful deterrent than the impossibility of wielding significant political power. The process also works in reverse. When "respectable" figures are able to join the party without suffering any adverse consequences, others are more likely to view the party as acceptable. Every radical right party has tried to attract such people, not only for their inherent abilities but also to convince the wider public that they are not a bastion of inveterate racists, conspiracy theorists, and uneducated hooligans.

It is worth noting that the Nazis also pursued the support of reputable notables in order to present a moderate face and that this strategy often worked. It is only one example, but the case of Walter Spannau, the Nazi bookstore owner in the town of Northeim in William Sheridan Allen's classic *The Nazi Seizure of Power*, is illustrative. Spannau was not an academic, but his profession gave him some degree of intellectual standing. Moreover, he was viewed as a pillar of the community. If Spannau supported the Nazis, the citizens of Northeim reasoned, then the party could not be all that bad.

Many Europeans are doubtless growing tired of analogies to the interwar period. Yet there are at least three reasons for the continuing influence of the legacies of fascism on contemporary politics. First, I have argued that the relative strength of the far right in the immediate postwar period helps explain the success of radical right parties several decades later – not in all cases, but certainly in some. Second, we have seen throughout this book that radical right parties in Western Europe have very different relationships to Nazism, fascism, and collaboration. For some, such as the Danish People's Party, the Norwegian Progress Party, and the Lega Nord, the past is largely irrelevant. Yet they are in the minority, and most parties have found it necessary, and sometimes electorally profitable, to engage in the politics of memory and revisionism. An example of the latter phenomenon is the Swiss People's Party, which had no discernible links with fascism, yet boisterously defended Switzerland's behavior during the Second World War. Most of the other parties we have analyzed contained at least some members of the "old right" in their ranks, which often led them to downplay, and sometimes deny, the crimes committed during the Second World War. Other parties openly glorified Nazism or fascism before trying to jettison, with various degrees of success, this type of ideology. Gianfranco Fini performed a 180-degree turn with his relationship to fascism in his attempt to position his party in the center-right and to improve his chances of eventually becoming prime minister. Third, mainstream parties and groups in civil society have tried to employ the fascist past as a weapon against the radical right. The Germans have gone the farthest in this regard, but the Swedes, Dutch, French, and others have done it as well. Perhaps it was just a coincidence that representatives from fourteen members of the European Union had just finished attending a conference on Holocaust memory in Sweden when they announced sanctions against Austria, following the formation of a government that included Haider's FPÖ. Yet the sequencing leaves room for a plausible alternative interpretation.

One can debate the degree to which these efforts have worked and whether it is even possible for elites to transform their societies by invoking the lessons of the past. Yet one thing is undeniable: the legacy of the Holocaust and its continued salience in political discourse, school curricula, and mass culture have contributed to a widely shared norm of antiracism in Western Europe (Ivarsflaten, Blinder, and Ford: 2008). This norm helps explain why no radical right party that was formed simply as part of an anti-immigrant backlash was able to succeed. Indeed, every successful radical right party came to the politics of anti-immigration through another route, either as the representative of a nationalist subculture or through party transformation. Thus, while scholars and observers regularly view the enduring success of some radical right parties as the political expression of widespread xenophobia, we should not forget that their failures far outnumber their successes. Nor should we forget that most voters in Austria, Denmark, France, and other countries where the radical right was successful do not vote for radical right parties and that their political opponents regularly refer to norms of tolerance and antiracism in their battles against them.

The question is whether these norms will become attenuated if and when the Second World War ceases to become a primary point of reference for political-moral arguments. We have seen how norms against radical right parties can change quite suddenly, as in Italy, or more gradually, as in the Netherlands. This will be particularly important, as debates about culture and ethnicity in Europe have become more complex than in the 1980s and 1990s, when the central issue was how many asylum seekers and immigrants to allow into the country. The economic integration of minorities and conflicts over political and cultural values have since replaced questions about numbers. The issue is no longer whether European states will become multiethnic societies, but how they will manage the politics that emerge from this transformation.

The financial crisis of 2008 and the ensuing Great Recession have ensured that these debates will be carried out in a climate of extreme economic insecurity and pain. It is tempting to view this period as a crisis of global capitalism that will, in a type of Polanyian double movement, produce a nationalist backlash in the form of radical right parties. One could certainly point to specific election results, such as the British National Party's breakthrough in the 2009 European Parliament elections, the Party of Freedom's (PVV) 17% in the same contest, and the Movement for a Better Hungary's (Jobbik) 16.7% in the 2010 parliamentary elections. But to restate one of the central arguments of this book, there is no automatic transmission mechanism between fear and anger on the part of voters, both of which are undoubtedly quite high, and the durability of radical right parties. At the end of the day, parties like Jobbik and the PVV will need to recruit and maintain the type of politicians who built successful radical right parties elsewhere and to avoid those who make party building next to impossible (witness the BNP's collapse on the 2010 general elections). The greatest economic downturn in the advanced industrialized world since the Great Depression will undoubtedly give radical right parties an opening, but it will be up to them to seize it.

In this sense, very little has changed since radical right parties first emerged more than a quarter-century ago. Party institutionalization remains a goal that most new parties are unlikely to achieve. Yet in another sense, the dynamics of party organization in Europe have shifted fundamentally. By the 1970s, the mass party, which maintained a strong organizational presence in society, was already moribund, but the process of organizational contraction intensified in the 1980s. One could argue that we have now reached a point where "nothing much remains to mediate relations between the voter and the voted" (Katz and Mair 2009: 761). The ultimate significance of Geert Wilders' PVV may lie less in its radical right ideology than in the attempt to build a political party with the absolute minimum number of members, activists, and staff, as well as to avoid any trappings of internal democracy. On the one hand, this reflects Wilders' direct observation of the collapse of the List Pim Fortuyn and his intuitions about the types of organizational pathologies I have presented in this book. On the other hand, this extreme example of a "party without partisans" (Dalton and Wattenberg 2002) reflects a broader trend toward the personalization of politics. The underlying forces that are reshaping party organization, perhaps even more than those that are fueling the radical right, are unlikely to attenuate in the future. Indeed, the growing reliance on the media, electoral dealignment, and political professionalization look to be no less reversible than immigration, globalization, and European integration. Under these conditions, the skills and qualities of a smaller and smaller group of politicians will continue to have a larger and larger effect on electoral outcomes and policy making. Troubling as the rise of the radical right has been for many Europeans over the past several decades, the implications of this development for the quality and practice of parliamentary democracy are more worrisome still.

Appendix A

Percentage of the Vote for Radical Right Parties in National Parliamentary Elections

TABLE A.I. *Cases Coded as Successful*

	AN	DF	FN	FrP	FPÖ	LN	SVP	VB
1985				3.7				1.4
1986			9.7		9.7			
1987								1.9
1988			9.7					
1989				13.0				
1990					16.6			
1991							11.9	6.6
1992						8.7		
1993			13.8	6.3				
1994	13.5				22.5	8.4		
1995					22.0		14.9	7.8
1996	15.7					10.1		
1997			15.0	15.3				
1998		7.4						
1999					26.9		22.5	9.9
2000								
2001	12.0	12.0		14.6		3.9		
2002			11.3		10.0			
2003							26.6	11.6
2004								
2005		13.2		22.1				
2006	12.3				11.0	4.1		
2007		13.8	4.3				28.9	12.0
2008					17.5	8.3		
2009				22.9				

TABLE A.2. *Cases Coded as Failures*

	BNP	CD	DVU	FNb	LPF	ND	NPD	REP	SD
1985				0.1					
1986		0.1							
1987	0.0			0.1			0.6		
1988									0.0
1989		0.9							
1990							0.3	2.1	
1991				1.1		6.7			0.2
1992	0.1								
1993									
1994		2.5				1.2		1.9	0.2
1995				2.3					
1996									
1997	0.1								
1998		0.6	1.2				0.3	1.8	0.4
1999				1.5					
2000									
2001	0.2								
2002					17.0		0.4	0.6	1.4
2003				2.0	5.7				
2004									
2005	0.7						1.6	0.6	
2006									2.9
2007				2.0					
2008									
2009							1.5		

Appendix B

Coding Procedure for Radical Right Party Lists

I obtained a party list for an election between 2005 and 2007 for radical right parties in states that require candidates for public office to list their occupations along with other personal data. The following states have such a requirement: Austria, Belgium, Denmark, Germany, France, Sweden, and Switzerland. I chose the party list that would maximize the number of observations for each radical right party. For all parties except the Belgian National Front and the Sweden Democrats, where the lists for the regional and municipal elections, respectively, contained more candidates, this was the list for the national parliamentary election. Using the International Standard Classification of Occupations (ISCO-88), a native speaker of the relevant language assigned the corresponding numerical code to the occupation of each candidate. Separate codes were assigned to the following: students, pensioners, homemakers, self-employed (when there was no further specification), and unemployed. These categories were not included in the percentages reported in Appendix C, although they were counted toward the total number of observations.

In Austria, it was necessary to recode the large percentage of candidates who described themselves as either *angestellte* (employee) or *beamten* (civil servant). It was possible to give approximately half of these candidates more specific codings by consulting the party Web site or through a general Internet search; otherwise, such candidates were assigned the code 4.

Appendix C

ISCO Codes for Radical Right Candidates for Office

TABLE C.1. *Percentage of Total for Different ISCO Codes*

Party	Year	1	2	3	4	5	6	7	8	9	N
DF	2007	7	43	15	10	13	0	5	7	0	82
FN	2007	20	22	25	22	3	1	6	2	0	557
FNb	2006	0	22	0	13	30	0	9	22	4	68
FPÖ	2007	6	32	20	15	15	5	4	2	0	300
NPD	2005	0	22	24	11	9	2	29	3	0	214
REP	2005	1	17	24	14	8	2	21	8	4	98
SD	2006	3	17	18	9	12	6	15	13	6	224
SVP	2007	13	32	12	14	6	11	10	2	1	420

ISCO codes:
1. Managers
2. Professionals
3. Technicians and associate professionals
4. Clerks
5. Service workers and shop and market sales workers
6. Skilled agriculture and fishery workers
7. Craft and related trades workers
8. Plant and machine operators and assemblers
9. Elementary occupations

Bibliography

Aardal, Bernt. 1994. "The 1993 Storting Elections: Volatile Voters Opposing the European Union." *Scandinavian Political Studies* 17(2): 171–180.

Abramowicz, Manuel. 1996. *Les rats noirs*. Brussels: Luc Pire.

Albertazzi, Daniele, and Duncan McDonnell. 2005. "The Lega Nord in the Second Berlusconi Government: In a League of Its Own." *West European Politics* 28(5): 952–972.

Algazy, Joseph. 1989. *L'Extrême-droite en France de 1965 à 1984*. Paris: L'Harmattan.

Allen, William Sheridan. 1984. *The Nazi Seizure of Power: The Experience of a Single German Town, 1922–1945*, rev. ed. New York: Franklin Watts.

Altermatt, Urs, and Damir Skenderovic. 1995. "Die Extreme Rechte: Organisationen, Personen und Entwicklungen in den achtziger und neunziger Jahren." In *Rechtsextremismus in der Schweiz. Organisationen und Radikalisierung in den 1980er und 1990er Jahren*. Edited by Urs Altermatt and Hanspeter Kriesi. Zürich: Verlag Neue Zürcher Zeitung, pp. 11–155.

Andersen, Jørgen Goul, and Tor Bjørklund. 2000. "Radical Right-Wing Populism in Scandinavia: From Tax Revolt to Neo-Liberalism and Xenophobia." In *The Politics of the Extreme Right: From the Margins to the Mainstream*. Edited by Paul Hainsworth. New York: Pinter, pp. 193–223.

Art, David. 2006. *The Politics of the Nazi Past in Germany and Austria*. New York: Cambridge University Press.

2007. "Reacting to the Radical Right: Lessons from Germany and Austria." *Party Politics* 13(3): 331–349.

2008. "The Organizational Origins of the Contemporary Radical Right: The Case of Belgium." *Comparative Politics* 40(4): 421–440.

Arzheimer, Kai. 2009. "Contextual Factors and the Extreme Right Vote in Western Europe, 1980–2002." *American Journal of Political Science* 53(2): 259–275.

Arzheimer, Kai, and Elisabeth Carter. 2006. "Political Opportunity Structures and Right-Wing Extremist Party Success." *European Journal of Political Research* 45(3): 419–444.

Backes, Uwe, and Cas Mudde. 2000. "Germany: Extremism Without Successful Parties." *Parliamentary Affairs* 53(3): 457–468.

Bailer, Brigitta, and Wolfgang Neugebauer, eds. 1994. *Handbuch des Österreichischen Rechtsextremismus.* Vienna: Stiftung Dokumentationsarchiv des österreichischen Widerstandes.

Balace, François. 1994. "Le tournant des années soixante, de la droite réactionnaire à l'extrême droite révolutionnaire." In *L'Extrême droite en Belgique francophone. De l'avant à l'après-guerre.* Edited by François Balace et al. Brussels: De Boeck, pp. 107–211.

Bale, Tim. 2003. "Cinderella and Her Ugly Sisters: The Mainstream and Extreme Right in Europe's Bipolarizing Party Systems." *West European Politics* 26(3): 67–90.

      2008. "Turning Round the Telescope: Centre Right Parties and Immigration and Integration Policy in Europe." *Journal of European Public Policy* 15(3): 315–330.

Bardi, Luciano, and Leonardo Morlino. 1992. "Italy." In *Party Organizations: A Data Handbook on Party Organizations in Western Democracies, 1960–1990.* Edited by Richard S. Katz and Peter Mair. London: Sage, pp. 458–618.

Berezin, Mabel. 2009. *Illiberal Politics in Neoliberal Times.* New York: Cambridge University Press.

Berggren, Lena. 2002. "Swedish Fascism – Why Bother?" *Journal of Contemporary History* 37(3): 395–417.

Berman, Sheri. 1997. "The Life of the Party." *Comparative Politics* 30(1): 101–122.

Betz, Hans-Georg. 1993. "The New Politics of Resentment: Radical Right-Wing Populist Parties in Western Europe." *Comparative Politics* 25(4): 413–427.

      1994. *Radical Right-Wing Populism in Western Europe.* New York: St. Martin's Press.

      1998a. "Against Rome: The Lega Nord." In *The New Politics of the Right: Neo-Populist Parties and Movements in Established Democracies.* Edited by Hans-Georg Betz and Stefan Immerfall. New York: St. Martin's Press, pp. 45–57.

      1998b. "Introduction," In *The New Politics of the Right: Neo-Populist Parties and Movements in Established Democracies.* Edited by Hans-Georg Betz and Stefan Immerfall. New York: St. Martin's Press, pp. 1–10.

Betz, Hans-Georg, and Stefan Immerfall, eds. 1998. *The New Politics of the Right: Neo-Populist Parties and Movements in Established Democracies.* New York: St. Martin's Press.

Billig, Michael. 1978. *Fascists: A Social Psychological View of the National Front.* London: Academic Press.

Biorcio, Roberto. 1997. *La Padania Promessa.* Milan: Il Saggiatore.

Birenbaum, Guy. 1992. *Le Front National en politique.* Paris: Éditions Balland.

Birenbaum, Guy, and François Bastien. 1989. "Unité et diversité des dirigeants frontistes." In *Le Front National à découvert.* Edited by Nonna Mayer and Pascal Perrineau. Paris: Presses de la Fondation Nationale Des Sciences Politiques, pp. 83–106.

Bizeul, Daniel. 2003. *Avec ceux du FN: Un sociologue au Front National.* Paris: Éditions la Découverte.

Bjørklund, Tor. 2007. "Unemployment and the Radical Right in Scandinavia: Beneficial or Non-Beneficial for Electoral Support?" *Comparative European Politics* 5(3): 245–264.

Bjørklund, Tor, and Jørgen Goul Andersen. 2002. "Anti-immigration Parties in Denmark and Norway: The Progress Parties and the Danish People's Party." In Martin Schain, Aristide Zolberg, and Patrick Hossay, eds., *Shadows over Europe: The Development and Impact of the Extreme Right in Western Europe*. New York: Palgrave, pp. 107–136.

Bjørklund, Tor, and Jo Saglie. 2004. "The Norwegian Progress Party: Building Bridges Across Old Cleavages." Paper presented at the 12th Nasjonal fagkonferansei statsvitenskap, Trømso, January 7–9.

Bleich, Erik. 2008. "Immigration and Integration Studies in Western Europe and the United States: The Road Less Traveled and a Path Ahead." *World Politics* 60(3): 509–538.

Bornschier, Simon. 2009. "Cleavage Politics in Old and New Democracies: A Review of the Literature and Avenues for Future Research." EUI Working Papers, Max Weber Programme, European University Institute.

2010. *Cleavage Politics and the Populist Right: The New Cultural Conflict in Western Europe*. Philadelphia: Temple University Press.

Bossi, Umberto (with Daniele Vimercati). 1992. *Vento dal Nord: La Mia Lega la Mia Vita*. Milan: Sperling and Kupfer Editori.

Bossi, Umberto. 1996. *Il mio progetto: Discorsi su federalismo e Padania*. Milan: Sperling and Kupfer Editori.

Brady, Henry E., Kay Lehmann Schlozmann, and Sidney Verba. 1999. "Prospecting for Participants: Rational Expectations and the Recruitment of Political Activists." *American Political Science Review* 93(1): 153–168.

Braunthal, Gerard. 1990. *Political Loyalty and Public Service in West Germany: The 1972 Decree against Radicals and Its Consequences*. Amherst: University of Massachusetts Press.

Bréchon, Pierre, and Subrata Kumar Mitra. 1992. "The National Front in France: The Emergence of an Extreme-Right Protest Movement." *Comparative Politics* 25(1): 63–82.

Bueno de Mesquita, Ethan. 2005. "Conciliation, Counterterrorism, and Patterns of Terrorist Violence." *International Organizations* 59(1): 145–176.

Bull, Anna Cento. 1993. "The Politics of Industrial Districts in Lombardy: Replacing Christian Democracy with the Northern League." *Italianist* 13(1): 209–229.

Bull, Anna Cento, and Mark Gilbert. 2001. *The Lega Nord and the Northern Question in Italian Politics*. New York: Palgrave.

Bull, Martin, and James Newell. 1995. "Italy Changes Course: The 1994 Elections and the Victory of the Right." *Parliamentary Affairs* 48(1): 72–99.

Cachafeiro, Margarita Gómez-Reino. 2002. *Ethnicity and Nationalism in Italian Politics: Inventing the Padania – Lega Nord and the Northern Question*. Aldershot: Ashgate.

Camus, Jean-Yves. 1998. *Front National: Eine Gefahr für die französische Demokratie?* Bonn: Bouvier Verlag.

Capoccia, Giovanni. 2005. *Defending Democracy: Reactions to Extremism in Interwar Europe*. Balitmore: Johns Hopkins University Press.

Carioti, Antonio. 1996. "From the Ghetto to Palazzo Chigi: The Ascent of the National Alliance." In *Italian Politics: The Year of the Tycoon.* Edited by Richard Katz and Piero Ignazi. Boulder, CO: Westview Press, pp. 57–78.

Carson, Jamie L., Erik Engstrom, and Jason M. Roberts. 2007. "Candidate Quality, the Personal Vote, and the Incumbency Advantage in Congress." *American Political Science Review* 101(2): 289–301.

Carter, Elisabeth. 2002. "Proportional Representation and the Fortunes of Right-Wing Extremist Parties." *West European Politics* 25(3): 125–146.

2005. *The Extreme Right in Western Europe: Success or Failure?* Manchester: Manchester University Press.

Chiarini, Roberto. 1995. "The Italian Far Right: The Search for Legitimacy." In *The Far Right in Western and Eastern Europe.* Edited by Luciano Cheles, Ronnie Ferguson, and Michalina Vaughan. London: Longman, pp. 20–40.

Chiroux, René. 1974. *L'Extrême-droite sous la Ve République.* Paris: Librarie Générale de Droit et de Jurisprudence.

Chorus, Jutta, and Menno De Galan. 2002. *In de ban van Fortuyn. Reconstructie van een Politieke aardschok.* Amsterdam: Mets and Schilt.

Church, Clive. 2000. "The Swiss Elections of October 1999: Learning to Live in More Interesting Times." *West European Politics* 23(3): 215–230.

2004. "The Swiss Elections of October 2003: Two Steps to System Change?" *West European Politics* 27(3): 518–534.

Coffé, Hilde. 2005. "Do Individual Factors Explain the Different Success of the Two Belgian Extreme Right Parties?" *Acta Politica* 40(1): 74–93.

Cole, Alexandra. 2005. "Old Right or New Right? The Ideological Positioning of Parties of the Far Right." *European Journal of Political Research* 44(2): 203–230.

Colignon, Alain. 1996. "Les commémorations en Belgique francophone." In *Commémoration. Enjeux et débats.* Edited by Alain Colignon, Chantal Kesteloot, and Dirk Martin. Brussels: Centre de recherche et d'études historiques de la seconde guerre mondiale, pp. 13–65.

Conway, Martin. 1993. *Collaboration in Belgium: Léon Degrelle and the Rexist Movement, 1940–1944.* New Haven, CT: Yale University Press.

Copsey, Nigel. 2004. *Contemporary British Fascism: The British National Party and the Quest for Legitimacy.* London: Palgrave Macmillan.

Cox, Gary. 1997. *Making Votes Count.* New York: Cambridge University Press.

Cox, Gary W., Frances M. Rosenbluth, and Michael F. Thies. 1998. "Mobilization, Social Networks, and Turnout: Evidence from Japan." *World Politics* 50(3): 447–474.

Crenshaw, Martha. 1981. "The Causes of Terrorism." *Comparative Politics* 13(4): 379–399.

Dalton, Russel J., and Martin P. Wattenberg, eds. 2002. *Parties Without Partisans.* New York: Oxford University Press.

Dalton, Russel J., Ian McAllister, and Martin P. Wattenberg. 2002. "Political Parties and Their Publics." In *Political Parties in the New Europe: Political and Analytical Changes.* Edited by Kurt Richard Luther and Ferdinand Müller-Rommel. Oxford: Oxford University Press, pp. 19–42.

Damen, Sofie. 2001. "Strategieën tegen Extreem-Rechts. Het Cordon Sanitaire." *Tijdschrift voor Sociologie* 22(1): 89–110.

Decker, Frank. 2004. *Der neue Rechtspopulismus.* Opladen: Leske + Budrich.

DeClair, Edward G. 1999. *Politics on the Fringe: The People, Policies, and Organization of the French National Front.* Durham, NC: Duke University Press.

De Felice, Renzo. 1969. *Le interpretazioni del Fascismo.* Bari: Laterza.

De Lange, Sarah. 2007a. "A New Winning Formula? The Programmatic Appeal of the Radical Right." *Party Politics* 13(4): 411–435.

2007b. "From Pariah to Power Broker: The Radical Right and Government in Western Europe." In *Extrême droite et pouvoir en Europe.* Edited by Pascal Delwit and Philippe Poirier. Brussels: Editions de l'Université de Bruxelles, pp. 21–41.

Delwit, Pascal. 2007. "The Belgian National Front and the Question of Power." In *The Extreme Right Parties and Power in Europe.* Edited by Pascal Delwit and Philippe Poirier. Brussels: Éditions de l'Université de Bruxelles, pp. 141–167.

Deschouwer, Kurt. 2008. *New Parties in Government.* London: Routledge.

De Witte, Hans. 2006. "Extreme Right Activism in the Flemish Part of Belgium." In *Extreme Right Activists in Europe.* Edited by Bert Klandermans and Nonna Mayer. New York: Routledge, pp. 127–151.

De Witte, Hans, and Bert Klandermans. 2000. "Political Racism in Flanders and the Netherlands: Explaining Differences in the Electoral Success of Extreme-Right Parties." *Journal of Ethnic and Migration Studies* 26(1): 699–717.

Dézé, Alexandre. 2004. "Between Adaptation, Differentation and Distinction: Extreme Right-Wing Parties Within Democratic Political Systems." In *Western Democracies and the New Extreme Right Challenge.* Edited by Roger Eatwell and Cas Mudde. London: Routledge, 19–40.

Diamanti, Ilvo. 1993. *La Lega. Geografia, storia e sociologia di un soggetto politico.* Rome: Donzelli Editore.

Dittmer, Lowell. 1969. "The German NPD: A Psycho-Sociological Analysis of Neo-Nazism." *Comparative Politics* 2(1): 79–110.

Downs, Anthony. 1957. *An Economic Theory of Democracy.* New York: Harper and Row.

1967. *Inside Bureaucracy.* Boston: Little Brown.

Drummond, Andrew J. 2006. "Electoral Volatility and Party Decline in Western Democracies: 1970–1995." *Political Studies* 54: 628–647.

Eatwell, Roger. 2004. "The Extreme Right in Britain: The Long Road to Modernization." In *Western Democracies and the New Right Challenge.* Edited by Roger Eatwell and Cas Mudde. London: Routledge, pp. 62–81.

Eatwell, Roger. 1995. *Fascism: A History.* London: Chatto and Windus.

Eatwell, Roger, and Cas Mudde, eds. 2004. *Western Democracies and the New Extreme Right Challenge.* London: Routledge.

Ellinas, Antonis. 2007. "Phased Out: Far Right Parties in Western Europe." *Comparative Politics* 39(3): 353–371.

2010. *The Media and the Far Right in Western Europe.* New York: Cambridge University Press.

Erk, Jan. 2005. "From Vlaams Blok to Vlaams Belang: Belgian Far-Right Renames Itself." *Western European Politics* 28(3): 493–502.

Evans, Jocelyn A. J. 2005. "The Dynamics of Social Change in Radical Right-Wing Populist Party Support." *Comparative European Politics* 3(1): 76–101.

Faux, Emmanuel, Thomas Legrand, and Gilles Perez. 1994. *La Main droite de Dieu. Enquête sur François Mitterrand et l'extrême droite*. Paris: Seuil.

Favier, Pierre, and Michel Martin-Roland. 1990. *La Décennie Mitterrand*, vol. 1. Paris: Seuil.

Fearon, James D., and David D. Laitin. 2003. "Ethnicity, Insurgency, and Civil War." *American Political Science Review* 97(1): 75–90.

Finkel, Steven E., and Peter R. Schrott. 1995. "Campaign Effects on Voter Choice in the German Election of 1990." *British Journal of Political Science* 25(3): 349–377.

Frei, Norbert. 1999. *Vergangenheitspolitik. Die Anfänge der Bundesrepublik und die NS Vergangenheit*. Munich: Deutscher Taschenbuch Verlag.

Friedrich, Jörg. 1984. *Die Kalte Amnestie: NS-Täter in der Bundesrepublik*. Frankfurt am Main: Fischer Taschenbuch Verlag.

Gallagher, Tom. 2000. "Exit from the Ghetto: The Italian Far Right in the 1990s." In *The Politics of the Extreme Right: From the Margins to the Mainstream*. Edited by Paul Hainsworth. New York: Pinter, pp. 64–86.

Gardberg, Annvi. 1993. *Against the Stranger, the Gangster and the Establishment: A Comparative Study of the Swedish Ny Demokrati, the German Republikaner, the French Front National and the Belgian Vlaams Blok*. Helsinki: Helsinki University.

Gärtner, Reinhold. 1989. "Right-Wing Student Politics in Austria after 1945." In *Conquering the Past: Austrian Nazism Yesterday and Today*. Edited by F. Parkinson. Detroit: Wayne State University Press, pp. 279–294.

Gaspard, Françoise. 1995. *A Small City in France*. Translated by Arthur Goldhammer. Cambridge, MA: Harvard University Press.

Gentile, Pierre, and Hanspeter Kriesi. 1998. "Contemporary Radical-Right Parties in Switzerland: History of a Divided Family." In *The New Politics of the Right*. Edited by Hans-Georg Betz and Stefan Immerfall. New York: St. Martin's Press, pp. 125–141.

Gerber, Alan S., and Donald P. Green. 2000. "The Effects of Canvassing, Telephone Calls, and Direct Mail on Voter Turnout: A Field Experiment." *American Political Science Review* 94(3): 653–663.

Gibson, Rachel. 2002. *The Growth of Anti-Immigrant Parties in Western Europe*. Lewiston, NY: Edwin Mellen.

Gijsels, Hugo. 1992. *Het Vlaams Blok*. Leuven: Kritak.

Gijsels, Hugo, and Jos Vander Velpen. 1994. *Le Chagrin des Flamands: Le Vlaams Blok de 1938 a nos jours*. Berchem: EPO.

Gilbert, Mark. 1995. *The Italian Revolution: The End of Politics Italian Style?* Boulder, CO: Westview Press.

Ginsborg, Paul. 1990. *A History of Contemporary Italy: Society and Politics, 1943–1988*. New York: Penguin.

2004. *Silvio Berlusconi*. New York: Verso.

Givens, Terri E. 2004. "The Radical Right Gender Gap." *Comparative Political Studies* 37(1): 30–54.

2005. *Voting Radical Right in Western Europe*. New York: Cambridge University Press.

Glaus, Beat. 1969. *Die Nationale Front. Eine Schweizer Faschistische Bewegung, 1930–1940*. Zürich: Benziger.

Gold, Thomas W. 2003. *The Lega Nord and Contemporary Politics in Italy*. New York: Palgrave MacMillan.

Golder, Matthew. 2003. "Explaining Variation in the Success of Extreme Right Parties in Western Europe." *Comparative Political Studies* 36(4): 432–466.

Goodwin, Matthew. 2007a. *The BNP and Party Activists*. Ph.D. Dissertation, University of Bath.

2007b. "Research, Revisionists and the Radical Right." *Politics* 28(1): 33–40.

2010. *The New British Fascism: Rise of the British National Party*. London: Routledge.

Gryzmala-Busse, Anna M. 2002. *Redeeming the Communist Past: The Regeneration of Communist Parties in East Central Europe*. Cambridge: Cambridge University Press.

Hafeneger, Benno. 2000. *Die Republikaner in Stadtallendorf. Eine Lokalstudie*. Schwalback: Wochenschau Verlag.

Hagelund, Anniken. 2003. "A Matter of Decency? The Progress Party in Norwegian Immigration Politics." *Journal of Ethnic and Migration Studies*, 29(1): 47–66.

Hainsworth, Paul, ed. 1992. *The Extreme Right in Europe and the USA*. New York: St. Martin's Press.

2000. *The Politics of the Extreme Right: From the Margins to the Mainstream*. London: Pinter.

Hamilton, Richard. 1982. *Who Voted for Hitler?* Princeton, NJ: Princeton University Press.

Harmel, Robert, and John D. Robertson. 1985. "Formation and Success of New Parties: A Cross National Analysis." *International Political Science Review* 6: 501–523.

Hartmann, Hans, and Franz Horvath. 1995. *Zivilgesellschaft von rechts. Die unheimliche Erfolgsstory der Zürcher SVP*. Zurich: Realotopia Verlagsgenossenschaft.

Heidar, Knut, and Jo Saglie. 2003. "Predestined Parties? Organizational Change in Norwegian Political Parties." *Party Politics* 9(2): 219–239.

Heinisch, Reinhard. 2002. *Populism, Proporz and Pariah – Austria Turns Right: Austrian Political Change, Its Causes and Repercussions*. Huntington, NY: Nova Science Publishing.

2003. "Success in Opposition: Failure in Government Explaining the Performance of Right-Wing Populist Parties in Public Office." *West European Politics* 26(3): 91–139.

Hillygus, D. Sunshine. 2005. "Campaign Effects and the Dynamics of Turnout Intention in Election 2000." *Journal of Politics* 67(1): 50–68.

Höbelt, Lothar. 2003. *Defiant Populist: Jörg Haider and the Politics of Austria*. West Lafayette, IN: Purdue University Press.

Hoffman, Stanley. 1956. *Le Mouvement Poujade*. Paris: Armand Colin.

Hooghe, Marc, Dietlind Stolle, and Patrick Stouthuysen. 2004. "Head Start in Politics: The Recruitment Function of Youth Organizations of Political Parties in Belgium (Flanders)." *Party Politics* 10: 193–212.

Hossay, Patrick. 2002. "Why Flanders?" In *Shadows over Europe: The Development and Impact of the Extreme Right in Western Europe*. Edited by Martin Schain, Aristide Zolberg, and Patrick Hossay. New York: Palgrave Macmillan, pp. 159–185.

Hossay, Patrick, and Aristide Zolberg. 2002. "Democracy in Peril." In *Shadows Over Europe: The Development and Impact of the Extreme Right in Western Europe*. Edited by Martin Schain, Aristide Zolberg, and Patrick Hossay. New York: Palgrave Macmillan, pp. 301–316.

Howard, Marc. 2000. "Can Populism Be Suppressed in a Democracy? Austria, Germany, and the European Union." *East European Politics and Society* 14(2): 18–32.

2009. *The Politics of Citizenship in Europe*. New York: Cambridge University Press.

Huckfeldt, Robert, and John Sprague. 1992. "Political Parties and Electoral Mobilization: Political Structure, Social Structure, and the Party Canvass." *American Political Science Review* 68(1): 70–86.

Hug, Simon. 2001. *Altering Party Systems: Strategic Behavior and the Emergence of New Political Parties in Western Democracies*. Ann Arbor: University of Michigan Press.

Husbands, Christopher. 1992. "The Netherlands: Irritants on the Body Politic." In *The Extreme Right in Europe and the USA*. Edited by Paul Hainsworth. New York: St. Martin's Press, pp. 95–125.

Ignazi, Piero. 1989. *Il Polo Escluso. Profilo storico del Movimento Sociale Italiano*. Bologna: Società Editrice Il Mulino.

1992. "The Silent Counter-revolution: Hypotheses on the Emergence of Extreme Right Parties in Europe." *European Journal of Political Research* 22(1): 3–34.

1998. "MSI/AN: A Mass Party with the Temptation of the Führer-Prinzip." In *The Organization of Political Parties in Southern Europe*. Edited by Piero Ignazi and Colette Ysmal. Westport, CT: Praeger, pp. 157–177.

2003. *Extreme Right Parties in Western Europe*. Oxford: Oxford University Press.

2005. "Legitimation and Evolution on the Italian Right Wing: Social and Ideological Repositioning of Alleanza Nazionale and the Lega Nord." *South European Politics and Society* 10(2): 333–349.

Ignazi, Piero, and Colette Ysmal, eds. 1998. *The Organization of Political Parties in Southern Europe*. Westport, CN: Praeger.

Inglehart, Ronald. 1977. *The Silent Revolution*. Princeton, NJ: Princeton University Press.

Ivaldi, Gilles. 1994. *Les Cultures politiques des sympathisants et adhérents du Front National. Enquêtes dans le département de L'Isère*. Ph.D. dissertation, University of Grenoble.

1996. "Conservation, Revolution, and Protest: A Case Study in the Political Cultures of the French National Front's Members and Sympathizers." *Electoral Studies* 15(3): 339–362.

1998. "The Front National: The Making of an Authoritarian Party." In *The Organization of Political Parties in Southern Europe.* Edited by Piero Ignazi and Colette Ysmal. Westport, CT: Praeger, pp. 43–69.

2008. "Inequality, Identity, and the People: New Patterns of Right-Wing Competition and Sarkozy's 'Winning Formula' in the 2007 Presidential Election." Paper presented at the annual meeting of the American Political Science Association, Boston, August 28.

Ivarsflaten, Elisabeth. 2005. "The Vulnerable Populist Right Parties: No Economic Realignment Fuelling Their Electoral Success." *European Journal of Political Research* 44(3): 465–492.

2008. "What Unites Right-Wing Populists in Western Europe? Re-examining Grievance Mobilization Models in Seven Successful Cases." *Comparative Political Studies* 41(1): 3–23.

Ivarsflaten, Elisabeth, Scott Blinder, and Robert Ford. 2008. "The Anti-Racism Norm in West European Immigration Politics." Paper presented at the Annual Meeting of the American Political Science Association, Boston, August 28.

Iyengar, Shanto, and Adam F. Simon. 2000. "New Perspectives and Evidence on Political Communication and Campaign Effects." *Annual Review of Psychology* 51(1): 149–169.

Jackman, Robert W., and Karin Volpert. 1996. "Conditions Favouring Parties of the Extreme Right in Western Europe." *British Journal of Political Science* 26(4): 501–521.

Jacobson, Gary, and Samuell Kernell. 1983. *Strategy and Choice in Congressional Elections,* 2d ed. New Haven, CT: Yale University Press.

Jaschke, Hans-Gerd. 1993. *Die "Republikaner." Profile einer Rechtsaußen-Partei,* 3d ed. Bonn: Dietz.

John, Peter, and Helen Margetts. 2009. "The Latent Support for the Extreme Right in British Politics." *West European Politics* 32(3): 496–513.

Kalvyas, Stathis. 2006. *The Logic of Violence in Civil War.* New York: Cambridge University Press.

Karpantschof, Rene. 2002. "Populism and Right Wing Extremism in Denmark, 1980–2001." *Sociologist Rapportserie* 4. Department of Sociology, University of Copenhagen.

Katz, Richard S., and Piero Ignazi, eds. 1996. *Italian Politics: The Year of the Tycoon.* Boulder, CO: Westview Press.

Katz, Richard S., and Peter Mair, eds. 1994. *How Parties Organize: Change and Adaptation in Party Organizations in Western Democracies.* London: Sage.

Katz, Richard S., and Peter Mair. 1995. "Changing Models of Party Organization and Party Democracy: The Emergence of the Cartel Party." *Party Politics* 1(1): 5–28.

2009. "The Cartel Party Thesis: A Restatement." *Perspectives on Politics* 7(4): 753–766.

Kedar, Orit. 2005. "When Moderate Voters Prefer Extreme Parties: Policy Balancing in Parliamentary Elections." *American Political Science Review* 99(2): 185–199.

Kestel, Laurent, and Laurent Godmer. 2004. "Institutional Inclusion and Exclusion of Extreme-Right Parties in Austria, Germany and France." In *Western Democracies and the New Extreme Right Challenge*. Edited by Roger Eatwell and Cas Mudde. London: Routledge.

Key, V. O., Jr. 1958. *Politics, Parties and Pressure Groups*, 4th ed.. New York: Thomas Crowell.

Kitschelt, Herbert. 1989. *The Logics of Party Formation*. Ithaca, NY: Cornell University Press.

   1994. *The Transformation of European Social Democracy*. New York: Cambridge University Press.

   1995. *The Radical Right in Western Europe: A Comparative Analysis*. Ann Arbor: University of Michigan Press.

   2007. "Growth and Persistence of the Radical Right in Postindustrial Democracies: Advances and Challenges in Comparative Research." *West European Politics* 30(5): 1176–1206.

Klandermans, Bert, and Nonna Mayer eds. 2006. *Extreme Right Activists in Europe: Through the Magnifying Glass*. London: Routledge.

Knigge, Pia. 1998. "The Electoral Correlates of Right-Wing Extremism in Western Europe." *European Journal of Political Research* 34(2): 249–279.

Kooiman, K. 1994. "Undercover in de CD." *De Groene Amsterdammer* 118(12): 6–11.

Koopmans, Ruud. 2001. "Rechtsextremismus und Fremdenfeindlichkeit in Deutschland. Probleme von Heute – Diagnosen von Gestern." *Leviathan* 29(4): 469–483.

Krasno, Jonathan S. 1994. *Challengers, Competition and Reelection: Comparing Senate and House Elections*. New Haven, CT: Yale University Press.

Kriesi, Hanspeter. 2001. "The Federal Parliament: The Limits of Institutional Reform." In *The Swiss Labyrinth. Institutions, Outcomes and Redesign*. Edited by Jan-Erik Lane. Special issue of *West European Politics* 24(2): 59–76.

Kriesi, Hanspeter, et al. 2008. *West European Politics in the Age of Globalization*. Cambridge: Cambridge University Press.

Kühnl, Reinhard, Rainer Rilling, and Christine Sager. 1969. *Die NPD. Struktur, Ideololgie und Funktion einer neofaschistischen Partei*. Frankfurt: Suhrkamp Verlag.

Kydd, Andrew, and Barbara F. Walter. 2002. "Sabotaging the Peace: The Politics of Extremist Violence." *International Organization* 56(2): 46–79.

Lafont, Valérie. 2006. "France: A Two-Centuries-Old Galaxy." In *Extreme Right Activists in Europe*. Edited by Bert Klandermans and Nonna Mayer. New York: Routledge, pp. 93–127.

Larsson, Stieg, and Mikael Ekman. 2001. *Sverigedemokraterna*. Stockholm: Ordfront.

Le Pen, Jean-Marie. 1984. *Les Français d'abord*. Paris: Carrère-Lafon.

Lewis, Paul. 2001. *Political Parties in Post-Communist Eastern Europe*. London: Routledge.

Linden, Annette, and Bert Klandermans. 2006. "The Netherlands: Stigmatized Outsiders." In *Extreme Right Activists in Europe*. Edited by Bert Klandermans and Nonna Mayer. New York: Routledge, pp. 172–203.

Lindquist, Hans. 1979. *Fascism I Dag*. Stockholm: Federativ.

Linz, Juan J., and Alfred Stepan, eds. 1978. *The Breakdown of Democratic Regimes*. Baltimore: Johns Hopkins University Press.

Lipset, Seymour Martin. 1960. *Political Man: The Social Bases of Politics*. Garden City, NY: Doubleday.

Lipset, Seymour Martin, and Stein Rokkan. 1967. *Party Systems and Voter Alignments: Cross National Perspectives*. Toronto: Free Press.

Lodenius, Anna-Lena, and Stieg Larsson. 1994. *Extremhögern*. Stockholm: Tidens Förlag.

Lööw, Helene. 1999. *Nazismen i Sverige, 1980–1999*. Stockholm: Ordfront.

Lubbers, Marcel. 2001. "Exclusionist Electorates: Extreme Right-Wing Voting in Western Europe." Ph.D. dissertation, Radbout University, Nijmegen.

Lubbers, Marcel, Mérove Gijberts, and Peer Scheepers. 2002. "Extreme Right-Wing Voting in Western Europe." *European Journal of Political Research* 41(3): 345–378.

Lucardie, Paul. 1998. "The Netherlands: The Extremist Center Parties." In *The New Politics of the Right*. Edited by Hans-Georg Betz and Stefan Immerfall. New York: St. Martin's Press, pp. 111–124.

Lucardie, Paul, and Gerrit Voerman. 2002. "Liberal Patriot or Nationaal Populist? Het gedachtegoed van Pim Fortuyn." *Socialisme en Democratie* 59(4): 32–42.

2006. "From Challenger to Government Partner Without a Party: The List Pim Fortuyn." Unpublished paper.

Luchinni, M. 1992. "Il militante: Questo sconosciuto." *Lega Lombarda*, supplement to no. 18 of *Lombarda Autonomista*, August–September, pp. 2–8.

Luebbert, Gregory. 1991. *Liberalism, Fascism, or Social Democracy*. New York: Oxford University Press.

Luther, Kurt Richard. 1997. "Die Freiheitlichen." In *Handbuch des Politischen Systems Österreichs*. Edited by Herbert Dachs et al. Vienna: Manz, pp. 286–303.

2003. "The Self-Destruction of a Right-Wing Populist Party? The Austrian Parliamentary Election of 2002." *West European Politics* 26(2): 136–152.

2006a. "Die Freiheitliche Partei Österreichs (FPÖ) und das Bündnis Zukunft Österreich (BZÖ)." In *Politik in Österreich: Das Handbuch*. Edited by Herbert Dachs et al. Vienna: Manzsche Verlags-und Universitätsbuchhandlung, pp. 364–389.

2006b. "Strategien und (Fehl-)Verhalten. Die Freiheitlichen und die Regierungen Schüssel I und II." In *Schwarz-Blau: Eine Bilanz des "Neu-Regierens."* Edited by Emmerich Tálos and Marcel Fink, Vienna: LIT Verlag, pp. 19–38.

2007. "Wahlstrategien und Wahlergebnisse des österreichischen Rechtspopulismus, 1986–2006." In *Wechselwahlen. Analysen zur Nationalratswahl 2006*. Edited by Fritz Plasser and Peter A. Ulram. Vienna: Facultas Verlag, pp. 231–255.

Mair, Peter. 2008. "Electoral Volatility and the Dutch Party System: A Comparative Perspective." *Acta Politica* 43(2–3): 235–253.

Mannheimer, Renato, ed. 1991. *La Lega Lombarda*. Milan: Feltrinelli.

Marcus, Jonathan. 1995. *The National Front and French Politics: The Resistible Rise of Jean-Marie Le Pen*. New York: New York University Press.

Markovits, Andrei. 2002. "Austrian Exceptionalism: Haider, the European Union, the Austrian Past and Present." In *The Haider Phenomenon in Austria*. Edited by Ruth Wodak and Anton Pelinka. New Brunswick, NJ: Transaction, pp. 95–119.

Martin, Virginie. 2002. *Toulon sous le Front National. Entretiens non-directifs*. Paris: L'Harmattan.

Mayer, Nonna, and Pascal Perrineau, eds. 1989. *Le Front National à découvert*. Paris: Presses de la Fondation Nationale des Sciences Politiques.

Mazzoleni, Oscar. 2003. *Nationalisme et populisme en Suisse. La radicalisation de la 'nouvelle' UDC*. Lausanne: Presses polytechniques et universitaires romandes.

McAdam, Douglas. 1982. *The Political Process and the Development of Black Insurgency*. Chicago: University of Chicago Press.

McAllister, Ian. 2007. "The Personalization of Politics." In *Oxford Handbook of Political Behavior*. Edited by Russell J. Dalton and Hans-Dieter Klingemann. Oxford: Oxford University Press, pp. 571–589.

McDonnell, Duncan. 2006. "A Weekend in Padania: Regionalist Populism and the Lega Nord." *Politics* 26(2): 126–132.

McGann, Anthony J., and Herbert Kitschelt. 2005. "The Radical Right in the Alps: The Evolution of Support for the Swiss SVP and the Austrian FPÖ." *Party Politics* 11(2): 147–171.

Meguid, Bonnie M. 2005. "Competition Between Unequals: The Role of Mainstream Party Strategy in Niche Party Success." *American Political Science Review* 99(3): 347–359.

Merkl, Peter H., and Leonard Weinberg, eds. 2003. *Right-Wing Extremism in the Twenty-First Century*. London: Frank Cass.

Messina, Anthony. 2007. *The Logics and Politics of Post-WWII Migration to Western Europe*. New York: Cambridge University Press.

Milza, Pierre. 1987. *Fascisme Français. Passé et présent*. Paris: Flammarion.

Minkenberg, Michael. 2001. "The Radical Right in Public Office: Agenda Setting and Policy Effects." *West European Politics* 24(4): 1–21.

Moore, Barrington. 1966. *Social Origins of Dictatorship and Democracy*. Boston: Beacon Press.

Mudde, Cas. 2000. *The Ideology of the Extreme Right*. Manchester: Manchester University Press.

    2004. *The Populist Zeitgeist: Government and Opposition*. Oxford: Blackwell Publishing.

    ed. 2005. *Racist Extremism in Central and Eastern Europe*. New York: Routledge.

    2007. *Populist Radical Right Parties in Europe*. New York: Cambridge University Press.

Mudde, Cas, and Joop van Holsteyn. 1994. "Over the Top: Dutch Right-Wing Extremist Parties in the Elections of 1994." *Politics* 14(3): 127–134.

2000. "The Netherlands: Explaining the Limited Success of the Extreme Right." In *The Politics of the Extreme Right: From the Margins to the Mainstream.* Edited by Paul Hainsworth. London: Pinter, pp. 144–171.

Nagle, John David. 1970. *The National Democratic Party: Right Radicalism in the Federal Republic of Germany.* Berkeley: University of California Press.

Newell, James, ed. 2002. *The Italian General Election of 2001: Berlusconi's Victory.* Manchester: Manchester University Press.

Niggli, Peter, and Jürg Frischknecht. 1998. *Rechte Seilschaften.* Zurich: Rotpunktverlag.

Niven, David. 2004. "The Mobilization Solution? Face-to-Face Contact and Voter Turnout in a Municipal Election." *Journal of Politics* 66(3): 868–884.

Noelle, Elisabeth, and Erich Peter Neumann, eds. 1967. *The Germans: Public Opinion Polls 1947–1966.* Westport, CT: Greenwood Press.

Norris, Pippa. 2005. *Radical Right: Voters and Parties in the Electoral Market.* Cambridge: Cambridge University Press.

Panebianco, Angelo. 1988. *Political Parties: Organization and Power.* Cambridge: Cambridge University Press.

Pastore, Ferrucio. 2004. "Italy's Migration Contradiction." *Open Democracy.* http://www.opendemocracy.net/debates/article.jsp?id+10&debateId= 96&articleId=1744.

Pedahzur, Ami, and Avraham Brichta. 2002. "The Institutionalization of Extreme Right-Wing Charismatic Parties: A Paradox?" *Party Politics* 8(1): 31–49.

Pederson, Karina, and Jens Ringsmosse. 2005. "From the Progress Party to the Danish People's Party: From Protest Party to Government-Supporting Party." Paper presented at the Joint Sessions of the European Consortium for Political Research, April 13–18, Uppsala.

Pederson, Mogens N. 1982. "Towards a New Typology of Party Lifespans and Minor Parties." *Scandinavian Political Studies* 5: 1–16.

Pelinka, Anton. 1998. *Austria: Out of the Shadow of the Past.* Boulder, CO: Westview Press.

Peterson, Roger. 2001. *Resistance and Rebellion: Lessons from Eastern Europe.* New York: Cambridge University Press.

Poguntke, Thomas. 2002. "Party Organizational Linkage: Parties Without Firm Social Roots?" In *Political Parties in the New Europe: Political and Analytical Challenges.* Edited by Kurt Richard Luther and Ferdinand Müller-Rommel. Oxford: Oxford University Press, pp. 43–62.

Poguntke, Thomas, and Paul Webb. 2005. *The Presidentializtion of Politics: A Comparative Study of Modern Democracies.* Oxford: Oxford University Press.

Ramet, Sabrina, ed. 1999. *The Radical Right in Central and Eastern Europe since 1989.* University Park: Pennsylvania State University Press.

Rea, Andrea. 1996. "Le Front National. Faiblesse institutionnelle et force électorale" In *Les Partis politique en Belgique.* Edited by Pascal Delwit and Jean Michel De Waele. Brussels: Editions de l'Université de Bruxelles.

Rensen, Peter. 1994a. "Een partij van fascisten, criminelen en tuig." *Nieuwe Revu,* 2–9, February: 41–58.

　　1994b. *Dansen met de duivel. Undercover bij de Centrumdemocraten.* Amsterdam: L. J. Veen.

Rensmann, Lars. 2006. "From High Hopes to On-going Defeat: The New Extreme Right's Political Mobilization and Its National Electoral Failure in Germany." *German Politics and Society* 24(1): 67–92.

Riedlsperger, Max. 1978. *The Lingering Shadow of Nazism: The Austrian Independence Party Movement since 1945.* New York: Columbia University Press.

　　1989. "The FPÖ: Liberal or Nazi?" In *Conquering the Past: Austrian Nazism Yesterday and Today.* Edited by F. Parkinson. Detroit: Wayne State University Press, pp. 257–279.

Ruzza, Carlo, and Oliver Schmidtke. 1993. "Roots of Success of the Lega Lombarda: Mobilisation Dynamics and the Media." *West European Politics* 16(2): 1–23.

Rydgren, Jens. 2002. "Radical Right Populism in Sweden: Still a Failure, but for How Long?" *Scandinavian Political Studies* 26(1): 26–57.

　　2004a. *The Populist Challenge: Political Protest and Ethno-Nationalist Mobilization in France.* New York: Berghahn.

　　2004b. "Explaining the Emergence of Radical Right-Wing Populism: The Case of Denmark." *West European Politics* 27(3): 474–502.

　　ed. 2005a. *Movements of Exclusion: Radical Right-Wing Populism in the West.* Hauppage: Nova Science.

　　2005b. "Is Extreme Right-Wing Populism Contagious? Explaining the Emergence of a New Party Family." *European Journal of Political Research* 44(3): 413–437.

　　2006. *From Tax Populism to Ethnic Nationalism.* New York: Berghahn.

　　2008. "Immigration Skeptics, Xenophobes, or Racists? Radical Right Wing Voting in Six Countries." *European Journal of Political Research* 47: 737–765.

Scaliati, Giuseppe. 2006. *Dove va la Lega Nord. Radici ed evoluzione politica di un movimento populista.* Milan: Zero in Condotta.

Scarrow, Susan E. 1996. *Parties and Their Members: Organizing for Victory in Britain and Germany.* New York: Oxford University Press.

Schain, Martin. 1987. "The National Front in France and the Construction of Political Legitimacy." *West European Politics* 10(2): 229–252.

　　1999. "The National Front in the French Party System." *French Politics and Society* 17(1): 1–16.

　　2002. "The Impact of the French National Front on the French Political System." In *Shadows over Europe: The Development and Impact of the Extreme Right in Western Europe.* Edited by Martin Schain, Aristide Zolberg, and Patrick Hossay. New York: Palgrave MacMillan, pp. 223–243.

　　2006. "The Extreme Right and Immigration in Policy-Making: Measuring Direct and Indirect Effects." *Western European Politics* 29(2): 270–289.

Schain, Martin, Aristide Zolberg, and Patrick Hossay, eds. 2002. *Shadows over Europe: The Development and Impact of the Extreme Right in Western Europe.* New York: Palgrave MacMillan.

Seberechts, Frank. 1992. "Beeldvorming over collaboratie en repressie bij de naoorlogse Vlaams-nationalisten." In *Herfsttij van de 20ste Eeuw. Extreemrechts in Vlaanderen, 1920–1990*. Edited by Rudi van Doorslaer et al. Leuven: Kritak, pp. 65–82.

Shields, J. G. 2007. *The Extreme Right in France: From Pétain to Le Pen*. New York: Routledge.

Simmons, Harvey. 1996. *The French National Front: The Extremist Challenge to Democracy*. Boulder, CO: Westview Press.

Skenderovic, Damir. 2007a. "Immigration and the Radical Right in Switzerland: Ideology, Discourse, and Opportunities." *Patterns of Prejudice* 41(2): 154–176.

  2007b. "Changing Political Campaigning in Switzerland: The Case of the Swiss People's Party." Paper prepared for the conference "Les partis politiques suisses: permanences et mutations," Bellinzona, November 30–December 1.

Smoydzin, Werner. 1969. *NPD: Partei mit Zukunft?* Nachdruck: Ilmgau Verlag Pfaffenhofen A.D. ILM.

Statham, Paul. 1996. "Berlusconi, the Media, and the New Right in Italy." *Harvard International Journal of Press and Politics* 1(1): 87–105.

Staud, Toraluf. 2005. *Moderne Nazis. Die Neuen Rechten und der Aufstieg der NPD*. Cologne: Kiepenheuer & Witsch.

Stenner, Karen. 2005. *The Authoritarian Dynamic*. New York: Cambridge University Press.

Stöss, Richard. 1989. *Die Extreme Rechte in der Bundesrepublik. Entwicklung, Ursachen, Gegenmassnahmen*. Opladen: Westdeutscher Verlag.

Svåsund, Lars. 1998. "Scandinavian Right-Wing Radicalism." In *The New Politics of the Right*. Edited by Hans-Georg Betz and Stefan Immerfall. New York: St. Martin's Press, pp. 77–93.

Swyngedouw, Marc, 1998. "The Extreme Right in Belgium: Of a Non-existent Front National and an Omnipresent Vlaams Blok." In *The New Politics of the Right*. Edited by Hans-Georg Betz and Stefan Immerfall. New York: St. Martin's Press, pp. 59–75.

  2000. "Belgium: Explaining the Relationship Between Vlaams Blok and the City of Antwerp." In *The Politics of the Extreme Right: From the Margins to the Mainstream*. Edited by Paul Hainsworth. New York: Pinter, pp. 121–143.

Swyngedouw, Marc, and Maarten Van Craen. 2002. *Het Vlaams Blok. Een overzichtsstudie*. Leuven: K. U. Leuven, Departement Sociologie/ISPO.

Taggart, Paul. 1995. "New Populist Parties in Western Europe." *West European Politics* 18(1): 34–51.

  1996. *The New Populism and the New Politics: New Protest Parties in Sweden in a Comparative Perspective*. Basingstoke: Macmillan.

Tambini, Damian. 2001. *Nationalism in Italian Politics: The Stories of the Northern League, 1980–2000*. London: Routledge.

Tarchi, Marco. 1997. *Dal MSI ad AN. Organizazzione e strategie*. Bologna: Società Editrice Il Mulino.

Tavits, Margit. 2006. "Party System Change: Testing a Model of New Party Entry." *Party Politics* 12 (1): 99–119.

Tillie, Jean, and Boris Slijper. 2007. "Immigrant Political Integration and Ethnic Civic Communities in Amsterdam." In *Identities, Affiliations, and Allegiances.* Edited by Seyla Benhabib, Ian Shapiro, and Danilo Petranovic. New York: Cambridge, pp. 206–225.

Togeby, Lise. 1997. *Fremmedhed og fremmedhad i Danmark.* Copenhagen: Columbus.

Van den Brink, Rinke. 1994. *De Internationale van de haat. Extreem-rechts in Europa.* Amsterdam: SUA.

   1996. *L'Internationale de la Haine: Paroles d'extrême droite – Belgique, France, Italie.* Brussels: Editions Luc Pire.

Van der Brug, Wouter. 2003. "How the LPF Fuelled Discontent: Empirical Tests of Explanations of LPF support." *Acta Politica* 38(1): 89–106.

Van der Brug, Wouter, and Meindert Fennema. 2003. "Protest or Mainstream? How the European Anti-immigrant Parties Developed into Two Separate Groups by 1999." *European Journal of Political Research* 42(1): 55–76.

Van der Brug, Wouter, and Joost Van Spanje. 2004. "Consequences of the Strategy of a 'Cordon Sanitaire' Against Anti-immigrant Parties." Paper presented at the ECPR Joint Sessions of Workshops, Uppsala, April 13–18.

   2009. "Immigration, Europe, and the 'New' Cultural Dimension." *European Journal of Political Research* 48 (3): 309–334.

Van Donselaar, Jaap. 1991. *Fout na de oorlog. Fascistische en racistische organisaties in Nederland 1950–1990.* Amsterdam: Bert Bakker.

   1993. *De staat paraat? De bestrijding van extreem-rechts in West Europa.* Amsterdam: Babylon de Geus Bakker.

   2000. *Monitor racisme en extreem-rechts. Derde rapportage.* Leiden: Universitiet Leiden.

Van Doorslaer, Rudi. 2003. "Gebruikt verleden. De politieke nalatenschap van de Tweede Wereldoorlog in België, 1945–2000." In *Geschiedenis Maken.* Edited by Gita Deneckere and Bruno De Wever. Ghent: Liber Amicorum Herman Balthazar, pp. 227–249.

Van Holsteyn, Joop, and Galen Irwin. 2003. "Never a Dull Moment: Pim Fortuyn and the Dutch Parliamentary Election of 2002." *West European Politics* 26(2): 41–66.

Van Hout, Bas. 1994. "De dodenlijst van de Centrum Democraten." *Panorama* 81(12): 12–17.

Spanje, Joost van. 2010. "Contagious Parties: Anti-immigration Parties and Their Impact on Other Parties' Immigration Stances in Contemporary Western Europe." *Party Politics* 16(5): 563–586.

Van Spanje, Joost, and Wouter van der Brug. 2007. "The Party as Pariah: The Exclusion of Anti-immigration Parties and Its Effect on Their Ideological Positions." *West European Politics* 30(5): 1022–1040.

Vanvaeck, Mark. 1987. *'t Pallieterke van Bruno De Winter 1945–1955.* Antwerp: De Nederlanden.

Verzichelli, Luca. 1996. "The New Members of Parliament." In *Italian Politics: The Year of the Tycoon.* Edited by Richard Katz and Piero Ignazi. Boulder, CO: Westview Press, pp. 115–133.

Veugelers, Jack. 2005. "Ex-colonials, Voluntary Associations, and Electoral Support for the Contemporary Far Right." *Comparative European Politics* 3(1): 408–431.

Veugelers, Jack, and Roberto Chiarini. 2002. "The Far Right in France and Italy: Nativist Politics and Anti-Fascism." In *Shadows over Europe: The Development and Impact of the Extreme Right in Western Europe*. Edited by Martin Schain, Aristide Zolberg, and Patrick Hossay. New York: Palgrave MacMillan, pp. 83–107.

Vimercati, Daniele. 1990. *I Lombardi alla nuova crociata*. Milan: Mursia.

Voerman, Gerrit, and Paul Lucardie. 1992. "The Extreme Right in the Netherlands: The Centrists and Their Radical Rivals." *European Journal of Political Research* 22(1): 35–54.

Vos, Louis. 1992. "De politieke kleur van jonge generaties. Vlaams-nationalisme, Nieuwe Orde en Extreem-Rechts." In *Herfsttij van de 20ste Eeuw. Extreem-rechts in Vlaanderen, 1920–1990*. ed. by Rudi van Doorslaer et al. Leuven: Kritak, pp. 15–46.

Weinstein, Jeremy. 2007. *Inside Rebellion: The Politics of Insurgent Violence*. New York: Cambridge University Press.

Westlind, Dennis. 1996. *The Politics of Popular Identity: Understanding Recent Populist Movements in Sweden and the United States*. Lund: Lund University Press.

Whitely, Paul F., and Patrick Seyd. 1994. "Local Party Campaigning and Mobilization in Britain." *Journal of Politics* 56(1): 242–252.

2003. "How to Win a Landslide by Really Trying: The Effects of Local Campaigning on Voting in the 1997 British General Election." *Electoral Studies* 22(1): 301–324.

Widfeldt, Anders. 1997. *Linking Parties with People? Party Membership in Sweden, 1960–1995*. Gothenburg: Gothenburg University.

2000. "Scandinavia: Mixed Success for the Populist Right." *Parliamentary Affairs* 53(3): 486–500.

2007. "The Sweden Democrats: The New Kid on the Block?" Paper prepared for the conference of the Political Studies Association, University of Bath, April 11–13.

Wielhouwer, Peter W. 1999. "The Mobilization of Campaign Activists by the Party Canvass." *American Politics Quarterly* 27(2): 177–200.

Williams, Michelle Hale. 2006. *The Impact of Radical Right-Wing Parties in West European Democracies*. New York: Palgrave MacMillan.

Winkler, Jürgen, and Siegfried Schumann. 1998. "Radical Right-Wing Parties in Contemporary Germany." In *The New Politics of the Right*. Edited by Hans-Georg Betz and Stefan Immerfall. New York: St. Martin's Press, pp. 95–110.

Winter, Franz Florian. 1968. *Ich glaubte an die NPD*. Mainz: v. Hase und Koehler Verlag GmbH.

Wlezien, Christopher, and Robert S. Erikson. 2001. "Campaign Effects in Theory and Practice." *American Politics Research* 29(5): 419–436.

Wood, Elizabeth. 2003. *Insurgent Collective Action and Civil War in El Salvador*. New York: Cambridge University Press.

Young, Brigitte. 1995. "The German Party System and the Contagion from the Right." *German Politics and Society* 13(1): 62–78.

Ysmal, Colette. 1984. *Demain la droite*. Paris: B. Grasset.

1989. "Sociologie des Élites du FN." In *Le Front National à decouvert*. Edited by Nonna Mayer and Pascal Perrineau. Paris: Presses de la Fondational Nationale Des Sciences Politiques, pp. 107–118.

Zaslove, Andrej. 2004. "The Dark Side of European Politics: Unmasking the Radical Right." *Journal of European Integration* 26(1): 61–81.

2007. "Alpine Populism, Padania and Beyond: A Response to Duncan McDonnell." *Politics* 27(1): 64–68.

Index

How do you solve a problem like UKIP? the Oxbridge?
It simply is the growth of UKIP and it's sustained by far government.

UKIP: Reality to govern? or doomed to fail
~~destined for the scrap heap?~~
It simply of UKIP's resemblance to the radical right
in Europe and an ascinct of its structural and policy
similarity for government.

The strength of UKIP rests on its divorcing of the people.
· the callow windees.
· historical legacy.

It's credulous so are structed to its history.
It's crashing is not really light to have it been in part, it's manifesto in clear.

CPSIA information can be obtained at www.ICGtesting.com
Printed in the USA
BVOW070348140212

282802BV00003B/3/P

9 780521 720328